a POCK

SHORT HISTORY
OF THE
ANGLO-SAXONS

a POCKET ESSENTIAL

SHORT HISTORY
OF THE
ANGLO-SAXONS

GILES MORGAN

Oldcastle Books

First published in 2018
by Pocket Essentials,
an imprint of Oldcastle Books Ltd,
Harpenden, UK

www.pocketessentials.com
Editor: Nick Rennison

ISBN
978-0-85730-166-6 (print)
978-0-85730-167-3 (epub)

Typeset by Avocet Typeset, Somerton, Somerset, TA11 6RT
in 13.25pt Garamond Pro
Printed and bound by Clays Ltd, Elcograf S.p.A

For Georgina

No man is an *Iland*, intire of it selfe; every man is a peece of the *Continent*, a part of the *maine*; if a *Clod* bee washed away by the *Sea*, *Europe* is the lesse, as well as if a *Promontorie* were, as well as if a *Mannor* of thy *friends* or of *thine owne* were; any mans *death* diminishes *me*, because I am involved in *Mankinde*; And therefore never send to know for whom the *bell* tolls; It tolls for *thee*.

John Donne
Meditation 17
Devotions upon Emergent Occasions
1624

Contents

CONTENTS

Introduction

History tells us that the Anglo-Saxon period ended at the Battle of Hastings in 1066. Whilst the power of the Anglo-Saxon aristocracy was fundamentally destroyed by the Norman Conquest and its aftermath, Anglo-Saxon culture and its influence has arguably survived in many ways right up until the present day. The most obvious example of this is the widespread use and impact of English as a globally understood language with its roots in the Old English language used by Anglo-Saxon peoples.

In the centuries following William the Conqueror's victory at the Battle of Hastings, perhaps understandably, Anglo-Saxon achievements and history have been largely overshadowed by the story of the Normans and their successors. However, in recent years exciting new discoveries such as the Staffordshire Hoard and the Lenborough Hoard have cast a new light upon Anglo-Saxon culture and reinvigorated interest in and study of this historical period. The Staffordshire Hoard in particular, discovered in a field near Lichfield in Staffordshire in 2009, is the greatest hoard of Anglo-Saxon gold and silverwork ever found and has captivated the public and academics alike. Indeed, widespread popular interest in the Anglo-Saxons, their origins and culture has arguably never been higher.

The Anglo-Saxons were early European migrants from Germanic tribes such as the Angles, Saxons and Jutes who came to Britain following the end of Roman Rule in 410 AD. They were from geographical regions that today correspond with Germany, Denmark and Holland. The early British chronicler Gildas (500-570) records that they came to Britain at the invitation of the British King Vortigern to serve as mercenaries. However, they soon reneged on this arrangement and took lands for themselves, settling particularly in the south-east of Britain. Later history and myth claim that the Anglo-Saxon invaders were halted by the legendary figure of King Arthur who marshalled the Britons against these incomers. Although there is some evidence that the Anglo-Saxon advance into Britain was stopped for several decades, many believe that King Arthur is largely a fictional construct and never existed at all.

The Anglo-Saxons who travelled to Britain were a pagan people who were converted to Christianity in the sixth century by St Augustine and others. Following this conversion monastic settlements began to develop in Britain which served as centres for learning and education leading to the production of artistic masterpieces such as the Lindisfarne Gospels. Interestingly, missionaries from Britain such as St Boniface who enjoyed close links with the papacy travelled back to Europe to convert their continental relatives in areas such as Frisia.

In England, over the centuries following the arrival of the Anglo-Saxon incomers, a number of separate but interconnected kingdoms such as Wessex and Mercia developed. The Kingdom of Mercia reached its apex of prestige and influence during the reign of Offa in the late eighth century. Probably the best-known action of this powerful Mercian king was to create the major defensive earthwork of Offa's Dyke. Its purpose was to act as a border between Mercia and the Kingdom of Powys, controlling the movement of people and trade and also serving as a means to halt aggressive raids by the Welsh and mobilise Mercian forces along its length.

As Anglo-Saxon kingdoms in England prospered and developed they themselves came under attack from European peoples such as the Norwegians and the Danes. In 851, a great army of these Viking invaders over-wintered in Britain and increasingly large numbers of incomers started to settle in England. It was against this backdrop of Viking expansionism that Alfred the Great emerged as one of English history's most significant rulers. Alfred was king of Wessex from 871 to 899 and his reign saw Anglo-Saxon power reach a dramatic low point when the territory that he controlled effectively shrank to a few acres of marshland in Somerset. However, Alfred fought back. He defeated the Danes in battle and then effectively started a peace process with them. The treaties signed by Alfred and the Viking leader Guthrum divided England between the Anglo-Saxon kingdoms and the northern and eastern areas controlled by the Vikings. This arrangement is often referred to as the Danelaw. As well as military successes Alfred's reign was also characterised by a commitment to spreading literacy and education amongst his subjects. Alfred's children, King Edward the Elder and Aethelflaed, Lady of the Mercians, worked hard to make a reality of Alfred's vision of a united England, with prosperous economic towns that also served as military strongholds against the Vikings. That vision would reach its apex during the rule of King Athelstan who would become the first Anglo-Saxon king to rule the whole of England.

However, during the reign of Ethelred the Unready (ruled 978-1013 and 1014-1016), the Viking threat to English power returned and led ultimately to the rule of the Danish King Canute from 1016 to 1035. Danish power in England would continue until 1042 when Edward the Confessor was crowned King of England. Edward the Confessor was the son of Ethelred the Unready and successor to the House of Wessex. Edward's death in 1066 without issue led to the power struggle between King Harold of Wessex and William, Duke of Normandy and the

Anglo-Saxon defeat at the Battle of Hastings.

It is often said that history is written by the victors and, in many ways, that appears to have been the case with the Norman Conquest and its aftermath. In the modern era interest in the Anglo-Saxon period appears to have steadily increased from the Victorian fascination with Anglo-Saxon culture to the sensational discovery in the late 1930s of the ship burial at Sutton Hoo in Suffolk.

The Old English epic poem *Beowulf* has enjoyed growing popularity in modern times, serving as inspiration to the author JRR Tolkien and more recently to the Irish poet Seamus Heaney who produced an acclaimed translation of it in 1999. Heaney drew parallels between the events of *Beowulf* and the history of the Irish Troubles. Its enduring popularity is further reflected in the numerous film and television adaptations based on the poem which have been produced in recent decades. Coming right up to date, the American author George RR Martin drew heavily on Anglo-Saxon and Medieval history for his best-selling fantasy books *Game of Thrones* and the blockbuster television series based upon them.

The incredible archaeological discovery of the Staffordshire Hoard in 2009, as mentioned earlier, sparked a new-found fascination with the Anglo-Saxon period on an international level. Other important finds, such as the Lenborough Hoard which was unearthed in 2014, have only added to this fascination. Such discoveries, coupled with historical reassessments of the achievements and significance of the Anglo-Saxon period, are finally helping to bring the compelling story of these Dark Age people into the light of modern understanding and appreciation.

Chapter One

The First Anglo-Saxon Settlers in Britain

Roman Britain

During the third and fourth centuries the Roman Empire underwent a series of invasions and attacks from barbarian tribes and was also badly weakened by internal leadership conflicts. In Roman Britain during the fourth century there was an increasing wave of raids from the Saxon tribes on the east coast and also from the Irish to the west of the island. A critical event in this period of increased pressure from external peoples was the so-called 'Barbarian Conspiracy' or 'Great Conspiracy' of 367-368. The Great Conspiracy involved a combined attack on Britain by Saxons, Picts, Scotti, Attacotti, Franks and Roman deserters. They were able to capitalise on a depleted Roman military presence in the province in the aftermath of the Battle of Mursa Major which took place in 351. The battle followed a conflict between the usurper Magnentius, who had overthrown and killed the Western Emperor Constans, and the ruler of the Eastern Empire Constantius II. Constantius II was the son of the Roman Emperor Constantine the Great and the brother of Constans and he inflicted a severe defeat on Magnentius at the Battle of Mursa Major. However, both sides suffered heavily in the fighting, resulting in an estimated 50,000 casualties at a time when the empire was under pressure from external barbarian forces. The chaos and disorder of the Great Conspiracy was ended by a force led by Count Theodosius in 368 which restored order, drove out the invaders and recaptured Hadrian's Wall. However, in 383 another rebellion took place involving Magnus Maximus who attempted to claim the title of Western Emperor and took troops from Britain across the English Channel into Europe to support his bid for power. It is thought that many of these troops never returned to Britain, leaving it once again vulnerable to attack. Further raids took place in 396 which were met by Roman actions against them and control was regained for a few years.

Another usurper of the imperial throne emerged in 407 when Constantine III was declared emperor in Britain by the army. He also crossed the Channel to Europe to confront the Emperor Honorius, taking most if not all of Britain's troops with him. Following a serious Saxon attack on Britain in 408 which was repelled by the Romano-British population, Roman magistrates representing Constantine III were expelled from the province by its inhabitants who felt that they had been abandoned by the empire and resorted to their own defence. The ancient historian Zosimus records that the Britons appealed for aid to the embattled Emperor Honorius who was fighting the Visigoths and their leader Alaric at the time. His conflict with the Visigoths would ultimately lead to the sacking of Rome on 24 August 410. He advised them to look to their own defences against the barbarian raids. (However, some historians think that Honorius may have actually been addressing the region of Bruttium in southern Italy and not Britain.) The sixth-century monk and historian Gildas states in his historical work *De Excidio et Conquestu Britanniae* (*On The Ruin and Conquest of Britain*) that, in 446, the Britons made a further appeal to the Roman general Aetius for military aid which was never answered. This appeal is often referred to as 'The Groans of the Britons' and concerns raids which were being made on Britain by the Picts, Scots and Saxons.

King Vortigern

Gildas also recorded that the British invited a group of Saxons to settle in Britain. Gildas is thought to have been born in 500 and died in 570 in Rhuys in Brittany. In *De Excidio et Conquestu Britanniae*, he describes events happening during the early decades of the fifth century. According to his account a group of councillors and their leader, whom Gildas terms a 'usurper', offered the Saxons a place to settle in return for military aid in fighting the Scots and the Picts. Gildas writes that they settled on the 'east of the island' which has led to considerable speculation about where he actually meant. However, the initial group offered settlement in Britain became larger as more of their countrymen joined them until eventually they demanded greater payments to serve as mercenaries and were refused by the leaders of the British. They then reneged on their agreements and began to attack and plunder the lands and property of their former employers. Gildas describes the leader of the British as being unlucky and lacking in judgement. He goes on to describe the raids of the Saxons as becoming like a devastating fire that burned from one side of Britain to the other, even reaching the west coast of the island.

Gildas's account of the history of the beginnings of the Saxon invasion and settlement of Britain was to prove an important source for the writings of the Venerable Bede who wrote his own history of the period during the eighth century. This work, entitled *Historia Ecclesiastica Gentis Anglorum* or the *Ecclesiastical History of the English People* and completed in 731, is the first account of this period to give a name to the leader of the British. Bede calls him Vurtigernus even though Gildas does not specifically name him. Importantly, Bede also gives names to the leaders of the Saxons who were invited to Britain, calling them Hengist and Horsa. He also states that the tribes that they represent are the Saxons, the Angles and the Jutes. Gildas also states that Vurtigernus (or Vortigern as he is better known today) was the king of the British and claims that these events took place in 449, a view which is now largely contested. Bede stated that Hengist and Horsa were the sons of a man called Wictgils and that he could trace his ancestry back to the god Woden. According to Bede, Horsa was killed during fighting with the British and his body was buried somewhere in east Kent.

In the *Anglo-Saxon Chronicle*, written during the ninth century, Hengist and Horsa are described as having sailed to Britain at the request of Vortigern in order to help him fight the Picts. The *Anglo-Saxon Chronicle* states that they arrived at Ebbsfleet on the Isle of Thanet in Essex and, like Bede, it records these events as taking place in 449. The *Chronicle* describes Hengist and Horsa as being successful in their work as mercenaries fighting against the Picts and that they were contemptuous of the British, sending word to Germany and the tribes living there to come and settle in Britain. The different tribes are described by the *Anglo-Saxon Chronicle* as being the Saxons, the Angles and the Jutes. The Jutes are said to have settled in Kent and Hampshire and the Saxons in Sussex, Wessex and Essex. East Anglia, Mercia and Northumbria were colonised by the Angles. Like Bede the *Anglo-Saxon Chronicle* has Horsa die during fighting with the British and gives the year 455 as the date of the battle against Vortigern at Aylesford in which he was killed. Two years later a force led by Hengist defeated the British at Crayford and as a result the Britons were pushed out of Kent and travelled to London. The final time that the *Anglo-Saxon Chronicle* refers to Hengist is in the entry for the year 473 when it is recorded that the invaders have captured a huge amount of plunder and that the British fled from them.

According to the *Historia Brittonum* or *The History of the Britons*, written by Nennius during the ninth century, Vortigern is said to have attended a feast with Hengist and Horsa when they were still serving him as mercenaries. During the feast Vortigern met the beautiful daughter of Hengist and, under the influence of drink supplied by his hosts, promised to give Hengist the Kingdom of Kent in return for her hand in marriage. However, Vortigern made his promise without consulting the British ruler of Kent. Hengist and Horsa sent for reinforcements from Germania intent on taking more land and power from the Britons. As relations soured between the incoming tribes and the British (as in the earlier accounts), war broke out between them. Vortigern's own son Vortimer is said by Nennius to have fought against Hengist and Horsa. Vortimer pushed them back to the Isle of Thanet and fought four battles against them. During the third battle Horsa was killed, as was Vortimer's brother Catigern. Finally, Vortimer defeated the Saxons and pushed them back to the sea where they fled in their ships. However, Vortimer died shortly afterwards and later the Saxons returned. Hengist then extended an offer of peace to Vortigern, suggesting that they hold a meeting and feast together. Hengist proved to be untrustworthy. He ordered his men to conceal their knives under their feet during the feast and then shouted for them to get their weapons and seize the British. Many were killed but Vortigern was spared in return for agreeing that the Saxons could have lands including Sussex, Essex and Middlesex.

According to Nennius, Germanus the Bishop of Auxerre then became the leader of the Britons. As a result of his appeals to God and a fightback against the invaders by the Britons, the Saxons were forced to take to their ships once again. Germanus then travelled to the castle in which Vortigern was taking refuge and prayed to God for three days and nights until the Almighty rained down fire on the occupants. Vortigern and his several wives including Hengist's pagan daughter were said to have all been killed. But the Saxons returned and in greater numbers and when Hengist died they were led by his own son Ochta.

King Arthur

Perhaps no other figure in early British history has caused greater controversy and speculation than King Arthur. Opinion has been divided as to whether King Arthur ever actually existed as a Romano-British leader or was essentially a mythological figure that emerged from folklore and was transformed into a literary tradition. The earliest recorded reference to him can be found in the *Historia Brittonum* which, as we have seen, is credited to the Welsh cleric Nennius and was written during the ninth century. In the pages relating to the history of Britain during the fifth century Nennius writes:

'At that time the English increased their numbers and grew in Britain. On Hengist's death, his son Ochta came down from the north of Britain to the kingdom of the Kentishmen, and from him are sprung the kings of the Kentishmen. Then Arthur fought against them in those days, together with the kings of the British; but he was their leader in battle.'

(Nennius, *Historia Brittonum*, p.35).

Nennius goes on to say that Arthur fought twelve separate battles against the Anglo-Saxons. He is described as a Christian war leader who carries the image of the Virgin Mary on his shield as he fights against the heathen Anglo-Saxon invaders. The most famous of the twelve battles listed by Nennius is the Battle of Mount Badon during which it is claimed that Arthur personally killed 960 men. Nennius tells us that Arthur was victorious in all his campaigns against the Anglo-Saxons.

However, it is now widely thought that Nennius's account of British history is unreliable. Arthur is not mentioned by the *Anglo-Saxon Chronicle* or in Bede's *Ecclesiastical History of the English People*, written during the eighth century. However, the *Anglo-Saxon Chronicle* does record that, in 519, Cerdic and Cynric obtained the kingdom of the West Saxons and fought a battle against the British at a place called Cerdicesford. That battle appears to have ended with a truce between the two sides that lasted for around 30 years. The truce was briefly interrupted in 530 when the Saxons captured the Isle of Wight. This period may possibly be the basis for the accounts of the Battle of Mount Badon. However, it is not clear exactly where in Britain the battle is meant to have taken place. Bede does refer to the Battle of Mount Badon in his work and placed it in the last decade of the fifth century. The earliest mention of the Battle of Mount Badon can be found in Gildas's *De Excidio et Conquest Britanniae* (*On The Ruin and Conquest of Britain*), written during the early to mid-sixth century. Gildas tells us that the British were led into battle by a man named Ambrosius Aurelianus and that he won a significant victory against the Anglo-Saxons. He is described as born of a noble Romano-British family and Gildas also tells us that his parents were slain by the Anglo-Saxons but that he was able to galvanise and reorganise the British in the defence of their country. Gildas also says that he won his victories 'with God's help' and so was presumably a Christian.

It is possible that the figure of King Arthur could have been based on Ambrosius Aurelianus as there are a number of clear parallels between them. Interestingly, neither Nennius's *Historia Brittonum* nor the later *Annales Cambriae*, written during the tenth century, describes Arthur as a king. Nennius describes him as '*dux bellorum*' which translates as a 'leader of battles' and the *Annales Cambriae* refers to him as '*miles*' meaning soldier. It seems likely that the title of king was added later to the story of Arthur which appears to have originated with

Nennius who was influenced by the work of Gildas. Arthur's name is also referenced in the Welsh poem *Y Gododdin* which is thought to have been written by the sixth-century poet Aneirin but this may well be an interpolation made during later centuries. The legend of King Arthur reached something of a peak in popularity during the twelfth century due in large part to Geoffrey of Monmouth's colourful and largely imaginative *History of the Kings of Britain*. This work contained many of the key elements of Arthurian lore such as Arthur's sword Excalibur, the wizard Merlin and the Isle of Avalon. Later writers such as Chretien de Troyes writing in the late twelfth century and Wolfram von Eschenbach in the early thirteenth century introduced the concept of the quest for the Holy Grail into the Arthurian stories.

Northumbrian Kingdoms

In the north of England two separate kingdoms called Bernicia and Deira were conquered by the Angles from the sixth century onwards. The

Angles take their name from the district of Angeln in Southern Schleswig in Germany, close to the border with Denmark. The ancient territory of the Angles probably encompassed areas that are now part of both countries. Some Angles were probably employed as mercenaries along Hadrian's Wall in the late Roman period whilst more migrated to Britain in the early sixth century, settling in areas such as East Anglia, the Midlands and northern England. The word England derives from the Angles as does the name for the English language although clearly this is comprised of many different influences and origins.

The Kingdom of Bernicia covered a territory between the Forth and Tees rivers and would have included Northumberland, Durham, East Lothian and Berwickshire. The first Anglian king to conquer Bernicia whose name was recorded in written sources was King Ida. He came to power there in around 547. The Kingdom of Deira occupied territory between the River Humber and the River Tees and its first recorded Anglian king was named Aella who, according to the *Anglo-Saxon Chronicle*, came to power in 560.

Aella was said to have reigned for around 30 years and, like many Anglo-Saxon royal families, claimed a genealogy stretching back to the god Woden. When Aella died in 588 he was succeeded by Aethelric who ruled for five years. In 593, Aethelfrith succeeded to the throne of Bernicia. Aethelfrith was the grandson of King Ida and he forcibly united the kingdoms of Bernicia and Deira in about 604. Whilst details about the lives of his predecessors are scant, more is known about King Aethelfrith and he effectively founded the Anglo-Saxon kingdom of Northumbria. He was a pagan ruler who was successful in his military campaigns against the Britons and the Gaels of Dál Riata. However, he was finally killed fighting a battle with King Raedwald of East Anglia at the River Idle in 616. Following his defeat and death, Aethelfrith was succeeded as king of Northumbria by Edwin, who was the son of Aella, on the orders of Raedwald. Edwin was to be the first king of Northumbria to convert to Christianity in 627 although this new religion was not immediately accepted by his subjects.

Chapter Two

The Conversion to Christianity

St Augustine

In 596, Pope Gregory the Great selected the prior of a monastery in Rome called Augustine to lead a mission of monks to bring Christianity to the Anglo-Saxons in Kent. Augustine had been a monk at the monastery of St Andrew before becoming its prior. It is likely that Gregory sent the monks to England because King Ethelbert of Kent had recently married a Christian princess called Bertha from Paris. Whilst travelling through Gaul the party led by Augustine wanted to return to Rome but Gregory insisted that they carry on and gave Augustine greater powers and authority by having him consecrated as a bishop. Gregory also instructed a number of Frankish priests to join the group so that when they arrived at Ebbsfleet in Kent in 597 there were forty people in their party. Initially King Ethelbert provided them with accommodation in Canterbury and the freedom to preach the Christian doctrine. However, the mission took some years to establish itself and Ethelbert required persuasion and time to reflect on the new religion before he was finally baptised in 601.

Augustine went on to found the monastery of St Peter and St Paul close to Canterbury and founded a see at Rochester and one at London. At that time London was a town ruled by the East Saxons although Ethelbert was considered their overlord. Augustine also played an important role in helping Ethelbert to produce the earliest written Anglo-Saxon laws that have survived to the present day. Pope Gregory instructed Augustine that he should not attempt to destroy any pagan temples or sites, only the idols within them. An interesting example of a site that appears to reflect this policy can be found at the church of St Giles, Barrow, near Much Wenlock in Shropshire. It has been suggested that the chancel of St Giles dates to the eighth century which makes it one of the oldest churches in Britain. It is thought that a small chapel was built here at that time, probably as a 'cell' of the nearby Wenlock Abbey, at the command of St Mildburg. The chapel was dedicated to St Giles, a hermit and abbot who is recorded as dying in 712. He is the patron saint of cripples and beggars. There are Saxon windows in the chancel and in the exterior of the north-east wall there is evidence of a Saxon pilaster strip. The nave is a Norman rebuilding of a Saxon original and a tower was added in around 1100.

The church is located upon a raised circular graveyard which, in a number of other examples (such as Ysbyty Cynfyn in west Wales), indicates that the site had pre-Christian, pagan origins. The Rev John Woods of Much Wenlock has identified an unusual stone in the graveyard. He describes the stone as being, 'still set upon a sandstone stipes (stem-like structure) which in turn is still set into a pedestal. The stipes in particular has the appearance of a British cromlech and thus may be pre-Saxon. The whole assembly is some 30 inches too high for an altar...(and) gives the impression that it may originally have been a memorial dolmen...' (Sarah

Zaluckyj, *Mercia: The Anglo-Saxon Kingdom of Central England*, p.98). The Rev Woods has also argued that the site is the burial ground of St Owen and that is why St Mildburg had a chapel built here. Following her death St Mildburg's bones were deposited in the church but were later destroyed during the Reformation.

King Raedwald

Following the migration of the Anglo-Saxon peoples to Britain in the sixth century a number of kingdoms emerged as they began to achieve dominance over the British. The Kingdom of East Anglia formed one of the kingdoms that were traditionally referred to as the Anglo-Saxon Heptarchy. The term itself derives from the Greek word for the number seven which is 'hepta'. Although East Anglia was one of these early seven Anglo-Saxon kingdoms much information about its foundation has been lost. A likely explanation for this gap in the historical written record is that, during the ninth century, Viking attacks on the region led to the destruction of many of the Anglo-Saxon monasteries and their contents, including written records such as genealogies and royal charters. However, the Venerable Bede and the *Anglo-Saxon Chronicle* provide us with an insight into the early formation of East Anglia.

According to Nennius, its first ruler was Wehha in the early to mid-sixth century. His son Wuffa ruled East Anglia from around 571 and the Wuffinga dynasty of important early rulers of the East Angles was named after him. The name Wuffinga means 'son of the wolf' and Wuffa was succeeded by his son Tytila who ruled from around 578. Little is known about these rulers but more details have survived through Bede of Tytila's son Raedwald who was born sometime between 560 and 580. He ruled from about 599 and, according to Bede, he married a pagan woman during the 590s. Together they had two sons called Eorpwald and Ragenhere, and possibly more.

Raedwald's early reign coincided with the arrival in Kent of St Augustine of Canterbury in 597. King Ethelbert of Kent and King Saeberht of Essex both converted to Christianity during this period and created bishoprics in their territories. At the beginning of his reign Raedwald recognised Ethelbert as his overlord. Raedwald and his son Eorpwald both converted to Christianity through the influence of Ethelbert somewhere around 604, probably in part in an attempt to strengthen ties between East Anglia, Essex and Kent. However, Raedwald did not commit fully to the new religion and continued to keep a pagan altar in his temple, perhaps because of pressure from his council or his wife. Raedwald was to play an important part in the politics of Northumbria when he offered protection to its future king Edwin. Edwin had been driven out of Northumbria by Aethelfrith who had fathered a son called Oswald with Acha, Edwin's sister. In order to ensure that Oswald would become king of the northern Northumbrian kingdom of Bernicia, Aethelfrith tried to kill Edwin. When he discovered that Edwin had taken shelter at Raedwald's court, he offered money and treasure for his murder. Raedwald refused to kill Edwin and Aethelfrith then threatened him with a war between the two kingdoms. It was during his time at the court of Raedwald that Edwin was introduced to

Christianity by Paulinus of York. When threatened with war Raedwald initially offered to have Edwin killed or delivered to Aethelfrith but changed his mind, perhaps through the influence of his wife.

Instead he marched north with an army in around 616 and fought a battle with Aethelfrith's forces on the western boundary of the Kingdom of Lindsey on the east bank of the River Idle. Although his son Ragenhere died during the fighting, Raedwald defeated and killed Aethelfrith. Edwin then became the new king of Northumbria under the control of Raedwald. Following the death of Ethelbert of Kent, his sons reverted to paganism but Raedwald maintained his Christian altar throughout this period. In the aftermath of Ethelbert's death and the Battle of the River Idle, Raedwald became the most powerful Anglo-Saxon ruler south of the Humber and was described by the *Anglo-Saxon Chronicle* as a 'bretwalda' meaning 'Britain ruler' or 'wide ruler'. Bede also called him 'Rex Anglorum', meaning 'King of the Angles', and he exercised power and influence over Edwin who unified the kingdoms of Bernicia and Deira in Northumbria. Raedwald died in about 624 and was succeeded by his son Eorpwald. It is now generally thought that Raedwald is the most likely historical figure to have been buried at the internationally famous Anglo-Saxon ship burial at Sutton Hoo near Woodbridge in Suffolk which is examined in greater detail in Chapter 7.

St Aidan and the foundation of Lindisfarne

Today St Aidan is viewed as having played an important role in converting the pagan Anglo-Saxons of northern England to the new religion of Christianity. Most of what is known about St Aidan is recorded in Bede's *Ecclesiastical History of the English People* which was completed in about 731. Aidan was born in Ireland, although little else is known of his early life, and he became a monk on the island of Iona. He travelled to England in 635 at the invitation of King Oswald of Northumbria who had spent a period of time in exile on Iona after being driven out of his kingdom by Mercian attacks. The first monk from Iona who had attempted to convert the Anglo-Saxons had given up, finding them to be barbaric and unreceptive to his message. It was hoped that St Aidan would prove a more persuasive and successful missionary. To assist him in his work, Oswald gave St Aidan the island of Lindisfarne which was located near to the king's royal palace at Bamburgh. Oswald hoped that he would be able to evangelise the northern area of Northumbria then known as Bernicia because St Paulinus of York had already evangelised the southern area of Northumbria called Deira. St Aidan became the first bishop and abbot of Lindisfarne and, following the death of Oswald in 642, was a friend and supporter of King Oswine of Deira.

St Aidan developed a reputation for living a life of frugality and poverty and for chastising the rich and powerful when he felt it was appropriate. During the period of Lent in 651 he is said to have travelled to Inner Farne Island to pray. Whilst he was staying there the royal palace at Bamburgh was attacked by King Penda of Mercia who set fire to it. It is said that when St Aidan prayed for the wind to change so that Bamburgh would be saved, it did so. However, on 20 August in the same year, King Oswine of Deira was murdered by the soldiers of King Oswiu who ruled Bernicia the northern kingdom of Northumbria. St Aidan died eleven days after Oswine. He had become ill whilst carrying out missionary work and is said to have died whilst leaning against the wall of the church at Bamburgh. He was buried in the cemetery at Lindisfarne.

When his bones or relics were translated into the church some were taken to Ireland by Colman who was a bishop of Lindisfarne. Although St Aidan's cult seems to have been slow to develop, in the tenth century some monks from Glastonbury claimed to have obtained relics of the saint and, as a result of this, his feast day was recorded in some early Wessex calendars. When Bede wrote his *Ecclesiastical History of the English People* he particularly praised St Aidan for his humility and dedication to his work and for helping the poor and the sick. During the nineteenth century, Irish and English Christian scholars such as Joseph Lightfoot recognised St Aidan's achievements, with Lightfoot describing him as 'the apostle of the English'.

St Cuthbert

St Cuthbert is perhaps the most important saint to have emerged from the early Northumbrian church. He was born around 634 in Dunbar in what is now East Lothian in south-east Scotland. At the time of his birth Dunbar was part of the shifting territories of the Kingdom of Northumbria. His family were from the Anglo-Saxon nobility and Cuthbert became a monk at Melrose Abbey in 651. During this period, the early church in northern England experienced inner turmoil as a result of differences between the church in Rome and Irish traditions. The baptism of King Edwin had been carried out by an emissary of Pope Gregory called Paulinus of York and so the Roman tradition had a strong influence on the development of the church in this region. However, it was monks from Ireland such as St Aidan who had founded Lindisfarne and carried with them their differing Christian traditions. When Alcfrith, son of King Oswiu, donated lands for the foundation of a monastery at Ripon, Cuthbert became its guest master serving under Abbot Eata. However, Alcfrith went on to instruct the monastery at Ripon that it must follow the traditions of the Roman church. Eata and Cuthbert travelled back to Melrose Abbey and they were replaced by St Wilfrid who was a strong proponent of Roman customs. The most significant difference between the two traditions was the way in which they calculated Easter.

Cuthbert became prior of Melrose Abbey in 661 and he then spent much of his time carrying out missionary work in the local area. Following the Synod of Whitby in 663 to 664 (which is explored in greater detail later in this chapter), Cuthbert accepted Roman customs and he became the prior of Lindisfarne where he introduced them on the instruction of Eata. Cuthbert is credited with patiently persuading the monks to accept these changes and he gained a reputation as a charismatic leader who was kind to the poor and had healing abilities. As well as serving as prior of Lindisfarne he continued his missionary work throughout the region and founded an oratory at Dull in Scotland. For a while Cuthbert became a hermit on an island, now known as St Cuthbert's Isle, close to Lindisfarne. In 676, Cuthbert stepped down as prior of Lindisfarne and moved to Inner Farne where he lived a life of austerity and solitude. But Cuthbert's reputation as a holy man grew to the extent that, in 685, King Ecgfrith and members of his council chose him to become Bishop of Hexham. He was initially reluctant to accept any title but finally agreed to become Bishop of Lindisfarne whilst Eata became the Bishop of Hexham. As Bishop of Lindisfarne Cuthbert channelled his energies into preaching and travelling throughout his diocese and it was also claimed that he was able to prophesy the future and heal the sick. However, his time as a bishop was to be short-lived. He died on Inner Farne on 20 March 687 to which he had returned after Christmas 686, following a painful illness.

He was buried at Lindisfarne. According to Bede, when his body was elevated to a shrine in the church, it was found to be incorrupt and this was interpreted as a miracle and a clear sign of his holiness. Following the destruction of Lindisfarne in 875 by the Vikings, his relics were moved by members of the monastic community to a number of different sites in order to protect them from desecration and damage. These sites included

Northam-on-Tweed, Ripon and famously Chester-le-Street. Durham was chosen to be Cuthbert's final resting place after the cart in which his coffin was being carried became stuck in the road there and this was believed to have expressed the will of the saint. A shrine was established in Durham in 995 and a Saxon church built on the site in 999. Cuthbert became a very significant figure for the Anglo-Saxons and in particular the kings of Wessex following numerous miracles that were attributed to him. He would also come to represent a unifying figure for the English of the southern and northern kingdoms against the ongoing incursions of the Danes.

Lindisfarne Gospels

One of the greatest achievements of the monastic community at Lindisfarne was the creation of the Lindisfarne Gospels. This illuminated manuscript containing the gospels of Matthew, Mark, Luke and John, along with other material often found in medieval copies of the gospels, was produced about 715. It is believed that they were written and illustrated by Eadfrith who was Bishop of Lindisfarne from 698 to 721. The Lindisfarne gospels are written in Latin and, in the tenth century, Aldred, the provost of the monastic community of St Cuthbert at Chester-le-Street, carried out a word-for-word translation into Anglo-Saxon or Old English between the lines of the Latin text. Aldred the Scribe, as he is sometimes known, added a brief statement or colophon about the Lindisfarne Gospels, recording that they had been produced by Eadfrith and that the original binding for the gospels had been provided by Bishop Ethelwald in 921. Aldred also wrote that an anchorite called Billfrith had made a leather binding for the gospel which was originally set with jewels and precious metals.

However, following the later Viking attacks on Lindisfarne, this covering has not survived. Aldred also wrote that the gospels had been written in honour of St Cuthbert and God. During the tenth century the cult of St Cuthbert had grown rapidly in northern England. The Lindisfarne Gospels are regarded as a masterpiece of their kind and interestingly combine Anglo-Saxon and Celtic styles as well as the influence of Mediterranean cultures. Parallels have been drawn between the interlaced patterns and spirals found in Anglo-Saxon jewellery and the elaborate lettering of the gospels. It is thought that the Lindisfarne Gospels may have been used for missionary work as well as by the community at the monastery because its colourful, beautifully illustrated pages, filled with biblical figures, birds and animals, would have probably been found astonishing and awe-inspiring by many people at the time.

Synod of Whitby

The Synod of Whitby is often seen as one of the most significant events to take place in the development of Christianity during the Anglo-Saxon period. During the seventh century two forms of Christian practice had operated in Britain although they had not necessarily been in conflict with one another. The two differing practices were the 'Ionan' and 'Roman' traditions, both of which had important supporters and adherents amongst the Anglo-Saxon nobility. King Edwin, as we have seen, had been converted to Christianity in 627 by Paulinus of York who was a representative of the Roman church and an emissary of Pope Gregory I, and had been sent to Britain to carry out work as a missionary in 601. Following Edwin's death at the Battle of Hatfield Chase in 633, in which he was defeated and killed by the forces of King Penda of Mercia and Cadwallon, the king of Gwynedd, the Kingdom of Northumbria was divided in two. Osric became king in the southern kingdom of Deira whilst Eanfrith ruled in the northern kingdom of Bernicia. Both kings became pagans again during their reigns until they were both also defeated and killed by Cadwallon who then ruled for a period of about a year.

However, Eanfrith's brother Oswald reunited the two kingdoms after killing Cadwallon at the Battle of Heavenfield in 633 or 634. Oswald had been introduced to Christianity by the Irish monks of Iona. He supported the spread of Christianity throughout his kingdom and gave Aidan the island of Lindisfarne close to his seat at Bamburgh to establish a Christian community. Following his death in 642 or 643, Northumbria was once again split in two. Bernicia was ruled by Oswiu, Oswald's brother, and Deira by Oswine. Oswiu's son Alcfrith is often seen as being of critical importance in bringing about the Synod of Whitby after he expelled Ionan monks, including St Cuthbert, from the monastery of Ripon and handed it over to Wilfrid who followed Roman customs.

It is thought Alcfrith persuaded his father Oswiu to call the Synod of Whitby to further the position and dominance of the Roman church. It was held in 664 at the monastery of a powerful Northumbrian noble called Hilda, a follower of the Ionan position, at a site then known as Streonshalh which would eventually become Whitby Abbey. The purpose of the Synod was to establish the proper calculation of Easter. The Ionan tradition followed a calculation devised by Bishop Augustalis in the third century and which involved an 84-year cycle. However, in Rome, the church was using a calculation devised by Dionysius Exiguus that followed a cycle of 532 years. At the synod Wilfrid was the advocate for the Roman position and Colman, Bishop of

Northumbria, represented the Ionan position. King Oswiu ruled over the proceedings and gave a judgement over which position Christianity in his kingdom would adopt. Wilfrid essentially argued that the church should adopt the practice of Rome and that it was universal even in Alexandria in Egypt whilst Colman argued that they followed the practice of St Columba who had founded the church in their region. Wilfrid countered that Columba had used such knowledge as was available to him but that no figure in the church had authority over St Peter and his successors in Rome.

Oswiu ruled in favour of adopting the Roman practice on the basis of the significance of St Peter and his status as the rock on which the church was to be built. Oswiu also said that they should adopt the Roman practice because Peter held the keys of the kingdom of heaven and he did not want to be turned away for failing to acknowledge the authority he had been granted by Christ himself. The Synod of Whitby also ruled that monks would adopt the tonsure favoured by Rome featuring the 'halo' or 'corona' of hair rather than diverging styles (whose nature is largely unclear today) adopted by the Ionan monks. The long-term significance of the Synod of Whitby has divided opinion. Some argue that it led to the Romanisation of the 'Celtic Church' in Britain, a view often favoured following the Protestant Reformation. Others claim that this viewpoint has largely developed in later centuries and that the move to adopt Roman practices was fairly inevitable. Specifically, Alcfrith's primary interest in the convocation of the Synod of Whitby may well have been to develop his own power and influence by appointing bishops with a greater loyalty to himself.

St Boniface

St Boniface is particularly important to the development and conversion to Christianity of the Anglo-Saxon people. He is known today as the 'Apostle of the Germans' and is the patron saint of Germany. Boniface is also credited with helping to shape Western Christianity and, arguably, the course of European history. More specifically he became the Archbishop of Mainz and ultimately a martyr to his faith. But for a saint so closely linked to the history of German Christianity it may come as a surprise to some to find that Boniface was actually born in Devon, possibly at Crediton in 675. His given name at birth was Wainfrith although variations of his name from various lives of the saint name him as Wynfryth or Wynfrith.

It is thought that he was the son of Anglo-Saxon peasants who nonetheless were free and owned their own land. In the earliest recorded life of St Boniface, composed by a priest called Willibald shortly after his death, Boniface is said to have been educated at a monastery in Exeter ruled by Abbot Wulfhard. Willibald's account of his life also says that Boniface showed a devotion to a monastic life from childhood and that this was against the wishes of his family. Following his time at Exeter, Boniface received a further education at Nursling near Winchester whose abbot at that time was called Winbert. At Nursling, Boniface became a monk and a teacher in the abbey school and also composed the first Latin grammar to be produced in England. He also wrote poetry and a series of riddles or acrostics inspired by Aldhelm, the abbot of Malmesbury and later Bishop of Sherborne.

He was ordained as a priest at the age of 30 and he was chosen by Ina, king of Wessex between 688 to 726, to be an envoy for his synod to Burchard, the Archbishop of Canterbury. Because of his reputation as a teacher and evangeliser and possibly because of family relations, Boniface was offered the position of abbot at Nursling following the death of Abbot Wynberth. However, Boniface chose instead to become a missionary and, in 716, he travelled to Frisia which is today a coastal region that incorporates large parts of the Netherlands and northern Germany and was home to a Germanic-speaking people. He sailed to Utrecht and joined Willibrord who had been working there as a missionary for some time.

However, the efforts to convert the pagan inhabitants of the region were interrupted by a war between the Frankish leader Charles Martel and the Frisian leader Radbod. Radbod succeeded in taking over control of the region and became king of the Frisians. He was a pagan and he persecuted many Christians, destroying churches and killing missionaries. In the circumstances Willibrord, his monks and Boniface were forced to flee the country. Boniface returned to Nursling and was once again offered the position of abbot. He refused it and instead travelled to Rome in 718, hoping to be given an instruction from Pope Gregory II to pursue his missionary work. Gregory renamed him as Boniface in honour of the fourth-century martyr Boniface of Tarsus and appointed him as missionary bishop for Germany, focusing on an area that had no diocese at that time.

Whilst travelling to evangelise in the areas of Bavaria and Hesse, Boniface learned that circumstances had improved in Frisia, following the death of King Radbod, and he rejoined Willibrord there for a period of three years. He then went on to evangelise the mainly pagan region of Hesse under the protection of Charles Martel. At the time the Frankish leader was aiming to conquer the pagan Saxons and expand his own Christian empire and the work of Boniface and others was useful to him in gaining supremacy in these regions. A famous incident from the life of Boniface has him felling the Donar Oak close to the modern-day town of Fritzlar. As Boniface was cutting down the sacred oak, it is said a great wind suddenly blew the tree down. The local inhabitants were amazed at this and also that their pagan gods did not punish Boniface for his actions. As a result, many converted to Christianity and Boniface built a chapel dedicated to St Peter on the site with the wood from the oak tree. Boniface then moved on to Thuringia to continue his work as a missionary, supported by letters of encouragement from Pope Gregory and Daniel, Bishop of Winchester. It is interesting to note that the monasteries that were set up in the region at this time were often run by English monks and nuns who intended to convert their continental Saxon cousins. The purpose of creating monasteries was to found centres of Christianity but also to act as civic centres.

Boniface received a promotion in 732 from Pope Gregory III who awarded him the pallium, an ecclesiastical vestment, and raised him to the position of Archbishop. This meant that Boniface now had the power to consecrate bishops within Germany beyond the line of the River Rhine. He went on to found many bishoprics such as Erfurt for Thuringia. When, in 738, Charles Martel defeated the Saxons of Westphalia, it appeared that new territories had been opened up for Christian conversion. It was at this time that Boniface wrote a letter to his fellow countrymen 'begotten of the stock and lineage of the English' asking for their support and prayers in the conversion of the pagan Saxons who 'are of one blood and one bone with you'. However, although Boniface's English Christian countrymen did help with new missionaries and gifts such as books and vestments, Charles Martel lost control of Westphalia and the new venture was ended until the reconquest of the Saxons by Charlemagne.

In 738 to 739, Boniface travelled to Rome and held a synod for the German Christians. Although he is primarily known for his work as a missionary, Boniface also spent a considerable amount of time reorganising those of the converted Germans who had followed heretical paths and leaders who were not approved by the Vatican. Four dioceses were set up in Bavaria with the aid of Charles Martel. Martel died in 741 and was succeeded by Carloman. During his reign, Boniface introduced monastic reforms including making the Rule of St Benedict the house rule for every Carolingian monastery.

Carloman himself retired to a monastery in 747 and was succeeded by Pepin, with whom Boniface had a stormier relationship. Pepin intervened in church matters and Boniface aimed to maintain some independence from him by appointing his own bishops and maintaining papal support.

However, in 754, Boniface decided to hand over the business of church reforms to others and set off for Frisia to continue his earlier missionary work there. He was able to reconvert part of Frisia which had previously been converted but had lapsed. He also moved into north-east Frisia which was still primarily pagan. Boniface baptised many during this time and called a meeting on 5 June 754 for new converts close to Dokkum on the banks of the River Borne. Before the baptisms of the new converts could take place a group of armed pagan robbers arrived and killed Boniface and his companions. Following his murder, the body of Boniface was taken to Fulda which became the focus of veneration for his subsequent cult. In England, shortly after his martyrdom, an English synod convened to approve and set the date of his feast day and during this time he was viewed as being as significant a figure as Augustine and Gregory. However, although his feast day was widely celebrated and he was revered by many of the English, over time his reputation diminished rather than grew in England with later figures such as St Edmund, St Edward the Confessor and St George becoming identified as patron saints of the English. During the nineteenth and twentieth centuries there was a reassessment of the achievements of St Boniface by historians such as Christopher Dawson and Norman F Cantor who argued that he had played a major role in European history. Dawson in particular believed that he had been the most influential English figure in the development of Europe.

Chapter Three

The Kingdoms of Mercia and Wessex

Mercia

The Kingdom of Mercia was one of the kingdoms to emerge following the end of Roman rule in Britain. Traditionally, historians have considered Mercia as one of the seven kingdoms often known as the Anglo-Saxon Heptarchy. The term Mercia comes from the Old English word 'Mierce' which refers to 'border people' or borderlands. Today the term the 'Welsh Marches' refers to English counties that lie on the border of England and Wales such as Herefordshire and Shropshire and, in the past, historians often argued that the Kingdom of Mercia developed on the borders between the Welsh and the expanding Anglo-Saxon tribes. However, today the origins of Mercia are thought to be less certain. In the document known as the *Tribal Hidage*, written sometime between the seventh and ninth centuries, it appears to correspond to such modern counties as Leicestershire, southern Derbyshire, Northamptonshire, Nottinghamshire, Staffordshire and parts of Warwickshire.

The *Tribal Hidage* is a document that lists 35 tribes and the size and value of the territories they occupied. There has been considerable variation in assessing what the dimensions of a 'hide' of land actually constitute but it is often referred to as the amount of land needed by a freeman in order to be able to feed himself and his family. Historian Sarah Zaluckyj argues that the 'boundary referred to may have been… roughly that between today's southern Staffordshire and north-western Warwickshire' (Sarah Zaluckyj, *Mercia: The Anglo-Saxon Kingdom of Central England*, p13). Alternatively, it has been argued by P Hunter Blair that the border in question was the frontier between Northumbria and the line of the Trent river valley. The first recorded king of Mercia was a man called Creoda who reigned between 585 and 593, according to the twelfth-century chronicler Henry of Huntingdon.

However, some historians dispute the reliability of this and other sources. They have suggested that an actual King Creoda never existed and that his identity represents an attempt to fill in the gaps in the history of Mercia. Despite these doubts, it is also thought that there is enough evidence to suggest that the Kingdom of Mercia was in existence by the end of the sixth century. Creoda was said to have been the great-grandson of Icel who himself was thought by the Anglo-Saxons to have been the great-grandson of Offa of Angel. This semi-mythical figure claimed to be a descendant of the god Woden and is now considered to be largely a symbol of the migration of the Anglo-Saxon peoples to Britain. Creoda, therefore, was of illustrious stock and traditionally was said to have built a fortress at Tamworth which became the capital of Mercia. Creoda was succeeded by his son Pybba in 593. Following the reign of Pybba, Cearl, a relative of Creoda, became king of Mercia but little is known about either figure. However, Cearl's successor King Penda was to become a very powerful and influential figure in the history of Mercia.

Penda

King Penda of Mercia is now remembered as a particularly significant ruler because, during his reign, Mercia became probably the most powerful kingdom within Anglo-Saxon England during the seventh century. Penda was also a pagan king at a time when many other Anglo-Saxon kingdoms were turning to Christianity. He is thought to have been born in 606 and, according to the *Anglo-Saxon Chronicle*, he was the son of Pybba. The *Anglo-Saxon Chronicle* describes him as being descended from the Iclingas dynasty with an ancestry stretching back through Icel to the pagan god Woden himself. It also records that he became king in 626. It is thought likely that Penda became king of Mercia after creating an alliance with Cadwallon ap Cadfan, the British king of Gwynedd, against King Edwin of Northumbria sometime in the 620s or 630s. Edwin was the most powerful ruler of the Anglo-Saxon kingdoms but, according to the Venerable Bede, the Northumbrians were defeated by the combined forces of Cadwallon ap Cadfan and Penda in October 633 at the Battle of Hatfield Chase.

Edwin was killed during the battle and Cadwallon and Penda are described by the *Anglo-Saxon Chronicle* as having ravaged the Kingdom of Northumbria. Penda is also said to have taken Edwin's son, Eadfrith, as his prisoner. However, around a year later, Cadwallon was himself slain at the Battle of Heavenfield. It appears that, by this point, Penda was not involved in the conflict and he may have returned to Mercia to strengthen his position as king. Following the death of Cadwallon, Oswald of Bernicia became the king of Northumbria.

At some point during the reign of King Oswald, Penda defeated the East Angles in battle, probably between 635 and 641. During his battle with the East Angles their ruler King Egric was killed as was their previous king Sigebert. Penda's victory over the East Angles may have led King Oswald of Northumbria to decide that the Mercians would have to be defeated for the Northumbrians to have power in the south of England. According to Bede, the Mercians and the Northumbrians clashed again on 5 August 642 at the Battle of Maserfield. Penda defeated the Northumbrians and Oswald was killed during the battle. Once again Penda allied himself with Welsh forces, on this occasion teaming up with men from the Kingdom of Powys. Tradition states that the Battle of Maserfield took place at Oswestry in Shropshire. At this point in history, it is thought that Oswestry lay within the Kingdom of Powys, suggesting that Oswald had entered the territory of his enemies. According to Bede, Oswald, who was a Christian, prayed for the souls of his soldiers when he realised that he was going to be killed. He was 38 at the time of his death and, on the order of Penda, his body was cut into pieces as a sacrifice to Woden. His arms and head were placed on poles but were recovered the following year by his own brother Oswiu who succeeded him as king. Following his death Oswald was venerated as a Christian saint and martyr who had died at the hands of the pagan King Penda. It is thought that the name of the town of Oswestry derives from this event and the mutilation of his body, translating as 'Oswald's Tree'. The Welsh name for Oswestry is 'Croes Oswallt' which means 'Oswald's Cross'.

In two later chronicles, the *Annales Cambriae* and the *Historia Brittonum*, it is recorded that

Penda's own brother Eowa was killed in the Battle of Oswestry. Perhaps surprisingly, he is said to have been fighting for King Oswald and the Northumbrians. It is unclear why this was so but it may be that Eowa had been king of the northern Mercians whilst Penda ruled those in the south and that Eowa had recognised Oswald as his overlord. The significance of Eowa's death for Penda seems to have been that it left him in the position of being the most powerful king of the Mercians of that period. The death of Oswald appears to have had a major impact on the Kingdom of Northumbria as it became divided into two separate kingdoms. The northern region of Bernicia, which had previously been the more powerful of the two under Oswald, chose his brother Oswiu as their king. The southern region of Deira chose a new king called Oswine. Interestingly, in the aftermath of the Battle of Maserfield, the pagan king of the West Saxons, Cenwealh, married Penda's sister. This would suggest a strengthening of alliances and recognition of Penda's status at this time but events did not run smoothly as Cenwealh went on to put aside Penda's sister in favour of another wife. As a result, Penda had Cenwealh exiled to East Anglia in 645 for three years. This further suggests that Penda was the most powerful ruler of his time.

Following the Battle of Maserfield, Penda continued to wage war against the Northumbrians and launched a number of attacks on King Oswiu of Bernicia. Bede records Penda laying siege to Bamburgh castle. After failing to capture the Bernician stronghold, he then attempted to burn it down. Bede credits St Aidan with saving Bamburgh by praying for the wind to change and so turning the fire on the invading Mercians. Penda continued to attack and harass King Oswiu who seems to have avoided any pitched battles which perhaps suggests that Penda had greater military power at this time. Given the ongoing hostilities between the Northumbrians and the Mercians, it is surprising to find that, according to Bede, a marriage took place between Penda's son Peada and Oswiu's daughter Alchflaed in 653. It is also interesting to note that, as part of the conditions of the wedding, Peada willingly converted to Christianity and Penda allowed missionaries to preach amongst the people of the Middle Angles and Mercians. This religious tolerance on Penda's part would seem to suggest that both sides had something to gain by co-operating in this way.

Nonetheless, Penda once again attacked the Kingdom of Bernicia in 655. He was supported in this by Cadafael ap Cynfeddw of Gwynedd and his men. The southern Northumbrian kingdom of Deira, led by King Aethelwald, son of Oswald, also joined forces with Penda together with Aethelhere, king of the East Angles. The reason for Penda's invasion is unclear but he may have wanted to prevent a reunification of the two kingdoms of Northumbria. Initially, Penda laid siege to Oswiu at a place called Iudeu, which is now thought to have been Stirling, but he was perhaps paid off by the king of Bernicia and moved his army southwards. A major battle then took place at a location close to a river called the Winwaed which may have been a tributary of the River Humber. The Winwaed was in flood at the time and many of Penda's allies appear to have left the Mercian army, perhaps because they were unhappy with the outcome of the siege of Iudeu. With the forces of the Welsh king and Aethelwald gone and Penda apparently caught in a position of strategic weakness by the river in flood, the Northumbrians inflicted a major defeat on the Mercian side. Penda was killed during the battle as was Aethelwald, his remaining ally. According to Bede, many of the Mercians simply drowned in the river attempting to escape. Penda's head was cut off, perhaps in retribution for the mutilation he had inflicted on the body of King Oswald. Following Penda's defeat and death, King Oswiu gained power over Mercia. However, he allowed Peada to rule over the southern area of Mercia and, during the late 650s, Northumbrian power in Mercia was defeated. Penda was eventually succeeded by his younger sons Wulfhere and Athelred but his line came to an end with the death of his grandson Ceolred in 716. From that point on the descendants of his brother Eowa ruled Mercia for most of the following century.

The Venerable Bede

As we have seen, one of the most important surviving records of Anglo-Saxon history is the *Ecclesiastical*

History of the English People, written by the Venerable Bede and completed in 731. He was a monk at Jarrow and was trained as a biblical scholar. He is often referred to as the father of English history and the first to chronicle the history of the English people. Bede was born in 673 near Sunderland and, from the age of seven, he received an education from Benedict Biscop at Wearmouth. The name Bede derives from the Anglo-Saxon word 'beodan' meaning to 'bid or command'. His education was continued by Coelfrith at Jarrow. Bede's *Ecclesiastical History of the English People* is a valuable source of information on early English history and offers an intriguing insight into the conversion of the Anglo-Saxons to Christianity. In Book 2, Chapter 13 of his history Bede describes a meeting between King Edwin of Northumbria and his chief men during which the king proposed that they convert to Christianity. Following a speech given by the head priest, Coifi, one of Edwin's chief men is said by Bede to have made the following speech:

'Your Majesty, when we compare the present life of man on earth with that time of which we have no knowledge, it seems to me like the swift flight of a single sparrow through the banqueting-hall where you are sitting at dinner on a winter's day with your thegns and counsellors. In the midst there is a comforting fire to warm the hall; outside, the storms of winter rain or snow are raging. This sparrow flies swiftly in through one door of the hall, and out through another. While he is inside, he is safe from the winter storm; but after a few moments of comfort, he vanishes from sight into the wintry world from which he came.

Even so, man appears on earth for a little while; but of what went before this life or of what follows, we know nothing. Therefore, if this new teaching has brought any more certain knowledge, it seems only right that we should follow it.'

(Bede, *Ecclesiastical History of the English People*, p.129).

Bede was ordained as a priest in 703 and he demonstrated a love of and aptitude for studying Scripture, learning and teaching. He produced a range of writing at Jarrow including studies of the lives of the saints, astronomical chronologies and commentaries on Scripture. However, he is now best remembered for his famous history of the English. For a man who wrote such an epic account of the twists and turns and intrigues of the story of England, Bede travelled very little. Most of the information for his history was obtained from books supplied by Abbots Benedict Biscop and Coelfrith. His devotion to his monastic duties and writing were famed in his own lifetime and he had a reputation for his scholarship and knowledge that was unsurpassed by his contemporaries. An account of his death by the monk Cuthbert relates that his final days alive were spent singing psalms and translating the Gospel of St John into Old English. He is said to have died singing 'Glory be to the Father and to the Son and to the Holy Ghost' on Ascension Day 26 May 735. Following his death his cult was promoted by Alcuin, Boniface and others. His relics were translated from, or (in modern terms) his body was moved, from Jarrow to Durham Cathedral in around 1020 and placed in the same shrine as St Cuthbert, a clear sign of his status after his death. Bede was first referred to as 'Venerable' during the ninth century. He was declared a Doctor of the Church by Pope Leo XIII in 1899 and he is the only British saint to have been given this title.

Offa

King Offa of Mercia is today best known for having given his name to the great earthwork of Offa's Dyke. Offa ruled the Kingdom of Mercia from 757 to 796. Much of what is known about Offa is found in later sources. Bishop Asser, the Welsh biographer of King Alfred the Great, wrote of Offa, 'In modern times in Mercia there ruled a mighty king called Offa, who struck all the kings and regions around him with terror. He it was who ordered the great dyke to be constructed between Wales and Mercia, stretching from sea to sea.' (On the Deeds of King Alfred, Michael Wood, *In Search of the Dark Ages*, p.81). The dyke that Offa is said to have built is 64 miles in length and runs from a point close to the town of Mold in North Wales southwards to the River Wye in an area close to Hereford. Strictly speaking it does not run from 'sea to sea' but its northern end is extended by Wat's Dyke which runs onwards north to the estuary of the River Dee. Offa claimed that he was descended from King Offa of Angel, a figure from the epic poem *Beowulf*. He is described in *Beowulf* as having raised a 'boundary between his own people and their neighbours' and it is possible that Offa of Mercia was influenced by the story of one of his own legendary forefathers.

Offa came to power in the Kingdom of Mercia following the assassination of King Aethelbald who was killed by his own guards in 757. His heir Beornred was defeated by Offa during a period of civil war. According to the Anglian collection, which records some Anglo-Saxon royal genealogies, Offa was descended from Eowa, the brother of King Penda of Mercia and the son of King Pybba. Offa's father Thingfrith was the son of Eanwulf who was the son of Osmod, son of Eowa. King Aethelbald was also descended from Eowa and ruled Mercia for around 40 years. Beornred went into exile in Northumbria after his defeat by Offa but is thought to have had children. Later accounts of Offa's victory describe Beornred as a tyrant who had usurped the throne but these are probably influenced by Offa's version of events and written in order to support his claim to the crown. Offa was married to Cynethryth and they had five children together. They had four daughters called Aelfflaed, Eadburh, Aethelburgh and Aethelswith and a son called Ecgfrith.

There were frequent clashes between the Mercians and the Welsh during the reign of Offa. For example, they fought in 760 at Hereford and the *Annales Cambriae*, dating from the tenth century, also states that Offa was fighting them again in the years 778, 784 and 796. The ongoing conflict with the neighbouring kingdoms of the Welsh is the likeliest reason for the construction of Offa's Dyke although there is no clear agreement amongst historians about what its actual purpose was. Clearly it formed some kind of barrier against the Welsh and marks a territorial border. The dyke would also have given the Mercians important sightlines into Wales in order to keep a watch on any approaching hostile forces. It would also have been possible to mobilise troops along its length should Mercia have come under attack from the Welsh. In addition, it could have acted as a border control for any other movement between the two peoples.

Its considerable scale and length would also appear to demonstrate that the ruler who had it built was someone of great power with both money and manpower at his disposal. Some Anglo-Saxon villages were left on the Welsh side of the border perhaps because the Welsh had already captured them. The dyke consists of a giant bank and ditch which was around sixty feet across and eight feet in depth. Although traditionally the dyke is associated with the reign of King Offa, recent carbon dating research at points along its length has suggested that it may, in fact, have been begun earlier and have been the product of the work of several Mercian kings.

Author and TV historian Michael Wood has suggested that Offa was also the patron responsible for the building of All Saints' Church at Brixworth in Northamptonshire. This is widely regarded as one of the most important surviving examples of early Anglo-Saxon architecture in England. Michael Wood has argued that the church was built at some point during the late eighth century. The church contains architecture from a range of different periods but its earliest elements remain in the nave and the lower parts of the tower. It is thought that it originally had aisles or side chapels and its main west doorway which had a balcony above it was remodelled in the tenth century, producing the tower and stair turret which is still in existence. Wood argues that this major Anglo-Saxon church dates from the period when Mercian power was at its pinnacle. Perhaps most interestingly, All Saints' has a ring crypt at its eastern end which originally would have been roofed over. It lies outside the main body of the church and is a covered circular corridor located below ground level. It is likely that it housed a shrine containing an important relic and that pilgrims travelled to the church to see it. They would have passed through a doorway in the church, walked down a short flight of steps and then circulated along the semi-circular corridor where they would have presumably knelt and prayed in front of the relic in its shrine. They would then have continued along the short corridor back into the main body of the church. The doorways into and out of the ring crypt are blocked today but their outline can still be seen in the church and would probably have led on to the external stairs down to the former shrine and back up into the building. It is thought that the ring crypt at All Saints' was modelled on the ring crypt at St Peter's in Rome that was built by St Gregory the Great in around 600. Michael Wood has suggested that the ring crypt was designed and built to hold a relic of St Boniface because surviving documents demonstrate a particular veneration for the saint at Brixworth. (St Boniface, as we have seen, was a saint from Devon who was martyred in Germany in 754 whilst attempting to convert pagans to Christianity.) Wood also states that Brixworth was later used as a royal residence and that it was a Mercian royal church.

Offa's influence extended into other regions such as Kent and Sussex where he was viewed as an overlord. In 785, Offa negotiated with Pope Adrian I to split the archdiocese of Canterbury and establish a new archdiocese at Lichfield. This created tensions between Offa and Jaenberht who was the archbishop of Canterbury. In 785, Offa's son Ecgfrith was also consecrated as king at Lichfield by Hygeberht, the man appointed archbishop there. Offa's daughter Eadburh was married to King Beorhtric of Wessex in 789. Beorhtric ruled from 786 to 802, had close ties to Offa and recognised Mercian supremacy during his reign. East Anglia also recognised him as an overlord and his control was such that the *Anglo-Saxon Chronicle* records in 794 that 'Offa, king of Mercia, ordered Aethelbert's head to be struck off', although it does not give a reason why.

During his reign, Offa reformed Anglo-Saxon coinage which, at the beginning of the eighth century, consisted mainly of small silver pennies called 'sceattas'. These coins did not always indicate which king or moneyer was responsible for their creation. Offa had coins minted that bore his name and that of the mint that had made them and he also produced some of the first gold coins to be issued in Britain. The quality of the coins from Offa's mints was comparable to Frankish coinage and indicate a powerful and influential ruler at the height of his powers. Even Charlemagne, who would become the Emperor of the Carolingian Empire based around the Frankish state, acknowledged Offa as an equal, giving an insight into how he was viewed by other rulers during this period. However, although Offa had influence over much of southern England, he never achieved overlordship of Northumbria.

When Offa died on 29 July 796, he was succeeded by his son Ecgfrith. However, Ecgfrith only ruled for a period of 141 days before dying of an illness in December 796. Offa is thought to have been buried at an unknown site in the town of Bedford. Ecgfrith was succeeded by Coenwulf who was only distantly related to Offa.

Wessex

The Anglo-Saxon kingdom of Wessex emerged during the chaotic post-Roman period which is often termed as the Dark Ages. The *Anglo-Saxon Chronicle* claims that Wessex or 'the kingdom of the West Saxons' was founded by Cerdic and Cynric and that they arrived there in 495, with a party of followers filling five ships. They are described as being two princes and Cynric was the son of Cerdic. They are thought to have landed somewhere on the coast of Hampshire and fought a battle against the Welsh on the day of their arrival. Cerdic and Cynric are said to have fought a major battle in 508 in which they killed an important British king called

Natanleod along with 5,000 of his troops.

The *Anglo-Saxon Chronicle* relates that Cerdic became the first king of Wessex in 519. In the same year, the West Saxons launched an attack against the Britons at Cerdicesford but neither side gained the upper hand. Unable to defeat the Britons it appears that the West Saxons were obliged to reach an agreement with them, probably because of the damage inflicted on their forces. According to Gildas, the Battle of Mount Badon was fought between the British and the Saxons at this time and the Saxons suffered a heavy defeat. The chronicler Nennius claims that King Arthur fought at the Battle of Mount Badon but the *Anglo-Saxon Chronicle* says nothing about it. However, the treaty between the two sides seems to have ended in 530 when Cerdic and Cynric invaded and conquered the Isle of Wight.

Following the death of Cerdic in 534, Cynric succeeded him as King of Wessex. He was then succeeded by Ceawlin in 560 who continued to expand his territory into British-held areas such as Gloucester and Somerset. In 577, Ceawlin conquered a number of British towns including

Bath, Cirencester and Gloucester. The *Anglo-Saxon Chronicle* describes Ceawlin as being a 'bretwalda', meaning 'wide-ruler' or 'high king' at this time in the south of England. But he was to be overthrown in 592, probably by his nephew Ceol whom the *Anglo-Saxon Chronicle* says ruled for a period of five years until 597. Ceol was then followed by Ceolwulf as ruler. Ceolwulf was succeeded by Cynegils in 611. Cynegils' time in power is significant because he became the first West Saxon king to be baptised. According to the *Chronicle*, this took place in 635. Cynegils was baptised by Birinus who was the bishop of Dorchester on Thames and King Oswald of Northumbria stood as his sponsor. It is likely that the conversion of Cynegils was part of a pact between Wessex and Northumbria to join forces against Penda the pagan king of Mercia. Cynegils was succeeded by Cenwealh, who may have been his son, in 642. Interestingly, Cenwealh was a pagan when he first came to the throne as were most of the people of Wessex at this time, even following the baptism of Cynegils. Although Cenwealh was to marry the daughter of Penda, hostilities began again when he later rejected her. Penda invaded

Wessex and forced Cenwealh into exile in East Anglia for a period of three years. Cenwealh became a Christian during his time in East Anglia and was baptised in 645. Although Cenwealh returned as ruler of Wessex, hostilities continued between him and Penda's successor, Wulfhere.

The domination and power of the Kingdom of Mercia to the north of Wessex led in many ways to the expansion of Wessex into the south-west, particularly into Somerset. During the reign of Cenwealh Wessex became a Christian kingdom and, because of the continuing expansion of Mercia, Dorchester on Thames ceased to act as a bishopric. A new bishopric was founded at Winchester. This development was of major significance because Winchester would later become the capital of Wessex and eventually the capital of England. Cenwealh died in 673 and, unusually, Wessex was ruled by his wife Seaxburh for a period of one year. Seaxburh was succeeded by a descendant of Ceawlin called Aescwine who ruled for two years and he was followed by Centwine in 676, the brother of Cenwealh. Centwine reigned from 676 to 686 and was succeeded by Caedwalla. Caedwalla went on to conquer Kent, Sussex and the Isle of Wight although Wessex was not able to retain Kent and Sussex for very long. Caedwalla abdicated in 688 and he was succeeded by King Ine who was to rule Wessex for 38 years, a relatively long period in comparison to some of the short-lived reigns of his immediate predecessors. During his reign, Ine established a new bishopric at Sherborne and he is also remembered for establishing a law code in 694 which is one of the oldest to have survived from this period in English history. King Ine abdicated in 726 and went on a pilgrimage to Rome. Those who followed him also claimed to be descendants of Cerdic but, during the eighth century, Wessex was overtaken in power and influence by the Kingdom of Mercia to the north of their borders. Wessex continued to expand into western England eventually absorbing most of Devon, or Dumnonia, as it was known. It is likely that the kings of Wessex had at times to acknowledge the overlordship of Mercian rulers who claimed Gloucestershire and Oxfordshire as their own.

King Egbert

King Egbert is today recognised as one of the most significant rulers in the history of the Kingdom of Wessex. He is thought to have been born in either 771 or 775 and was the son of Ealhmund of Kent. An early genealogy found in the *Anglo-Saxon Chronicle* claims that he was descended from Ingild, the brother of King Ine of Wessex who ruled from 688 to his abdication in 726. Like many West Saxon kings Egbert's family claimed that their ancestry could be traced all the way back to Cerdic the founder of Wessex but many historians now dispute this. As previously mentioned, Wessex tended to be dominated during much of the eighth century by the Kingdom of Mercia. The power of Mercia reached a peak during the rule of King Offa who reigned from 757 to 796. Wessex was ruled during much of this period by King Cynewulf (757 to 786), who appears to have succeeded in remaining independent of Offa's control. Egbert's father Ealhmund became the King of Kent in 784 according to the *Anglo-Saxon Chronicle*. Ealhmund is not mentioned again in the *Chronicle* and it seems likely that he was driven from the throne by Offa who is known to have exercised power and control in Kent during this period and who probably wanted to conquer it himself. When King Cynewulf was murdered in 786, Egbert was amongst the potential successors but he was not chosen as King of Wessex. Instead, Beorhtric took the crown probably with the aid of King Offa and Egbert was driven into exile in France for a period which has been disputed but was probably between three and thirteen years. Significantly, Beorhtric is known to have married Offa's daughter in 789 and this may be the year in which Egbert was driven into exile. During his time in France, Egbert came under the patronage of Charlemagne, and William of Malmesbury later wrote in the twelfth century that Egbert had received an education and training in governance whilst there.

Offa died in 796 and was succeeded by his son Ecgfrith who only reigned for five months before he was succeeded by Coenwulf. In Wessex, Beorhtric was to reign until his death in 802. Following his death Egbert took the Wessex throne and it is thought he received support in achieving this from

Charlemagne. Although there was opposition to him from the Kingdom of Mercia, Egbert appears to have maintained independence from their control. In 815, he launched attacks on Cornwall 'from east to west' according to the *Anglo-Saxon Chronicle*.

In 825, he was once again involved in conflict in Devon and Cornwall at the Battle of Galford. The outcome of these actions was that Egbert conquered the western Britons of Devon and became effectively overlord of the Cornish. Coenwulf was then succeeded in Mercia by his brother Ceolwulf who, in turn, was overthrown by Beornwulf. By this time, Mercian power had gone into decline and, in either 825 or 826, Egbert scored a major victory for Wessex by defeating Beornwulf at the Battle of Ellendun, close to modern day Swindon. Egbert was quick to take advantage of this change in fortunes and marched on Kent, which he seized, followed by Essex, Surrey and Sussex – all regions that had previously been controlled by the kings of Mercia. In 829, Egbert went further still by invading and conquering Mercia itself and forcing its then king, Wiglaf, into exile. Following this notable victory Egbert was acknowledged as overlord by the king of

Northumbria. The *Anglo-Saxon Chronicle* records that he became the eighth 'bretwalda' or wide-ruler of Britain in the year 829. However, Egbert's time as high king was brief and the following year saw Wiglaf return to power in Mercia. Nonetheless, Egbert's gains in the south-east were to prove largely enduring.

During the later years of Egbert's reign, Wessex began to suffer the first Viking raids which would have a profound and lasting impact on the history of Anglo-Saxon England. Egbert was defeated by the Danes at Carhampton in 835 but he went on to win a victory against them at the Battle of Hingston Down in 838. He died the following year and was succeeded by his son Aethelwulf. Faced with a major invading Danish force in 851, Aethelwulf won a significant victory against them at the Battle of Aclea. His son Aethelbald claimed the throne of Wessex in 855 whilst Aethelwulf was visiting Rome. However, on the latter's return it was agreed that Aethelbald would retain control of the western areas of Wessex whilst Aethelwulf ruled in the south-east. Following the death of Aethelbald, another of Aethelwulf's sons Ethelbert became ruler of all

Wessex. He was followed by his brother Aethelred who, in turn, was succeeded by the youngest son of Aethelwulf and perhaps the most famous Anglo-Saxon king of them all, Alfred the Great.

Chapter Four

Alfred the Great

Alfred was born in 849 in a village called Wanating, which grew into the modern town of Wantage. At that time this was located in Berkshire but today Wantage falls within the boundaries of Oxford. He was the youngest son of King Aethelwulf of Wessex and his first wife Osburh. The *Anglo-Saxon Chronicle* records that Alfred was sent to the city of Rome when he was just four years old where he was anointed as king by Pope Leo IV. Because he had three living brothers who were older than he was, this seems unlikely. It may be that, as a letter from Leo IV seems to show, he was in fact invested as a 'consul' and that confusion arose from this at a later date. When Alfred returned to England in 856, his father Aethelwulf was deposed by his own son Aethelbald.

The Great Heathen Army

In 865, the *Anglo-Saxon Chronicle* records that a Danish force, described as a 'Great Heathen Army', arrived in East Anglia and threatened the Anglo-Saxon territories. The East Anglians supplied them with horses in return for peace and they were allowed to winter at Thetford. They then moved north and captured the city of York in 866. The *Chronicle* describes Alfred joining his brother Aethelred of Wessex in a military campaign against the Danes in 868. They attempted to drive them from Mercia but were unable to do so. In 869, the Danes returned to East Anglia where they defeated the army of King Edmund. According to some traditions Edmund was beaten, shot with arrows and beheaded for refusing to renounce Christianity. Another even more grisly tradition states that Edmund was subjected to the Viking practice of the 'blood-eagle' or 'spread-eagle' as an offering to their gods. In this, a victim was laid on his stomach whilst his ribs were cut away from their spine and his lungs were pulled out from his body. The orders for his death were said to have been given by the Danish leaders Ivar the Boneless and his brother Ubba. Over time the martyred king would become a hero and a national patron saint for the English for fighting against the Vikings and for refusing to renounce his faith.

By late 870, the Danish army had invaded Wessex and Alfred fought in nine battles against them in the twelve months that followed. Seven of the locations of these battles are known but two are not. The Anglo-Saxons achieved a victory at the Battle of Englefield on 31 December 870 but were badly beaten at the Battle of Reading the following month. However, just days later, Alfred is recorded as having achieved a great success at the Battle of Ashdown. Bishop Asser famously recorded that Alfred charged uphill and attacked the Viking army 'like a wild boar'. The Anglo-Saxon success did not last, however. They were beaten by the Danes at the Battle of Basing later in January 871 and again in March at the Battle of Merton.

Alfred became the ruler of Wessex following the death of his brother King Aethelred in April 871. Aethelred had agreed that Alfred should become king following his death because his own sons were not old enough to rule. However, the Danes were unrelenting in their assault upon Wessex and inflicted a further defeat upon the Anglo-Saxon army whilst Alfred was attending Aethelred's funeral. When Alfred did lead his army against them at the Battle of Wilton in May 871, the Danes were again victorious. Alfred was forced to seek terms with them and, although the details of the agreement are uncertain, the Danes are known to have left Reading and spent the winter in London. It is likely that Alfred bought them off, since he did not have the military strength at this point to drive them out of Wessex.

The uneasy peace in Wessex that Alfred had achieved through paying off the Danes ended five years later when the Vikings attacked Wareham in Dorset in 876. They had a new leader called Guthrum at their head and, although the Anglo-Saxon army contained them at Wareham, it was unable to force them out. Once again Alfred was obliged to negotiate with the Danes and reached an agreement with them to cease hostilities. Both sides exchanged hostages and swore oaths to uphold this new agreement. The *Anglo-Saxon*

Chronicle reports that Alfred asked Guthrum, the leader of the Vikings, to swear his oath on a holy ring. It is thought that the ring was probably a sacred golden arm ring linked to the worship of the god Thor and usually held in pagan temples. Later sources such as the *Eyrbyggja Saga* from the thirteenth century describe the placing of such golden rings on temple altars in Iceland and men swearing oaths on them. They also describe local chiefs wearing the arm ring at important assemblies. It is interesting that Alfred chose to make the Danish leader swear on such a ring given that he was a Christian king but it suggests both that he was prepared to try new ways of solving this crisis and that he had an awareness of the culture of the enemy he faced.

However, the Vikings soon reneged on the deal, killed their hostages and then, leaving Wareham, travelled to Exeter at night to avoid Alfred's forces. But this time Alfred was able to gain the upper hand by blockading the Viking fleet in Devon and cutting them off from further reinforcements or supplies. Guthrum was forced to meet Alfred's terms, and the Viking army left Wessex and travelled to Gloucester in Mercia at the beginning of the harvest season which began on 7 August in 877. Alfred spent that winter at one of his royal estates at Chippenham. However, even as Alfred and his household were celebrating Christmas on Twelfth Night 878, the Vikings led by Guthrum made a sudden and unexpected attack that saw many of Alfred's retainers killed and forced the king to flee for his life with just a small group of survivors. Alfred then travelled to the marshes of Somerset where, hidden and protected by the swamps and woods of the local landscape, he had a fort built at Athelney. Athelney was effectively an island amongst the marshes close to North Petherton and proved to be an effective base to fight back against the Viking occupation. Alfred was also able to draw military support from the areas of Hampshire, Somerset and Wiltshire.

It is from this period when he was in hiding in the marshes of Somerset that a legend has developed that has survived to the present day. The famous story tells how Alfred, at the low point of his reign, was wandering in the Somerset Levels and came upon a lowly peasant hut. He knocked on the door of the hut seeking food and shelter. The hut belonged to a swineherd and his wife who did not recognise that he was their king but welcomed him in and offered him their hospitality. The wife of the swineherd left Alfred to look after some cakes (or bread) she was preparing for them to eat but he was so immersed in the problems and difficulties that he faced that he failed to notice that they were burning in the oven. Upon her return the swineherd's wife is said to have fiercely scolded Alfred for his negligence. Even though he was her king Alfred accepted the scolding and bowed his head and promised to take better care in future.

The legend of Alfred and the burning cakes is almost certainly untrue and first appears in the *Life of St Neot* written 100 years after Alfred's time in the wilderness. Other later variations of the tale describe Alfred as a philosopher studying scripture who lets the cakes burn or as a warrior who is fletching arrows and fails to notice them catching fire. In the opinion of author Justin Pollard, the legend preserves a deeper message than simply the humbling of a king. 'The purpose of the story of the cakes is not to encourage kings to be humble… but to portray the dangers of failing to tend to the needs of a kingdom. In the four years leading up to 878, Alfred had been given the opportunity to prepare better defences for Wessex and to secure his position, but he had wasted this.' (Justin Pollard, *Alfred the Great*, p.177).

Interestingly, in the *Life of St Neot* in which the story first appears, St Neot acts as a teacher of sorts to Alfred and warns him that intemperance will lead to trouble for him. After St Neot dies, Alfred is indeed sorely troubled by the Viking invaders as king and is humbled both by God and the wife of the swineherd. However, following the story of the cakes, Alfred is said to have been visited by a vision of St Neot in a dream. In the prophetic dream St Neot assures him that he will ultimately overcome his enemies and achieve victory with the help of God. Another vivid tale to have survived concerning Alfred's trials and tribulations dates from the eleventh-century *Chronicle of St Neot* and the twelfth-century chronicle written by William of Malmesbury. In this tale Alfred adopts the disguise of a wandering minstrel in order to gain access to the camp of the Viking leader Guthrum where he is able to wander freely unrecognised. According to the tale the king is even able to enter the tent where Guthrum and his chiefs are feasting and overhear the plans that they are drawing up against him. When he has learned their secrets he then travels back to Athelney, armed with this invaluable knowledge.

Alfred spent his time in the marshes of Somerset conducting guerrilla attacks and raids on the occupying Danes but, most importantly, planning a major counter-attack against them. During Whitsunstide, which took place between 4 and 8 May 878, Alfred travelled to a place called Egbert's Stone where he had planned that the 'fyrds' or peasant levies of three counties would meet him. The people of Somerset, Hampshire and Wiltshire who were still loyal to him had been called together to fulfil their oaths towards their king by providing him with military service. The thegns, whose duty it was to raise the fyrds, had mustered an estimated 4,000 men and boys to march against the Vikings under Alfred's leadership. The day after the muster at Egbert's Stone Alfred's forces moved in a north-easterly direction towards Iglea or 'Iley Oak', a location now thought to be close to Warminster at

Eastleigh Wood in Sutton Verney. The site was a traditional gathering point that was used in later centuries as a meeting place for the courts of the Hundreds of Heytesbury and Warminster. It is likely that Alfred chose the spot to bring together as many soldiers as possible and there he laid out his plans and prepared them for battle.

The Battle of Edington

When Guthrum learned that Alfred had raised an army against him he marched his men from their fortified position at Chippenham to the Iron Age hill fort of Bratton Camp at the edge of the Salisbury Plain escarpment. It is likely that Guthrum chose this point to assemble his troops because he would have known that Alfred would be passing by it on one of the routes that ran to Chippenham where he would confront the Danes. Alfred marched his army up the line of hills on which Bratton Camp stands and came into the view of the Vikings' assembled shield wall. It would have been significant to Alfred that the date in the Christian calendar upon which he was going into battle was Whitsun. Whitsun celebrates the meeting of the apostles 50 days after the resurrection of Christ when the Holy Ghost descended upon them and allowed them to speak in tongues as proof that he was risen again. It was also 50 days since Alfred had been in hiding at his fortified camp at Athelney and there must have been a sense of rebirth for the returning king who intended to take back his kingdom. Alfred moved his forces to the nearby location of Edington which lies below Bratton Camp. Both sides drew up into formation and formed their shield walls against each other. The following battle was a lengthy, brutal and stubborn meeting of the two opposing forces. There was no quick victory but, towards evening, the West Saxons broke through part of the Viking shield wall and the Danes began to give ground. Finally, Guthrum appears to have taken the decision to retreat and return to the fortified position he had been occupying at Chippenham. Alfred pursued the retreating Viking army, killing as many as possible, and followed them all the way to their stronghold.

It appears Guthrum and some of his men reached

Chippenham and barricaded themselves inside. Alfred surrounded them, killed any fleeing Vikings and removed any supplies that the trapped Danes could use to prolong the siege. After two weeks under siege, Guthrum sought terms with Alfred for the release of his men. Hungry and fearful, this time the Vikings made no demands against Alfred, a reflection of the desperation of their position. They agreed that Alfred would take as many hostages as he wanted whilst he would give none to Guthrum. Alfred was now in a position to have killed Guthrum, if he wanted, but he was also aware that this could lead simply to the emergence of another Viking leader and a continuation of the threat that plagued his reign. This time, rather than have Guthrum swear oaths on a gold arm ring, he insisted that the Viking leader convert to Christianity and made him swear to abide by a Christian peace. Although such a strategy could seem naïve, given Guthrum's behaviour in the past and his obvious willingness to break oaths, it seems that Alfred had a more complex plan in mind. He did not intend simply to convert Guthrum but actually to make him a Saxon prince, thus giving him land and power but within the Saxon system of loyalties and duties which would control his actions. This would mean Guthrum had more to lose by opposing Alfred than by supporting him. He was, in short, to be integrated into the existing system as an effective means of controlling him.

Three weeks after the surrender at Chippenham, Guthrum and 29 of his most important men were baptised at the royal estate of Wedmore, close to Athelney. Both leaders negotiated an agreement known as the Treaty of Wedmore. It initially appears to have been a verbal arrangement and a written treaty was not signed until 879 or 880. The Treaty of Wedmore demanded that the Vikings leave Wessex and return to East Anglia. In 879, the Vikings travelled to Cirencester and King Coelwulf II of Mercia was deposed the following year. The written treaty of Alfred and Guthrum then divided the Kingdom of Mercia between the two leaders. Its boundary ran along the Thames to the River Lea and along its length to a point close to Luton and then on to Bedford and along the River Ouse until it met Watling Street.

Alfred effectively took control of western Mercia

under the terms of their treaty and Guthrum ruled East Anglia and the eastern area of Mercia. This new kingdom became known as the Danelaw. Importantly, under the terms of the treaty, Alfred retained control over the city of London. It is also thought likely that Alfred continued to hold sway over most of Essex, although the treaty does not explicitly record this. In 879, a new Viking fleet had arrived in London and wintered there. However, following the Treaty of Wedmore and Guthrum taking up power in East Anglia, these Vikings appear to have decided to abandon any plans either to join him or to carry out attacks of their own. They sailed instead for Ghent where they raided and pillaged between 879 and 892.

Although Alfred had managed to overcome the Viking threat to his power, Wessex had suffered badly in the years of conflict. Monasteries had been destroyed and their possessions taken; Alfred's purse had been emptied paying off the Danes; farmers had neglected their work in order to fight for him; and law and education were both areas of serious concern for the king. The conflict had left Alfred's kingdom in a state of near ruin and it was now imperative that every effort be made to rebuild and, if possible, improve it. The greater significance of Alfred's reconstruction of Wessex in the years that followed the Treaty of Wedmore is that it is now viewed as marking the beginnings of the birth of England as a unified country in its own right.

The threat from Guthrum had been contained by Alfred but there would continue to be attacks mounted by other Danish raiders, albeit on a greatly reduced scale. For example, in 881, there was a sea battle between Anglo-Saxon and Danish ships during which two of the Danish vessels were destroyed and the other two surrendered. As this illustrates, Alfred had largely gained control of his kingdom but he would continue to be threatened by Danish incursions for the rest of his reign. One of the most important actions that Alfred took in this more peaceful period was to reorganise his old council, or witan, which had failed him during his period of exile in the marshes of Somerset and capitulated to the Danes. Documents and charters from this period show that most of the ealdormen who were called on to attest them were removed from their positions and new ealdormen put in their place. They were men that Alfred felt he could trust, probably because he had given them power, rather than those who had served before and who had acted in their own interests.

Because of Alfred's loyalty and financial support to the church in Rome, Pope Marinus sent the English king a number of gifts around 883. Alfred is said to have received a piece of the true cross and, as a recognition of the close relationship between the Pope and himself, all Anglo-Saxons then living in Rome were exempted from paying any form of taxes. In 886, Alfred began the task of resettling and reorganising the city of London which had been largely abandoned during the Viking attacks. Alfred established a market and a harbour in London so that trade could resume again. Significantly, he created a new street plan for the city and many of the streets in the city today follow the same pattern that he introduced. He also strengthened and fortified the existing Roman walls of the city located on the north bank of the Thames and may also have built fortifications on the south bank of the river. The work was carried out by his son-in-law Aethelred, who was an ealdorman of Mercia.

In 888, Aethelswith, who was the sister of Alfred, is recorded by Bishop Asser as having died whilst travelling to Rome. The following year, Guthrum, the king of East Anglia, also died and was buried in Suffolk. The death of Guthrum inevitably led to further trouble for Alfred as other Danish leaders set their sights on taking his place and began planning more attacks. During the early 890s, a Danish army sailed to England and landed in two separate groups at Appledore and Milton in Kent. The Danes were accompanied by their families which demonstrated to Alfred that they intended not simply to attack and plunder and then flee but to settle in England. The Danish force at Appledore struck out to the north of their position but were intercepted by Alfred's eldest son Edward who defeated them.

Simultaneously the East Anglian and Northumbrian Danes besieged Exeter and Alfred turned his attentions to their forces and broke the siege. The Danes who had landed in Kent attempted to join with the Danes in the west of England but were contained by the Anglo-Saxons. They did travel as far as Chester, which they occupied, but they were forced to leave because of a lack of food in either 894 or 895 and returned to Essex. Further manoeuvring took place between the Anglo-Saxons and the Danes but the latter abandoned any further attempts at conquest in 896 or 897 and instead retreated either to East Anglia, Northumbria or their homes in northern Europe. During the more peaceful years of his reign, Alfred had taken steps to reorganise the military defence of Wessex. The traditional system of the fyrd in Anglo-Saxon England involved local freemen responding to calls for military service when the king asked for it. However, one of its major disadvantages was that it was too slow to respond to the swift raids of the Danes who often chose vulnerable targets to attack and plunder and then withdrew to a fortified position where they could resist the Anglo-Saxons. When the Danes attacked again in the 890s, they were met by a standing army that could travel rapidly through England.

Alfred also set up a system of fortified towns with their own garrisons and reorganised his navy to patrol important rivers and their estuaries against Viking attacks. It is thought that Alfred may have been influenced in his restructuring of the defences of his kingdom by the Carolingian king Charles the Bald whom he had met during one of his visits to Rome. The Carolingians had also had to deal with Viking raids and it is likely that Alfred adopted some of their strategies in order to better organise and defend his own kingdom. Perhaps most famously, Alfred set up a series of fortified 'burhs', often based in former Roman towns which were refortified and strengthened against invasion. This network of burhs was laid out strategically, being about 30 miles apart from each other, so that the garrison of one burh could travel to the next in under a day's march. Alfred envisaged these towns as both places of military strength and flourishing sites of trade. Many of the burhs that Alfred established, or re-established, developed into market towns and cities that are still in existence and thriving today. They include Bath, Chichester, Cricklade, Hastings, Malmesbury, Shaftesbury, Southampton, Wallingford and Winchester. He was able to pay for his new military plans by changing the existing system of taxation. A tenant in Anglo-Saxon England was assessed for taxation and military service on their landholdings and how many 'hides' of land they possessed. A single hide was the minimum amount of ground that a family could live off. Alfred taxed his people financially and in terms of military service on the basis of how many hides of lands they held.

A document from this period, now referred to as the *Burghal Hidage*, has provided an insight into how Alfred's new system worked. For example, each hide of land was required to provide one man to defend a local burh. There is a formula in the appendix to the *Burghal Hidage* for calculating how many men would be needed to man a section of wall and how much land is needed to feed them: 'If every hide is represented by one man, then every pole (16.5 feet) can be manned by four men. Then for the maintenance of twenty poles of wall eighty hides are required.' (Justin Pollard, *Alfred the Great*, p.214). Wallingford is listed as having a hidage of 2,400 so the local landowners were required to provide and feed 2,400 men, because that was the number needed to man 9,900 feet or 3 kilometres of wall. Winchester also had 2,400 hides of land and 9,900 feet of wall to be defended. Interestingly, Winchester was rebuilt by Alfred within the ground plan of the old Roman walls which measures 9,954 feet, a close match for the recorded formula that Alfred used.

Laws and Learning

Alfred also took time to introduce legal reforms in his kingdom after the establishment of the Danelaw and the relative peace it provided. He produced a law code in the late 880s or early 890s based on his own judgements and those of his councillors but that also included a law code produced by King Ine of Wessex in the late seventh century. The whole work is made up of 120 chapters and was based on the laws of earlier rulers such as King Ine, King Offa and King Aethelbert of Kent. Alfred had a reputation for giving a great deal of thought to legal matters and Bishop Asser records that he would often personally review contested judgements in the interests of fairness and justice.

The Alfred Jewel

One of the most fascinating objects to have survived from the Anglo-Saxon period is the Alfred Jewel. It is a particularly fine example of Anglo-Saxon metalwork and is made from gold, quartz and enamel. It was discovered in 1693 at Petherton Park, North Petherton in Somerset. At that time, the land was owned by Sir Thomas Wroth. North Petherton is located around eight miles away from Athelney where Alfred the Great retreated from the Danish invaders and later founded a monastery. In the past, there was considerable speculation about what the Alfred Jewel actually was and suggestions ranged from some form of pendant to part of an elaborate headdress. However, it is now widely accepted that it is part of an 'aestel' or pointer which was used for the purpose of reading books. There are clear parallels between the Alfred Jewel and the Jewish implement known as the Yad that is used in Jewish synagogues to point at a copy of the Torah when it is being read or recited. There is a socket in the base of the jewel which, it is thought, would have held a pointer perhaps made of ivory that would have been pointed at the line of writing being read. The back of the Alfred Jewel is flat and made of gold and carries the engraving of some form of plant and may symbolise the tree of life. The jewel has a teardrop shape and it is now thought that it was created around an already existing piece of rock-crystal, perhaps from a recycled piece of Roman jewellery. In the past, there was speculation that the figure on the Alfred Jewel may have been St Cuthbert but it is much more likely to be a representation of Christ. The figure has large, stylised eyes and it seems likely that this is a reference to the sense of sight and the act of looking or reading which would, of course, be highly appropriate for such an object.

A silver brooch, made during the same period as the Alfred Jewel and now held at the British Museum, has been engraved with figures that represent the five senses and one of the figures representing the sense of sight is also holding two plant stems or flowers just as the figure on the Alfred Jewel does. The Alfred Jewel also features an inscription that reads 'AELFRD MEC HEHT GEWYRCAN' that translates as 'Alfred ordered me to be made'. Alfred produced a translation of Pope

Gregory the Great's *Pastoral Care* in 890 and had copies sent to monasteries around the country. He also sent an aestel with each copy for the purpose of reading it with great concentration and solemnity and perhaps also as a reminder of his authority and power. The Alfred Jewel is thought to be a surviving example of these aestels. It is currently on display at the Ashmolean Museum in Oxford and there is a replica at the Church of St Mary's in North Petherton, Somerset.

Beowulf

The oldest surviving example of Old English poetry is the epic story of *Beowulf*. Although its author is unknown, it is widely considered to be one of the most significant works to have survived from the Anglo-Saxon period. The poem is 3182 lines long and its events take place in Scandinavia. However, it was composed in England somewhere between the eighth and eleventh centuries but its narrative is set between the fifth and seventh centuries. *Beowulf* blurs the line between actual historical events, people and places and myth and legend.

The story centres on Heorot, the great hall of Hrothgar, the King of the Danes, which comes under a fierce attack by the grotesque monster Grendel. The king and his men are unable to rid themselves of Grendel so Beowulf, a warrior hero of the Geats, travels to Heorot and kills Grendel by tearing his arm off. He also pursues and kills the mother of Grendel with a giant's sword he finds in the cavern underneath a lake in which she lives. Beowulf finds the body of Grendel in the cavern and cuts off its head and returns to Heorot where he gives it to King Hrothgar. He finds great fame and honour through his deeds and later becomes King of the Geats. Beowulf's own kingdom comes under attack by a ferocious dragon because treasure from the dragon's hoard at Earnaness has been stolen by a slave which sends it into a terrible fury. Although Beowulf and his warriors attack the dragon they do not manage to kill it. So terrified of the dragon are the Geats that only Beowulf and his relative Wiglaf have the courage to follow the creature to its lair and attempt to put an end to its attacks. Beowulf finally succeeds in killing the dragon but suffers terrible wounds and dies soon afterwards. The Geats cremate their king and build a great burial mound close to the sea in remembrance of him.

There has been considerable debate about the origins and authorship of *Beowulf*. It has been suggested that the Beowulf story was carried to England with Geatish settlers. Others, including Sam Newton, have argued that Beowulf was written during the seventh century in East Anglia because the nearby Sutton Hoo burial mounds demonstrate strong ties to Scandinavian culture. However, it has also been suggested that *Beowulf* was composed at either the court of Alfred the Great or that of King Canute. The poem has survived as a single manuscript that is thought to date from around 1000. It was collected by the sixteenth-century scholar Laurence Nowell in a manuscript along with several other medieval works including *Wonders of the East* which is a fantastical account of overseas lands and people, a life of St Christopher and a version of the *Book of Judith*. The *Nowell Codex* as it is now known was acquired by Sir Robert Bruce Cotton who lived from 1570 to 1631. He was a member of parliament and an antiquarian who founded the Cotton library, a private library that housed a hugely important selection of early English manuscripts.

Kevin Kiernan argues that the *Beowulf* manuscript that has survived to the present day was, in fact, the work of two scribes who had themselves worked from an original source. One scribe had written up until line 1939 at which point the handwriting changes, demonstrating that another individual had taken over at that point. It has also been widely argued that the *Beowulf* manuscript had its origins in an oral, spoken tradition passed down over many generations before being written down in its surviving form. Scholars such as Albert Lord and DK Crowne have argued that *Beowulf* was composed orally and passed down in that form. Debate has focussed on whether *Beowulf* is largely a product of a pagan, Germanic, oral culture or that of a Christian worldview, strongly influenced by Latin and the written word, or is indeed a product of both cultures. The characters found in *Beowulf* are pagans from Scandinavia but the *Beowulf* manuscript was written by Anglo-Saxon scribes perhaps several centuries after the conversion to

Christianity during the seventh century. However, Anglo-Saxon and Scandinavian paganism have their roots in Germanic pagan beliefs and therefore have a shared history and culture.

Death of Alfred the Great

Alfred died on Friday 26 October 899 at the age of either 50 or 51. Although the cause of his death is not known, Bishop Asser recorded that he had suffered from an illness which caused him great pain and discomfort. In more recent years, it has been suggested that Alfred suffered from haemorrhoidal disease or Crohn's disease based on Asser's descriptions of his symptoms. He was initially buried in the Old Minster at Winchester in 899 but his body was moved to the New Minster in 903. The New Minster may have been specifically built for the purpose of housing his remains. In 1441, Henry VI of England attempted to persuade the church in Rome to have Alfred canonised but this was rejected. However, in the Anglican Communion, he is recognised as a Christian hero and has as his feast day 26 October. In many ways, Alfred's reputation is a product of the books of translations he produced in his lifetime that were known by historians and writers in the centuries following his death. He first came to be termed 'Alfred the Great' during the sixteenth century when his love of learning and his military achievements earned him his reputation as a wise and just king.

Chapter Five

The Rise of the Danish Invaders

King Edward the Elder and Aethelflaed, Lady of the Mercians

Following the death of Alfred the Great in 899, he was succeeded as king of the Anglo-Saxons by his son, Edward the Elder. However, although Edward inherited his father's throne many of the successes and victories that he went on to win would be due to the support and assistance of his sister, Aethelflaed. Aethelflaed, Lady of the Mercians, is one of the most significant and often overlooked figures of the Anglo-Saxon period. She was the eldest child of Alfred the Great and was born around 870. Her mother was Ealhswith, Queen of the Mercians, the daughter of Aethelred Mucel, an ealdorman of a Mercian tribe known as the Gaini. Aethelflaed's family background was important in forming an alliance through marriage between the kingdoms of Mercia and Wessex. She married Aethelred, Lord of the Mercians, in around 886. They had at least one child together, a daughter called Aelfwynn.

Aethelred joined King Alfred in his campaigns against the Vikings during the 890s. They were a powerful and influential couple and Athelstan, the son of Edward the Elder, grew up in their court. Aethelflaed and Aethelred worked hard together to strengthen Mercian power in a number of ways, including fortifying Worcester and giving money to the church in Mercia. However, Aethelred was older than his wife and, during the early 900s, his ill health meant that Aethelflaed became the main ruler of Mercia. After his death in 911, she became sole ruler under the title Lady of the Mercians. As ruler, Aethelflaed continued the work of her father who had fortified a number of towns or 'burhs'. She ordered the creation of defences for towns, including Tamworth, Bridgnorth, Stafford and Runcorn amongst others. At Bridgnorth in Shropshire, Aetheflaed built defences in 912 to protect a bridge on the River Severn. The following year, fortifications were constructed at Tamworth to provide protection from the Danish forces occupying Leicester.

She achieved a major military victory against the Vikings when her army seized Derby in 917 which, at that time, was one of the Five Boroughs of the Danelaw. This was followed by the submission of the Danes in East Anglia to her brother Edward the Elder and, in 918, Aethelflaed took control of Leicester. She continued to gain power in Danish-held regions but developing events such as the submission of York to her were cut short by her death. She died on 12 June 918 at Tamworth and was buried at St Oswald's Priory in Gloucester alongside her husband Aethelred. The couple had founded St Oswald's Priory and it appears to have been intended to serve as a royal mausoleum for them. Their burials were likely to have been close to the remains of St Oswald himself. Aetheflaed was initially succeeded as Lady of the Mercians by her daughter Aelfwynn. Her rule was to prove extremely short-lived as Edward the Elder removed her from power in December 918 and sent her to live in the Kingdom of Wessex. Mercia then came directly under the control of Edward himself.

King Athelstan

Following the death of Edward the Elder at Farndon in northern Mercia in July 924, he was succeeded by his son Athelstan as King of the Mercians. However, Athelstan's half-brother Aelfweard was initially recognised as King of Wessex. It is thought that Athelstan may have had to fight some form of civil war in Wessex in order to secure his claim to power there. However, Aelfweard died only three weeks after his father, Edward, and Athelstan was crowned on 4 September 925. At the time of his death, Edward had controlled all England south of the River Humber. The two separate kingdoms of Northumbria were being ruled by different kings at this stage. King Ealdred held power in the majority of the northern area of Northumbria known as Bernicia. York and the southern area of Northumbria was ruled by King Sihtric who was a Viking in origin. Scotland was ruled by King

Constantine II and Wales was formed of a number of separate kingdoms. Much of what is known about Athelstan was recorded by William of Malmesbury in his chronicle *Gesta Regum Anglorum* or *Deeds of the English Kings* which was completed in 1125. William of Malmesbury wrote that Athelstan was the oldest and tallest son of Edward the Elder and that he succeeded him as king in Wessex and Mercia when he was 30. Athelstan's mother was a consort of Edward called Ecgwynn and there has been disagreement about her background and social status.

William of Malmesbury claimed that, before he died, Alfred the Great had presented Athelstan with a scarlet cloak, jewelled belt and a Saxon sword with an elaborately designed scabbard as part of a special ceremony. Michael Wood has argued that the purpose of the ceremony was for Alfred to mark him out as a potential king to follow in the footsteps of his father Edward. Edward took another wife, perhaps around the time of the death of Alfred the Great, called Aelfflaed. This may have been because Ecgwynn died or it is possible that he simply chose to put her aside. This made

Athelstan's position as heir more precarious as his new stepmother had two sons called Aelfweard and Edwin who she hoped would succeed their father as king. However, Edward married for a third time in 920, putting aside Aelfflaed in favour of a new bride called Eadgifu. As previously mentioned, it is thought that Athelstan was educated at the court of Aethelred and Aethelflaed in Mercia. His aunt and uncle also provided him with military training and experience in their campaigns against the Vikings.

Following his father's death in 924, the dispute over whether Athelstan or his brother Aelfweard should succeed him was ultimately decided by Aelfweard's sudden death only 16 days after the death of his father. Athelstan had the backing of Mercia but appears to have been opposed in Wessex because his mother Ecgwynn was Edward's consort and not his wife at the time of Athelstan's birth. Edward's later wives were termed queens but Ecgwynn was not. It has been argued that Athelstan took the decision not to marry or have children in order to gain wider acceptance and to appear as a kind of caretaker king until the succession of his half-brothers Edmund and Eadred. It may be that the popular opinion was that the legitimate bloodline of King Alfred should be preserved. Alternatively, the historian Sarah Foot has argued that Athelstan's decision not to marry or have children was motivated by religious concerns and that he deliberately chose a life of celibacy. When Athelstan was crowned on 4 September 925, the coronation took place at Kingston upon Thames. This location may have been significant because it lay on the borders of the kingdoms of Wessex and Mercia and may have represented an attempt to symbolise the unification of the two regions under his kingship. However, the initial stages of his reign did not run smoothly. William of Malmesbury records that he narrowly avoided a plot to seize and blind him in Winchester organised by a nobleman called Alfred. If he had been blinded, he would have been viewed by Anglo-Saxon society as ineligible to rule as king. In 933, Athelstan's half-brother Edwin drowned in the North Sea whilst attempting to flee to France. It may be that he had been attempting some form of coup or rebellion against the king that had failed. In all likelihood, his death helped put an end to the opposition of Winchester to Athelstan's reign.

Athelstan had inherited territory from his father Edward that had been taken from the Danish settlers in East Anglia and Mercia. However, as previously mentioned, King Sihtric, who was of Danish descent, was the ruler of the Viking Kingdom of York. This territory was the kingdom formerly known as Deira, the ancient southern kingdom of Northumbria. In order to build an alliance with Sihtric, Athelstan arranged for one of his sisters to marry the Viking ruler in January 926. Both agreed that they would not attack their respective kingdoms or support others intent on wresting power from them. The agreement was to prove short-lived because Sihtric died the following year. Athelstan then invaded the Kingdom of York although he was challenged by a cousin of Sihtric called Guthfrith. It is not known whether Athelstan succeeded to the throne through force of arms or through the agreement of the leaders of the region. His succession may have proved controversial at the time as the north had traditionally resisted rule by southern kings. Athelstan also forced the Anglo-Saxon earl Ealdred Ealdulfing to submit to him by attacking his stronghold at Bamburgh. Ealdred had previously acted autonomously but accepted Athelstan as his overlord. The English king sent emissaries to the kings north of the border and in Wales, demanding that they submit to him with the threat that, if they failed to do so, he would declare war on them. Faced with such a powerful enemy, they accepted his terms. On 12 July 927, King Constantine of Scotland, King Hywel Dda of Deheubarth and King Owain of Strathclyde met with Athelstan at Eamont, close to Penrith, and acknowledged him as their overlord or high king.

Following this victory in the north, Athelstan moved his army southwards and focussed his attention on the kings of Wales. Although they had previously pledged their allegiance to Edward the Elder, Athelstan seems to have faced both hostility and resistance from them. Their leader was Idwal Foel of Gwynedd but Athelstan defeated them in battle in 927. (Hywel Dda, the king of Deheubarth, who strongly supported Athelstan and the kings of England, had not joined the rebellion.) Following these events, Athelstan summoned the kings of Wales to a meeting at Hereford. There they acknowledged him as 'mechteyrn', meaning 'great king', and accepted his authority over them. Athelstan demanded of them a very large annual tribute that consisted of 20 pounds of gold, 300 pounds of silver and 25,000 oxen. Additionally, they agreed that they would supply him with as many hounds and hawks as he demanded of them. Furthermore, Athelstan defined the border between England and Wales on the River Wye close to Hereford. Athelstan's victory over the Welsh secured peace between the two nations throughout his reign although many Welsh resented his power over them. In a Welsh poem of the time called 'Pyrdein Vawr', or the 'Great Prophecy of Britain', it was predicted that the peoples of Wales would eventually rise against the Anglo-Saxons and drive them out of their former territories.

Athelstan then set his sights on the kings of Cornwall who were often referred to as 'the West Welsh'. According to William of Malmesbury, he drove them from the city of Exeter and set a new boundary between Cornwall and Wessex at the River Tamar. Athelstan also restored the old Roman walls of Exeter and resettled the city with West Saxons. Significantly, he also established a new see in Cornwall at St Germans and appointed a bishop of his own choosing. Athelstan went on to visit Exeter on a number of occasions where a new minster was built and gifted with lands by him. This remarkable series of successes made Athelstan the first high king of all of the Anglo-Saxons and placed him as the effective overlord of all of Britain. He held a great court in Exeter at Easter 928 which was probably intended to mark this achievement. From this time onwards, the kings of Scotland and Wales would attend the assemblies that Athelstan held and would witness and sign his charters. He made attempts to strengthen his position in the north of England, giving gifts to his allies such as the territory of Amounderness in Lancashire which he handed to the Archbishop of York. Athelstan's achievement in unifying Britain under his rule cannot be underestimated. No other Anglo-Saxon king had achieved this and he was now the most powerful figure in British history since the days of the Roman emperors. His reputation spread far and wide as the rulers of Europe acknowledged his power and achievements. Athelstan also created and enforced new law codes during his reign, reflecting the fact that for the first time many disparate regions had been unified through him.

The relative peace of Athelstan's rule was broken in 934 when he invaded Scotland. It is unclear why he did so, but a likely explanation is that Constantine, the king of the Scots, broke his treaty and refused to pay Athelstan tribute. John of Worcester, writing in the twelfth century, recorded this as the reason for the invasion although another explanation could have been a dispute over territory between Constantine and Athelstan following the death of a ruler who may have been Ealdred of Bamburgh. Athelstan assembled an army at Winchester on Whit Sunday 934. It included the forces of four Welsh kings, Hywel Dda of Deheubarth, Morgan ap Owain of Gwent, Idwal Foel of Gwynedd and Tewdwr ap Griffri of Brycheiniog. He then travelled to Nottingham where he was met by six Danish earls from the east of England. On his journey north, Athelstan visited the shrine of St Cuthbert at Chester-le-Street which he reached in either June or early July. He prayed for the aid of the saint in his war against the Scots and gave rich gifts to the shrine. These included a stole and a maniple made of precious silks from the Byzantine Empire which have survived in part and are still held at Durham Cathedral today, together with the body of St Cuthbert. Athelstan promised further gifts if the invasion was a success and, perhaps highlighting his devotion to the cult of St Cuthbert, also asked his brother to bury him alongside the saint should he be killed during the conflict.

However, Athelstan's forces far outnumbered those of the Scottish king and, alongside those already mentioned, drawn from all over Britain, they were accompanied by a fleet of Mercian and West Saxon origin which travelled up the coast to Scotland. Athelstan ravaged the land as far north as Dunnottar, a fortress in north-east Scotland which is located south of Aberdeen. The English fleet sailed as far north as Caithness which they raided and which was probably a part of the Norse kingdom of Orkney. As part of his campaign of retribution, Athlestan took animal livestock from the Scots in compensation for the breach of his treaty. No battles are recorded during the campaign and it seems likely that Constantine was painfully aware that he could not challenge the military might of

Athelstan and submitted once again to his rule. As part of the renewal of his treaty with Athelstan, the Scottish king gave his son as a hostage and the two kings exchanged gifts. Having restored his control in the north, Athelstan rode south, accompanied by Constantine, who witnessed a charter at Buckingham on 12 September 934 in which he is described as 'subregulus' or an 'underking'. Athelstan was once again confirmed as effectively an emperor or high king over all the other kings of Britain.

Underneath the surface of imperial control, it appears that resentment of Athelstan's rule simmered amongst the Celtic peoples and Scandinavian settlers of Britain. In 934, Guthfrith, the Norse king of Dublin, died and was succeeded by his son Olaf Guthrithson. Constantine formed an alliance with Olaf which was confirmed by the marriage of the king of Dublin with Constantine's daughter. In 937, Constantine, Olaf and the Strathclyde Britons ruled by Owain formed a wider alliance against the English king, hoping that they could overthrow him by combining their forces. They invaded northern England and, although this has been disputed, it is probable that they landed a large fleet in the estuary of the River Humber. The invasion took place late in the year which was unusual in the medieval period when military campaigns were normally conducted in the summer. Constantine chose to invade northern England because they had more potential allies amongst the Anglo-Scandinavian aristocracy and chronicles of the time say that the region submitted to the invasion, and cooperated with the invaders. This allied force then ravaged English lands. A poem, preserved by William of Malmesbury, accuses Athelstan of being too slow to react to the threat to his kingdom and abandoning his duty to defend his people through force of arms. However, it may be that, in fact, Athelstan was wise to delay his response to this new threat to his rule. Gathering together an army was a time-consuming exercise and, in all probability, Athelstan was ensuring that he had as large a force as possible at his disposal before taking any action.

Drawing together an army made up primarily of Mercian and West Saxon troops, Athelstan marched north. (It appears that the Welsh did not participate on either side during the conflict.) Finally, the two forces met, probably later than the end of September of that year, although the date is not recorded. The battle took place at a location called Brunanburh which has not been identified but may have been somewhere on the southern border of Northumbria. Although the English won the battle, they suffered significant losses on their side including two of Athelstan's cousins, two bishops and two earls as well as many English troops. The invaders lost five kings, according to English sources, seven Earls loyal to Olaf and a son of Constantine. Following the battle, the survivors on the invading side fled under cover of night to their ships and escaped. Olaf Guthfrithson finally arrived back in Dublin in early 938 but, by that point, he had few men left. Brunanburh was viewed as a great victory at the time because it preserved the unity of English rule and territorial control. In the 980s, the chronicler Aethelweard recorded that the ordinary English people still referred to it as 'the Great Battle'. Later historians have been divided as to its importance with some seeing it as of national significance in the history of England and Britain whilst others argue its main impact was confined to the time of Athelstan's reign.

Although Athelstan had achieved a remarkable victory, he was only to rule for a further two years. He died at the royal palace of Gloucester on 27 October 939. He is thought to have been around 44 years old and had been king for 14 years. Interestingly, Athelstan chose not to be buried at Winchester, where many had been opposed to his succession to the throne, but was instead buried at Malmesbury alongside his cousins who were killed at Brunanburh. Following the death of Athelstan, the English suffered a reverse in the north of England when the city of York chose Olaf Guthfrithson to be their ruler. Athelstan had never married or had any children so, following his death, he was succeeded by his half-brother Edmund who ruled from 939 to 946. During Edmund's reign, Olaf took control of the East Midlands. When Olaf died in 941, Edmund was able to reconquer this area and he also regained control of the city of York in the same year. Edmund was succeeded by Eadred, who was also Athelstan's half-brother and who ruled from 946 to 955. In 947, the city of York once again switched sides to Viking rule and the Northumbrians took Eric Bloodaxe as their king. Eadred did not regain control over all of England until 954 when the Northumbrians finally expelled Eric Bloodaxe and submitted once again to the English. Following the death of Eadred in 955, England was ruled by Eadwig, the eldest son of Edmund, from 955 to 959.

His reign was characterised by internal feuds and disputes with members of the Anglo-Saxon church and aristocracy, including St Dunstan. Eadwig proved so unpopular that, in 957, the kingdom of England was split into two along the line of the River Thames. Eadwig retained control of Wessex and Kent whilst his more popular younger brother Edgar became the king in the north. When Eadwig died in 959, Edgar reunited the two halves of England under his sole control. Edgar ruled from 959 to 975 and, during his reign, England achieved a greater degree of stability and union than it had since the reign of Athelstan. It is because of his relatively long and stable reign that he is often referred to as King Edgar the Peaceful. Eadwig had exiled St Dunstan whilst he was king but Edgar recalled him and made him Bishop of Worcester. He later promoted him to Bishop of London and finally Archbishop of Canterbury. St Dunstan was to be Edgar's most important adviser. Edgar was crowned and anointed as king in 973 at Bath during a service, designed by St Dunstan, that forms the basis for the modern British coronation ceremony. It was intended not to mark the start of Edgar's reign but instead to be the culmination or high point of it. In the same year, Edgar was rowed on his royal barge on the River Dee at Chester by six or eight subkings from Scotland, Wales and the Western Isles. This public, symbolic act was intended to demonstrate that Edgar was the head of an Anglo-Saxon empire then at its peak. When he died in 975, he was succeeded by his eldest, but illegitimate, son, Edward the Martyr. Dunstan and Archbishop Oswald of Worcester supported Edward but many other Anglo-Saxon nobles supported his younger brother Ethelred, leading to a major dispute in England. Edward was murdered at Corfe Castle in 978, probably on the orders of Ethelred's mother Queen Aelfthryth. Following his murder, Ethelred became king of England.

Ethelred the Unready

Today, Ethelred the Unready has one of the worst reputations of any English king. His unflattering epithet evokes such negative connotations as laziness, cowardice or foolishness. However, there has been some recent reappraisal of Ethelred's reign, which lasted for 38 years. His nickname is, in fact, a play on words and was first written down in the twelfth century. The name Ethelred is formed of two Anglo-Saxon words, 'aethel' meaning noble and 'raed' meaning counsel. The modern term 'unready' is in fact a corruption of the Anglo-Saxon term, 'unraed', which means 'no council'. Therefore, it may be that earlier chroniclers were not describing him as 'unprepared' or 'unready' but recording that he was poorly advised by those around him. It is possible that this historical criticism of the royal council or witan has over time come to taint the king himself.

Ethelred was the son of King Edgar and Aelfthryth who had married in 964. Aelfthryth was the daughter of Ordgar the powerful ealdorman of Devon. Edgar had two sons, but his first son

Edward is thought to have been illegitimate. Following the sudden death of King Edgar in July 975 aged 32, Edward succeeded his father to the throne when he was still only a teenager but he had already divided opinion in the royal court. He had a reputation for being ill-tempered and liable to violent outbursts and had managed to offend many nobles before becoming king. Two factions emerged, one supporting Edward and the other Ethelred, although, since Ethelred was only around ten years old at the time, it seems unlikely that he played a major part in the infighting that followed Edgar's death. Edward's brief reign was an unhappy one and a comet which was seen in the sky during the autumn of 975 was widely interpreted as being an ill omen. In 976, England was struck by famine and the two royal factions began to fight amongst themselves. Many of the monasteries that were built by King Edgar were destroyed. Matters came to a head in 978 when Edward was murdered at the royal residence where Corfe Castle in Dorset now stands, by the retainers of Queen Aelfthryth. Although Edward had been an unpopular figure with an unstable character, the murder of an anointed king by those close to Ethelred was to cast a long shadow over his subsequent reign. Ethelred was crowned as Edward had been at Kingston a fortnight after Easter in 978. However, like that of his brother before him, the start of his reign was accompanied by an ill omen as a blood-red cloud was seen frequently in the skies over England. Many saw it as foreshadowing the coming vengeance of God for the murder of Edward.

During Edgar's reign, England had enjoyed a peaceful period as a result of his conquest of the Danelaw. But when Ethelred was still only very young, perhaps around 14 years old, Danish attacks on the English coast began again in 980. The first of these new raids was aimed at Cheshire, Thanet and Hampshire. The following year, Cornwall and Devon were attacked and, in 982, Dorset was also raided. These raids were carried out by relatively small groups of Danes and, although they had little overall impact on Ethelred's kingdom, they proved significant in that they brought England into a conflict of interest with Normandy. Because the Normans were descendants of Vikings who had settled in that part of France, they tended to have good relations with the Danish people and would often offer them safe harbour when they returned from their raids on Anglo-Saxon England. Hostility between the courts of England and Normandy reached such heights that Pope John XV intervened to create a peace accord between the two parties in 991. Nonetheless, the Danish raids on the coastline of England continued.

The Battle of Maldon

The *Anglo-Saxon Chronicle* records that, in the year 991, the Danes launched an attack on Ipswich and the eastern coast of England, and that ealdorman Byrhtnoth was slain at Maldon. Other documents detail that the Danes had a fleet of 93 ships and were led by Olaf Tryggvason who would become the King of Norway. The Danish fleet attacked a number of towns between Sandwich and Ipswich. After devastating the coastline between these two points, they sailed to Maldon in Essex to demand tribute from the local people. They were met by Earl Byrhtnoth and his thegns on either 10 or 11

August beside the River Blackwater, close to the town of Maldon. The events of that day are related in a surviving Old English poem entitled *The Battle of Maldon*.

According to the poem, the Danes sailed their fleet along the course of the River Blackwater which was then known as the Panta. On hearing news of their imminent arrival, Byrhtnoth had summoned the local fyrd or militia. During this period of Ethelred's reign, there was no uniform policy of how to respond to such attacks by the Vikings. Some favoured a military defensive strategy; others thought it wiser to simply pay them off. Byrhtnoth was determined to fight the Viking raiders and assembled his men close to a small island in the Blackwater River where the Danes had landed. The site of their arrival has now been identified as probably being Northey Island. During low tide, a causeway was accessible to the shoreline. Northey Island is around two miles to the south-east of the town of Maldon.

The leader of the Vikings, Olaf Tryggvason, sent a messenger to call out to the East Saxons that he would leave and sail his ships away if they would agree to pay him tribute in gold. However, Byrhtnoth was defiant and replied to the messenger:

'Do you hear, seaman, what this people says?
They wish to give you nought but spears for
   tribute,
Poisonous point and edge of tried old sword,
War-tax that will not help you in the fight.
Here stands an earl undaunted with his troop,
One who intends to save his fatherland,
Ethelred's kingdom, and my liege lord's land
And people.'

(Richard Hamer,
A Choice of Anglo-Saxon Verse, p.51).

Following this exchange of words, and as the tide began to recede, the Vikings launched an attack across the narrow causeway but their way was blocked by three Anglo-Saxon warriors. They were Wulfstan, Maccus and Aelfhere and they were able to stop the Vikings reaching the mainland because of the limited space they had to cross on. However, Olaf then asked that his men be allowed to cross over to the shoreline so that a battle could take place. Significantly, the Old English poem relates that Byrhtnoth, for his 'ofermode' (line 89), agrees to allow them to cross and meet his men in full battle. The meaning of this term has caused considerable debate amongst scholars as it may provide an important key to the overall meaning of the poem. It may mean 'over-heart' or 'having too much heart' or 'pride' but could also mean 'over-confidence'. A similar Swedish word, 'overmod', means 'recklessness' or 'hubris'. Some have seen the poem as depicting Byrhtnoth's stand as a heroic act intended to inspire others, perhaps in a similar way to the sacrifice of the 300 Spartans led by King Leonidas at the Battle of Thermopylae, but others, including the author JRR Tolkien, saw the meaning of the poem very differently. Tolkien felt that the author of the poem was writing about a terrible loss and an Anglo-Saxon defeat, and that its principal cause had been Byrhtnoth's sin of pride. Following Byrhtnoth's decision to let the Vikings cross, the battle began but an Englishman called Godric fled, riding on Byrhtnoth's horse, causing many of the English to think that their leader was deserting them. Many then fled themselves and the Vikings defeated the Anglo-Saxons and killed Byrhtnoth on the battlefield. It may be that the meaning or intention of the poem was to emphasise the importance of loyalty in the feudal culture of the Anglo-Saxons or that Byrhtnoth had too great a confidence in the loyalty of his own men.

Danegeld

Following the Anglo-Saxon defeat at Maldon, Archbishop Sigeric of Canterbury and other powerful members of the witan from the south-west advised the 24-year-old King Ethelred to pay the Vikings the tributes that they were demanding rather than to continue an armed struggle. By this time in his reign, many significant figures, such as Archbishop Dunstan, Bishop Aethelwold of Worcester and Aelfhere of Mercia, who had led the English armies, had died and it may be that Ethelred was lacking in the kind of strong counsel that would have helped him negotiate his way through this crisis. The tribute paid to the Danes amounted to £10,000. But paying tribute for peace appears to have had the opposite effect to that intended as the Danish fleet continued to attack the English coastline. The failure of the king and his government to tackle the problem only led to more and more recruits for the Viking attacks on what was then the wealthiest country in Europe.

In 994, the Danish fleet, led by Olaf Tryggvason of Norway and Swein of Denmark, attacked London. Although they failed to take the city, the countryside surrounding it was devastated. Ethelred reached a new agreement with Olaf. A treaty was drawn up and a further tribute of £16,000 was paid. Although Olaf then left, many Danes stayed on as mercenaries fighting for Ethelred. More raids followed in 997 and they were probably mounted by the mercenaries who had remained in 994. The Danes continued to raid areas including Hampshire, Dorset and Sussex the following year and then attacked Kent in 999. However, in 1000, the Danes left England and travelled to Normandy. This may have been because their demands for tribute, or 'Danegeld' as the payments became known in Anglo-Saxon terminology, had been refused. But there was little respite. In 1001, the Danish force returned to attacking the English coastline, using the Isle of Wight as a base. Starting with Sussex, the Danes then attacked the south coast as far as south Devon but were driven back from Exeter by the English. Faced with these renewed attacks, Ethelred once again agreed, in early 1002, to pay a tribute of £24,000 in exchange for a cessation of Danish raiding.

The *Anglo-Saxon Chronicle* reports that in the same year, 'the king gave orders for all the Danish people who were in England to be slain on St Brice's Day (13 November), because the king had been told that they wished to deprive him of his life by treachery and all his councillors after him, and then seize his kingdom...' (*Anglo-Saxon Chronicle*, p.135). The St Brice's Day Massacre, as it has come to be known, was probably limited in its scope to various towns such as Oxford and London because the Viking presence in the Danelaw would have been too large to displace. It seems likely that it was aimed mainly at the mercenaries who had turned on their employers but it is nonetheless a disturbing episode in Ethelred's reign. Unfortunately for Ethelred and his subjects, one of its victims was said to have been

Gunhilde who was the sister of Sweyn Forkbeard, the King of Denmark, and, perhaps motivated by revenge, he led an invasion of the west of England in 1003. The following year saw Sweyn and his forces in East Anglia but he met fierce opposition from the English who were led by Ulfcytel Snillingr, a local nobleman. Although the Danes ultimately defeated the English at Thetford, they suffered serious losses and, following a widespread famine, they left England in 1005 and returned to Denmark. The Danes returned to raiding again in 1007 and they were paid £36,000 by Ethelred to end their attacks. The payment appears to have secured two years of peace and an attempt was made to build a naval fleet for England, although one of its commanders then betrayed the trust of the king and took to raiding himself. The year 1009 saw a very large Danish force begin raids on Britain and its depredations only ended in April 1012 when a tribute of £48,000 was paid to them. In 1013, Sweyn Forkbeard returned again and the English defences crumbled in his path. This time Sweyn managed to conquer England and Ethelred fled his kingdom for the relative safety of Normandy.

King Canute

Although Sweyn Forkbeard had succeeded in conquering England, his victory was extremely short-lived. He died suddenly on 3 February 1014, creating a power vacuum in the kingdom. Whilst the Danes who had been supporters of Sweyn now swore allegiance to his son Canute (or Cnut), many Anglo-Saxon thegns looked to return Ethelred to the throne of England. Interestingly, these powerful Anglo-Saxon leaders offered to support Ethelred only if he agreed to govern them more justly and to forgive those of them who had submitted to Viking rule in preference to Ethelred.

Ethelred launched an attack on Canute's forces but Canute chose to leave England and avoid battle because he had not had time to prepare an effective resistance. Nonetheless, Ethelred ravaged the Danelaw and the Kingdom of Lindsey for supporting Sweyn and Canute. By late 1015, Edmund Ironside, Ethelred's son, had rebelled against the king and became the ruler of the Danelaw. Canute returned at this time and successfully set about reconquering England. Edmund was to rejoin his father in his defence of the kingdom but the situation once again changed suddenly following the death of Ethelred on 23 April the following year. Although Canute went on to defeat Edmund at the Battle of Ashingdon on 18 October 1016, he decided to offer his rival a treaty. Edmund would rule Wessex and Canute the rest of England. But just as before, events proved to be fast-moving. Edmund died on 30 November, leaving Canute as ruler of all England. In order to consolidate his claim to the throne, Canute married Emma of Normandy, the widow of Ethelred the Unready, in 1017. However, he also killed Ethelred's son Eadwig Atheling to remove him as a threat to his power. Ethelred's sons by Emma, Alfred Aetheling and Edward the Confessor, went into exile in Normandy, as did Edmund Ironside's sons. When Emma had another son during her marriage to Canute, who was named Harthacanute, he was chosen as his heir even though Canute already had children. In 1018, Canute extracted a huge Danegeld payment from England amounting to £72,000 as well as an extra payment of £10,500 from the city of London. Canute used the money to pay off the bulk of his army which returned to Denmark, although he kept 40 ships and their crews in England for defence. Canute held a meeting at Oxford where it was agreed that the English and the Danish would live together in peace under the laws of King Edgar.

With the death of Harald II in 1018, Canute sailed to Denmark to claim that throne. Harthacanute, who was still a child at the time, was made Crown Prince of the Kingdom of Denmark, although Ulf Jarl, the husband of Canute's sister, was entrusted to serve as regent. Although attempts were made to conquer Denmark by Norway and Sweden, Canute defeated his opponents at the Battle of the Helgea in around 1026. He was now the most powerful and dominant figure amongst the Scandinavian countries. He claimed the throne of Norway in 1028 and also took possession of the city of Sigtuna in Sweden. He was now ruler of an impressive North Sea Empire and one of the most powerful rulers in Europe. He also embraced Christianity and made a pilgrimage to Rome in 1027. Canute is often remembered today as the king who tried to turn back the waves on the seashore and this is often seen as an emblem of kingly folly, arrogance or delusion. However, the story was first recorded in the twelfth century and was intended to demonstrate the piety, humility and wisdom of Canute, who commanded the waves to turn back to demonstrate to his councillors the limitations of earthly kingship.

When Canute died in 1035, his son Harthacanute succeeded him as king of Denmark. However, because of the military threat posed by Magnus I of Norway, Harthacanute, who had ousted his half-brother Svein, remained in Denmark. England was ruled by Harold Harefoot who was the son of Canute and his first wife. Emma of Normandy retained control of Wessex. In 1036, her sons Alfred the Atheling and Edward the Confessor travelled to England from Normandy, independently of one another, to visit their mother. They were supposed to be under the protection of Harthacanute but, in his absence, Alfred was seized by Earl Godwin of Wessex who was acting for Harold Harefoot. Alfred was blinded with hot pokers so that he could not become king and died shortly afterwards from his wounds. Edward the Confessor escaped back to Normandy. Harold Harefoot ruled England for five years and died in 1040 at the same time as Harthacanute was preparing an invasion force to recapture England. Harthacanute then crossed with a war fleet to England, accompanied by his mother Emma. In 1041, he invited Edward the Confessor back to England, probably due to her influence. He did not have an heir when he died suddenly at a wedding in Lambeth in the following year, and Edward the Confessor succeeded him to the throne. Edward gained a reputation in his lifetime for being a holy and pious king which is where the sobriquet of 'Confessor' originated. He spent a great deal of his money on Westminster Abbey and was said to have had holy visions and been able to cure scrofula by his touch. Although he married Earl Godwin's daughter in 1045, they did not have any children and it was thought by many that this was because he was too holy to have been interested in anything as base as human desire. Although the *Anglo-Saxon Chronicle* portrays him as a strong king who ruled for a fairly long period of 24 years, he was to be the last king of the House of Wessex and his reign would mark the twilight of the Anglo-Saxon age.

Chapter Six

The Norman Conquest

The death of Edward the Confessor on 5 January 1066 was to precipitate a series of events that would change the future of England forever. Edward had married Earl Godwin's daughter Edith in 1045 but died childless which led to several figures stepping forwards to lay claim to the throne. Harold Godwinson, the Earl of Wessex, was elected by the witan of England to be the new king. He was the son of Earl Godwin of Wessex and part of one of the most powerful families in the kingdom. Harold acted swiftly and, with what seemed to many unseemly haste, was crowned the day after Edward's death, 'before the funeral meats were cold'. Harold was crowned by the Archbishop of York, Ealdred, at Westminster Abbey although his

Norman rivals later claimed that the coronation had been conducted by Stigand the Archbishop of Canterbury who had been elected uncanonically. Shortly after the coronation, two powerful and significant figures, both with designs on the English throne, were to contest Harold's right to it. Duke William of Normandy asserted that Edward the Confessor had promised him the throne during his exile in Normandy and further claimed that Harold Godwinson had personally sworn over sacred Christian relics that he supported William's claim.

The other claimant to the throne of England was Harald Hardrada, meaning 'hard ruler', also known as 'the ruthless'. Hardrada was the king of Norway and his claim derived from an agreement between Magnus I, the previous king of Norway, and Harthacanute. The terms of this agreement were that should either king die without having a recognised heir, the surviving king would become ruler of both kingdoms. Harold's own brother Tostig, who had been exiled from power in Northumbria by Harold, launched a series of raids against southern England in early 1066. He had raised a fleet in Flanders and Harold, thinking that it was the beginning of a

Norman assault on his kingdom, raised his forces against them. It was to be one of the greatest armies and navies that England had hitherto mustered and Tostig quickly retreated. Instead, he launched raids in East Anglia and Lincolnshire but he was forced to take flight in his ships after a counter-attack from Edwin, Earl of Mercia and his brother, Earl Morcar of Northumbria. Tostig lost many of his forces and he travelled north to Scotland to find new supporters. He then sailed to Norway to meet with Harald Hardrada, the formidable and seasoned warrior king, to pledge his support for Hardrada's claim to the throne of England and in order to take revenge against his brother Harold for his expulsion from Northumbria. In the spring of 1066, Hardrada assembled a large fleet in Trondheim in Norway and in the summer travelled to Scotland to join forces with Tostig. Hardrada then launched an invasion of northern England in early September 1066 with a force of between 10,000 and 15,000 men.

During the summer, Harold had moved his fleet to the Isle of Wight in preparation for the expected invasion from Normandy led by Duke William. However, William had been badly hampered in his plans by bad weather and the expected attack failed to materialise during the summer months. Because of the delay in William's invasion, King Harold was eventually forced to stand down his army and fleet because of the expenses involved in providing for them and because it was now harvest-time and his levies, many of whom were farmers, needed to return home to gather their crops. William's fleet had been prevented crossing the channel by the prevailing north winds but Harald Hardrada was to benefit from them as he travelled south to England from Norway. He arrived in the Tyne in early September with a fleet of 300 ships, going on to attack Cleveland and Scarborough, and sometime around 15 September 1066 he landed at Riccall in Yorkshire.

Hardrada and Tostig then advanced overland to York and, on 20 September, fought a battle at Fulford on the outskirts of the city against a northern English army led by Earl Edwin of Mercia and Earl Morcar of Northumbria. Although the English put up strong resistance, the Norwegians pushed their left wing into a nearby area of marshland where many were killed by drowning. The city of York then surrendered to Hardrada in the aftermath of the battle and accepted him as their king. The Vikings then offered a peace deal to the Northumbrians in return for support for the Norwegian king's claim to the English throne. As part of this deal, the Vikings took hostages and supplies from the city of York and demanded further hostages from the whole region. There has been much speculation about how quickly King Harold would have heard of the news of the Viking invasion of northern England and the capture of York. Messengers riding on horseback could have reached him in southern England within as little as three days but news could have travelled even faster if a system of beacons had been lit and observed. Upon receiving the news of Hardrada's invasion, Harold raced northwards to confront him and gathered forces as he travelled by raising the local levies as he went. He travelled so quickly that he arrived in Tadcaster on 24 September only four days after leaving London. Tadcaster is nine miles south of York and Hardrada was completely unaware at this point of the swiftness of the English advance.

The Battle of Stamford Bridge

On the morning of Monday 25 September, Harald Hardrada moved his army to a road junction called Stamford Bridge which lies seven miles to the east of York. The purpose of this was to meet and receive further hostages from the Northumbrians, and to obtain more supplies. King Harold learned that Hardrada had made this arrangement and, moving with lightning swiftness, travelled from Tadcaster through York to Stamford Bridge that morning, a distance of 16 miles. The Viking army was taken completely by surprise and only realised that the English army was even in that region when they saw them approaching their positions. In fact, the Vikings were expecting no opposition at this stage and had left a large part of their force with the ships at Riccall. They also had left behind their body armour and, as it was a hot day, many were simply lying in the sun or swimming in the River Derwent.

Accounts relating the course of the battle vary but there appears to be a strong tradition that part of the Viking army was located on the west bank of the River Derwent and the rest to the east of it.

Many of the Vikings on the west bank were killed by Harold's men whilst the rest fled across the bridge over the river. At this point, the English advance appears to have been delayed as Harold attempted to funnel his troops across the narrow crossing. The Vikings tried to hold the bridge against the English advance, probably in a bid to allow Hardrada to mobilise and organise his men and also as a delaying tactic to allow time for reinforcements to reach his position from Riccall. Famously, the *Anglo-Saxon Chronicle* describes how, at one stage, a single giant Norse berserker warrior blocked the English advance across the narrow bridge, wielding a double-headed battle axe. According to the story, the axeman cut down as many as 40 English soldiers in his heroic defence of the crossing. He was only stopped and removed from his position blocking the route when an English soldier climbed into a half barrel and, floating under the bridge, thrust his long spear up into the Viking through gaps in the planking. In the meantime, the Viking army had drawn up in a shield wall formation on the east bank of the river. After the English had crossed the river, they drew up in a battle line and charged the Viking army.

A fierce battle ensued but the Vikings were at a serious disadvantage because of their lack of chain mail body armour. Norwegian sources say that Hardrada was killed in the early stages of the battle after he was struck in the windpipe by an arrow. Tostig Godwinson was also killed during the battle and some accounts claim that he was killed by his own brother, King Harold.

Nonetheless, the battle raged on for several hours. The English army inflicted devastating losses on the Vikings but, during the final stages of the battle, Norse reinforcements arrived led by Eystein Orre who was Hardrada's prospective son-in-law. The reinforcements had raced to the battlefield in such haste that some are said to have died of exhaustion upon arrival. Norwegian accounts of the Battle of Stamford Bridge describe this phase of the fighting as 'Orre's Storm' and describe how Orre and his men inflicted serious losses on the English. However, the strain of rushing to battle from Riccall, coupled with the heat of the day, appears to have weakened their overall effectiveness. The Vikings were finally overwhelmed and defeated. Reportedly, so many men were killed during the battle in the confined space close to the Derwent that the battlefield was still covered with whitened bones even 50 years later. The surviving Vikings accepted a truce with King Harold and he allowed them to travel home after they agreed never to attack England again. The Vikings were led by Hardrada's son Olaf and Paul Thorfinnsson who was the Earl of Orkney. However, the Viking losses were so catastrophic it was said that, of the fleet of 300 ships in which they had arrived, only 24 were needed to transport them away. They were to spend the winter in Orkney and then, in spring, Olaf returned to Norway.

William the Conqueror

Duke William of Normandy spent the greater part of 1066 in putting together a fleet to carry his troops across the channel to England. His forces comprised elements from Normandy but also troops raised from Flanders and Brittany. He assembled a fleet on the estuary of the River Dives at Dives-sur-Mer that was intended not only to bring his army across to England but to carry a wide range of provisions and supplies including warhorses, food, metalworkers and large quantities of arms such as swords, spears and arrows. One medieval chronicler called William of Poitiers wrote that William gained the support of Pope Alexander II in pursuing his claim to the English throne and that the Pope supplied him with a papal banner as a sign of his approval. The Bayeux Tapestry, which was woven to commemorate the Norman invasion of England, records that a comet was seen in the skies above Europe in April 1066 and that many regarded it as a portent of the emerging conflicts created by Edward the Confessor's death without a clear heir. The comet in question was in fact Halley's Comet and it was visible from 24 April for a period of seven days. In August, William moved his base of operations to Saint-Valery-sur-Somme but found that he was unable to make the crossing to England because of bad weather and the prevailing winds blowing from the north.

However, the delay caused by the bad weather in the Channel was arguably to work to William's ultimate advantage. Whilst Harold was preoccupied with defeating the Viking invasion in the north of England, William was able to make the crossing unopposed and his fleet landed safely on the English south coast on 28 September 1066. Nonetheless, the crossing was not entirely without incident. Some of William's ships were blown off course and landed at Romney where they were attacked by local forces and, at one point, William's own ship became separated from the fleet in foggy conditions. The latter event is said to have caused consternation amongst the Normans but, when the fog cleared, William's ship once again became visible to the fleet. Even so, as William was landing on the beach at Pevensey, he stumbled in the shingle and fell to his knees. Once again, many in his army seem to have questioned whether their invasion was to be an ill-fated undertaking. With his customary confidence, William is said to have laughed off the incident and, holding beach pebbles in each hand, he declared that he was simply taking hold of his new kingdom. The Norman invaders then travelled to Hastings where they made a base of operations and built a wooden castle, perhaps having carried prefabricated materials with them for this purpose across the channel. They also created fortifications at Pevensey and used these points to raid the interior of the region.

Meanwhile, in the north of England, King Harold is thought by some to have heard the news of William's arrival on the south coast on Sunday 1 October. Alternatively, he may have received the news whilst heading south to London but it seems clear that many of the troops who had fought with him at the Battle of Stamford Bridge, supplied by Earls Morcar and Edwin, remained in the north. He appears to have travelled quickly to London which also suggests that he was accompanied by a stripped down elite force of housecarls, or household troops, who had horses to carry them south. Presuming that Harold left York on 2 October, then he could have reached London by 6 October. William of Malmesbury suggests that, apart from his elite fighting men and mercenaries, Harold had few men to support him from the local fyrds. Perhaps because he had already suffered losses at the Battle of Stamford Bridge and because he had had limited time to raise fresh levies, Harold had a smaller army at his disposal than might otherwise have been the case. The *Anglo-Saxon Chronicle* also claims that

Harold suffered from some desertions in the days leading up to the confrontation with William's forces at the Battle of Hastings.

Both Harold's mother and his brother Gyrth counselled him to avoid marching to fight William and both suggested that Gyrth should command a force against the Normans which would have allowed Harold time to raise more troops and regroup should his brother fail. The chroniclers Orderic Vitalis and William of Malmesbury wrote that Gyrth tried to persuade Harold not to fight William so that he would not break the oath he had made to him that he would support his claim to be king of England. Harold ignored them both and left London on 12 October. He camped at Caldbec Hill on the following night, close to a location where a hoar-apple tree stood. However, it has also been claimed by Norman sources that Harold arrived at the battlefield at Hastings on the morning of 14 October. Caldbec Hill is located about eight miles from where William had established his castle at Hastings. Based on contemporary accounts, it seems likely that representatives were sent between the two leaders to attempt to negotiate a settlement but no agreement was reached. The English king had been hoping to surprise William by his sudden arrival just as he had surprised the Viking invaders under Harald Hardrada only weeks before but the duke's scouts quickly alerted him to the presence of Harold's army. Harold then led his men to the upper part of Senlac Hill which is today located at Battle in East Sussex. William advanced his army from his castle at Hastings to meet the English army.

Harold chose a defensive position on a ridge which had slopes that ran down to watersheds on each flank and with a steep slope in front of it that also ran down to a marshy area. By choosing this spot, Harold was making it difficult for William to use his forces as effectively as he would have wanted to. Harold planted his standards on the ridge, one displaying the dragon of Wessex and another a banner of his own which depicted a fighting figure of some sort. The figure may have been of Christian origin or possibly a hero such as Hercules from Greek myth. Harold was accompanied by his housecarls and thegns who would have had the best armour and weapons and training. They fought mainly with battle axes, although some would have carried swords and they wore chain mail or scale mail. They were deployed in the front line of his army and together made up the shield wall formation for which the English were famous.

The English did not use cavalry in their battle tactics and used horses simply to travel to the battlefield. They had developed the shield wall formation over many years as a response to their wars with the Vikings who fought on foot. However, in addition to these seasoned, well-trained and well-equipped troops, supplemented with Danish mercenaries, Harold's army was made up of men from the local Sussex fyrds. In all likelihood, these were farmers who had no armour or weapons other than crude farming implements or perhaps simply clubs and stones attached to pieces of wood. Behind these lines of infantry, Harold would also have had some archers and men equipped with javelins. Estimates as to how many men were at Harold's disposal vary greatly. Some Norman chronicles claimed as many as 400,000 or more. However, it is much more likely that Harold had somewhere between 5,000 and 13,000 men. Similarly, it is not known how many men William commanded but it seems likely to have been between 7,000 and 12,000. Many of Harold's men may have been still arriving at the battlefield as the armies fought and it is possible though not certain that he was outnumbered.

The Battle of Hastings

Although much of the detail of the Battle of Hastings seems hazy and open to debate, there is a widespread agreement that the battle began at 9am. William's army was deployed below the English position on the north bank of a brook that ran along its base. His forces consisted of a core of Norman troops at the centre, controlled directly by William himself, with Bretons on the left, led by Alan the Red, and French and Flemish troops on the right under the control of William FitzOsbern and Count Eustace II of Boulogne. William deployed archers in front of these groups, backed by foot soldiers armed with spears. The Duke began the battle by ordering his archers to fire uphill at the densely packed English position in which men had locked their shields together and formed a formidable defensive target. This appears to have had little impact as the arrows mainly either struck the shields or overshot and carried on harmlessly over their heads. William then ordered his infantry to advance towards the English position but they were met by a rain of missiles consisting of spears, axes and stones, although relatively few arrows. When the Norman infantry reached the English line, with the intention of creating breaks in the shield wall into which Norman cavalry could be deployed, they were thrown back by the ferocity of the English and Danish troops, wielding their terrifyingly effective battle axes. The Norman cavalry were then sent up against the English line but were unable to fracture their formation because the horses tended to shy away from the densely packed shields. At this point the Bretons, fighting on William's left, appear to have suddenly turned and fled downhill. The English on the right of their battle formation seem to have taken this as a sign of general retreat, and broken ranks and chased them. A rumour quickly ran through the Norman forces that William had been killed, leading to some disorder and chaos. However, William was not dead and he rode through his troops, taking off his helmet to show his face and to prove that he was still alive.

William then ordered in cavalry who cut off the English pursuers, now dangerously isolated from the main body of Harold's army. Some were ridden down in the marshy area at the bottom of the battlefield while a small group is shown on the Bayeux Tapestry, which records the story of William's invasion, making a desperate last stand. These men were likely to have been the untrained and poorly equipped levies of the local fyrd and they were soon killed by William's troops. The tapestry also records that Harold's own brothers Gyrth and Leofwine died in this stage of the battle but whether they died on the hillock or in fighting with Norman cavalry on the ridge seems unclear. However, this phase of the battle proved highly damaging for Harold as it weakened the right wing of his army and deprived him of the critical support and leadership of his brothers. William appears to have responded quickly to what had just taken place and next ordered a full-scale cavalry charge against the English which resulted in another retreat by the Normans. But, once again, the English broke ranks to pursue their retreating enemy and they were quickly isolated and mown down by William's cavalry. The chronicler William of Poitiers states that William purposely used this tactic twice during the battle. The flexibility of William's battle tactics was to prove critical in breaking the strength of the English defensive position. Soon the English line was weakened to the extent that they could no longer effectively hold the command of the entire ridge.

William now ordered his archers to fire over the shield wall and into the massed ranks of the English and it is likely that they gained ground on the flanks of Harold's position. Even so, the core of Harold's army remained in a strong disciplined formation around the king. But the Bayeux Tapestry shows that the English were being struck from above by a rain of arrows. Famously, the tapestry shows a figure clutching an arrow which has hit him in the eye. Behind this figure the text on the tapestry states that, 'Here King Harold was killed'. However, it has been argued that the figure lying on the floor next to the man with the arrow in his eye is in fact

Harold. Current opinion has moved back to the traditional reading of the scene and it seems likely the artist behind the tapestry is showing a linear narrative where Harold is first struck in the eye then falls to the ground and is attacked by a Norman horseman. In defence of this reading, other figures in the tapestry are shown more than once in a scene and their identities are clearly indicated by nearby text. But the truth about Harold's fate may be darker still. A Norman account of the battle entitled 'Carmen de Hastingae Proelio', or the 'Song of the Battle of Hastings', which was written not long after the battle by Guy, Bishop of Amiens, records that he was killed by a party of four knights. The knights, who may well have included William himself, appear to have acted as a kind of execution squad which sought out the wounded Harold on the battlefield and broke through his loyal housecarls to reach him. After killing him, they badly mutilated and dismembered his body. His head was cut off, he was stabbed in the chest and then disembowelled and one of his legs was cut off. The account describes Harold being struck in the thigh but it is highly likely that this is a euphemism to disguise the fact that one of his attackers cut off the king's genitals. This level of violence against an anointed king was shocking even at this time in history and William of Malmesbury records that Duke William punished the knight responsible for the atrocity.

With the death of Harold and without clear leadership, the English defence began to fail. Many of the English began to flee from the battlefield but the loyal housecarls continued to fight on, surrounding Harold's body. By 5pm, as the sun was setting, the housecarls were pressed in so closely that accounts of the time state the dead were unable to fall to the ground from their ranks. Ultimately, in fulfilment of their oaths of loyalty, they would fight until all of them were killed. Other English troops who fled the battlefield were pursued by the Normans to a site known as the 'Malfosse' or 'evil ditch' where they appear to have turned on their pursuers and staged an ambush in a ravine where they killed a number of Norman cavalry. However, despite this last-minute and minor victory, the battle was effectively lost and the English army defeated with their king and other leaders lying slain by the Norman invaders.

The Domesday Book

The Battle of Hastings effectively removed any serious resistance to William's claim to the throne of England. The church leaders and remaining nobility met William at Little Berkhamstead which is located to the north of London. In the face of the Norman victory against their military forces, they accepted William as their new king. He was crowned on Christmas Day 1066 at Westminster Abbey by Archbishop Ealdred of York. However, although William's coronation followed English traditions, it soon became clear that Anglo-Saxon society was to be changed forever. Most dramatically, William rewarded his followers and backers, who had supported his bid for power, with the lands of the Anglo-Saxon nobility who were killed at Hastings. He also took the holdings of any Anglo-Saxon nobles who later rebelled against him and placed them in Norman hands. So great was the extent of his redistribution of land that it has been estimated that, by 1087, as little as eight per cent of it was owned by the Anglo-Saxon nobility. In 1085, William met with his councillors at Gloucester and ordered that a great survey be made of his kingdom. Its primary purpose was to determine a clear picture of land ownership and holdings throughout England both in the time of Edward the Confessor and under William's rule.

From this survey William wanted to establish in detail what taxes were due to him. It was carried out in 1086 and amounted to two volumes of work, consisting of a larger volume entitled *Great Domesday* and a smaller one called *Little Domesday*. Although it was ordered by the Norman ruler of England, it is thought that the *Great Domesday* was written by one man and that the enterprise was made possible by the already existing Anglo-Saxon governmental infrastructure. The man who compiled the great survey may well have already served Edward the Confessor as a secretary. Representatives of the king were sent to each shire and its land and holdings evaluated. This was done twice by separate enquirers to ensure that the king was not cheated of his dues. The detail of the survey also includes how many freemen, labourers or slaves an estate possessed. It also recorded whether estates had woodland, pasture, mills or fisheries. The survey then recorded the value of an estate at the death of Edward the Confessor, its value when William became king and its current value in 1086. However, it is clear that a further aim of the great survey was to determine what the lands in William's kingdom were capable of in terms of both revenue and produce and, if possible, whether they could yield more. The survey could not be appealed against or questioned. The 'dome' part of its name derives from an Old English term that indicates a statute or judgement. During the twelfth century, the great survey began to be referred to as the *Domesday Book* and it is still known as this today.

Hereward the Wake

Although the Normans had won a decisive victory at the Battle of Hastings, William faced continued resistance to his rule in its aftermath. One prominent leader of English resistance to Norman rule to emerge during this period was a nobleman who would become known in later centuries as Hereward the Wake. Although much of what is known about his life seems to have become intertwined with myth and legend, it is generally accepted that he was a real historical figure. The *Peterborough Chronicle*, which is a version of the *Anglo-Saxon Chronicle*, attests to his resistance against the Normans as does the *Domesday Book*. The most detailed account of his life is given in the *Gesta Herewardi* which was written around 1109 to 1131.

Much of the material within this account is thought to be fictional and embellished in the interests of storytelling and perhaps to promote an English national heroic figure. Nonetheless, there are considerable similarities between all of the sources that mention Hereward. There has been disagreement over the source of the epithet, 'the Wake'. It has been argued by some that it derives from the Old English term 'waecanan', meaning 'watchful'. The first recorded use of this epithet is in the fourteenth century. It has also been suggested that the Anglo-Norman Wake family, who gained his lands and who claimed their descent from him, gave him their name. This would have been a way of legitimising their claims to his former landholdings. Hereward is said to have been born in 1035 or 1036 into a noble Anglo-Saxon family. He was sent into exile as a young man by his father for disobeying him and causing trouble, and was declared an outlaw by Edward the Confessor. He then travelled to Flanders where he became a mercenary fighting for Baldwin V. He is said to have been in Europe during the Norman invasion but returned in 1069 or 1070. According to the *Gesta Herewardi*, he found that his family lands had been appropriated by the Normans. Hereward also discovered that they had killed his brother and mounted his head on a spike. He then swore revenge against them and is said to have killed those responsible for the crime. Hereward drew together a group of followers but returned to Flanders for a time. However, he returned in 1070 to join a small army sent by Sweyn Estrithson of Denmark who established a base of resistance to the Normans on the Isle of Ely. The *Peterborough Chronicle* says that Hereward, together with his own men and the Danish force, attacked Peterborough Abbey which was now in Norman hands. Hereward and his group then returned to the Isle of Ely and their position was strengthened by the arrival of a small army led by Earl Morcar of Northumbria, a

Saxon nobleman also displaced by William.

The *Gesta Herewardi* says that the Normans mounted an assault on their position on the Isle of Ely by building a mile-long timber causeway. However, the weight of the men and their horses meant that it sank and many of the Normans drowned in the surrounding marshes in their chain mail. The Normans then bribed the monks who were based on the island to show them a route that they could take through the marshes. With this information, they were able to capture the island. It is said that, although Earl Morcar was taken prisoner, Hereward and a band of men escaped and that they roamed the fens and continued a guerrilla-style war against the Norman invaders. It is unclear what Hereward's fate was after his escape from the Isle of Ely although the *Gesta Herewardi* claims that he eventually made peace with William. Hereward's life may have contributed to the later tales of Robin Hood and, during the Victorian period, Charles Kingsley wrote a novel about him called *Hereward the Wake: Last of the English* which popularised the idea of Hereward as a national English hero fighting against Norman injustice.

Wild Edric

Another prominent figure to lead English resistance
to Norman rule was the Anglo-Saxon nobleman
known as 'Wild Edric' or 'Eadric the Wild' who
was based in the West Midlands. Eadric appears
to have been one of the most powerful thegns in
the county of Shropshire where he held estates as
well as holding lands in the neighbouring county
of Herefordshire. In the D version of the *Anglo-
Saxon Chronicle* it is recorded that Eadric would not
accept Norman rule and had his lands laid waste
by Richard fitz Scrob, the commander of Hereford
Castle. In the *Worcester Chronicle*, based on a lost
version of the *Anglo-Saxon Chronicle*, Eadric is
described as the son of Aelfric, brother of Eadric
Streona.

The Anglo-Norman chronicler Orderic Vitalis
wrote that Eadric had submitted to William
following his coronation but that he later rebelled
as part of a much wider uprising amongst the
English. Joining forces with Bleddyn ap Cynfyn,
who was the prince of Gwynedd and Powys, and
his brother Riwallon in 1067, they launched an

attack on Hereford Castle. However, they were unable to defeat the Normans and travelled back over the border into Wales. The years 1069 and 1070 saw a more general rebellion across England against William the Conqueror and Eadric attacked the town of Shrewsbury at this time. He was able to set fire to the town itself but he was once again unable to take the Norman-held castle with the combined forces of insurrectionary Englishmen from the nearby county of Cheshire and Bleddyn ap Cynfyn. William also had to face a major uprising in Northumberland led by the former Earl of Northumberland, Morcar and his brother Earl Edwin of Mercia. They had the support of the King of Denmark, Swein Esthrithson and the Earls Waltheof and Gospatrick. Edgar Atheling, who was a claimant to the throne of England, was also involved in the uprising.

However, back in the border counties of England and Wales, Eadric's rebellion appears to have been relatively short-lived because William the Conqueror went on to defeat a combined English and Welsh force at the Battle of Stafford in 1069. It is thought by some that Eadric was amongst the defeated combatants and that he chose to submit to the king the following year. Eadric was to fight for William in 1072 when the Norman ruler attacked Scotland. The *Domesday Book* records that 'Edric salvage' was previously the tenant of six manors in Shropshire and one in Herefordshire but specific identification is difficult because Eadric was a popular Anglo-Saxon name before the arrival of the Normans. Eadric became known as 'Wild Edric' or 'Eadric Silvaticus' and, in some accounts, 'Edric the Forester'. Over time he has become something of a legendary character, merging with other folkloric traditions. For example, Walter Map wrote in the 1180s that Eadric was the lord of Lydbury North in Shropshire and that he married a fairy or elven maid. Perhaps more famously, Eadric is said to lead the Wild Hunt across the Stiperstones, a hill range in Shropshire, when England is threatened with invasion. Local legend has it that Eadric was seen riding with the Wild Hunt in the days before various major conflicts including the First and Second World Wars.

The appellation Wild Edric may derive from the fact that, like other English rebels, Eadric lived in woods and marshes during his resistance to Norman rule. Orderic Vitalis noted that the Normans referred to these English outlaws as 'Silvatici', a Latin term meaning 'men of the woods'. Vitalis wrote that many of the English rebels refused to sleep in houses for fear that they should become soft and purposely lived out in the wild. It seems likely that English rebels like Eadric and Hereward, who fought a guerrilla-style campaign from the woodlands and wild places of England against the Norman oppressors, form the basis for later tales of the legendary outlaw Robin Hood. It has also been suggested that the tales of Robin Hood have their origin in events of the 1330s but Susan Reynolds amongst others has argued that, 'they could have gained some of their unusual force from association with older stories of heroes who had once resisted foreign invaders...' (*Bulletin of the Institute of Historical Research*, Vol LIV, No129, 1981, *Edric the Wild* pp102-105, University of London).

Interestingly, the modern word 'murder' derives from the term 'murdrum' which was a fine imposed following the Norman Conquest with the intention of protecting the Norman followers of William the

Conqueror. If a Norman was killed and the killer remained unknown, a fine was then imposed on the area in which the murder had taken place. It was a law first introduced in England by the Danes in the Laws of Canute and was designed to protect them from English attacks. It was revived by William the Conqueror but did not apply to English victims who were killed by unknown persons. The reintroduction of the murdrum laws probably reflects the fact that guerrillas like the Silvatici were waging a campaign of violence against their Norman overlords.

The End of the *Anglo-Saxon Chronicle*

The *Anglo-Saxon Chronicle* was first compiled during the ninth century in Wessex on the instructions of King Alfred the Great. Following its completion, other copies were made and sent to monasteries around the country where scribes continued to update its entries year by year. The latest entry dates to the reign of King Stephen in 1154. Although it was originally written in Old English, the later entries found in the *Peterborough Chronicle* were written in a form of Middle English. The *Anglo-Saxon Chronicle* and Bede's *Ecclesiastical History of the English People*, completed in the eighth century, are widely considered to be the most significant records of Anglo-Saxon history before the arrival of the Normans. It was used as an important source of information by the Anglo-Norman chroniclers William of Malmesbury, John of Worcester and Henry of Huntingdon who were writing in the twelfth century. They had their own copies of the *Anglo-Saxon Chronicle* and used it as the basis for their own works. Later historians subsequently based their accounts on their predecessors' work and so the *Anglo-Saxon Chronicle* became a central pillar of knowledge concerning the history of the English. It is now considered to be an important source of information for understanding the continued development of the English language. More generally the influence of the Anglo-Saxon people can be seen to continue in many of our commonly used words. For example, the names of some of their pre-Christian gods form the basis for some of our modern names for days of the week. Wednesday derives from the god Woden or 'Woden's Day', Thursday derives from 'Thor's Day' and Friday from 'Freya's Day'. Although it is recognised that Anglo-Saxon rule in England ended in 1066 with the Norman Conquest, the legacy of the Anglo-Saxon period, particularly in the form of the English language, has in many ways survived right up until the present day.

Chapter Seven

Anglo-Saxons and the Modern Imagination

In the centuries following the Norman Conquest, views of the relative merits of Anglo-Saxon culture were mixed. Many historians viewed the Normans as having had a civilising influence on the Anglo-Saxons. Indeed, there was a widespread view that the Anglo-Saxons had been ruthless invaders and a generally barbarous people. The Scottish historian David Hume exemplifies this view of the Anglo-Saxons in his multi-volume series *The History of England from the Invasion of Julius Caesar to the Revolution in 1688*, first published in London in 1754-62, and subsequently republished in many editions. For Hume, the Anglo-Saxons were a people that were very much in need of improvement. He criticised them as illiterate, intemperate, violent and base, and was particularly dismissive of their 'barbaric' religion, worshipping the god Woden. This view tended to dominate English ideas of the Anglo-Saxons for many years and probably derives mainly from Norman propaganda following the Conquest. However, this fundamentally negative view was challenged by the historian Sharon Turner in his *History of the Anglo-Saxons*, first published in 1799-1805. The series was reprinted many times up until Turner's death in 1847. Turner offered a much more positive view of the Anglo-Saxons and he devoted a full 200 pages to the life of King Alfred whom he praised as an exemplary king and Englishman. Turner concluded that the Norman Conquest had been a divinely ordained event that served to bring England closer to the continent and that it had benefited England and indeed mankind as a whole.

But perhaps the most influential historian to bring about a change of thinking in England about the Anglo-Saxons was Edward Augustus Freeman. In his historical work *The History of the Norman Conquest: Its Causes and Results*, published in five volumes from 1867 to 1879, Freeman argued that an unbroken line of continuity could be traced in the English people and English institutions from the Anglo-Saxon period to the time in which he was writing. Indeed, he went so far as to say that to speak retrospectively of an Anglo-Saxon period was incorrect because in his view the Anglo-Saxon period was still going on. Perhaps most significantly, writers such as Freeman promoted the idea that Queen Victoria was a direct descendant of Alfred and other Saxon kings and that her rule represented a rightful return of Saxon blood to the throne of Britain. Similarly, the lineage of her German consort Prince Albert was traced to the continental Saxons and therefore validated and legitimised their claims to the throne. During the nineteenth century the desire to see in the reign of King Alfred the origins of many Victorian achievements and values led to some unlikely conclusions. For example, Sir Arthur Conan Doyle argued that King Alfred's plan to introduce higher standards of education to his royal court meant that he had intended that every boy and girl in his kingdom should be able to read and write, a claim echoing a Victorian ambition of the time.

In a striking marble sculpture executed between 1863 and 1867 by William Theed, Queen Victoria and Prince Albert are portrayed wearing Anglo-Saxon dress. This marble group was commissioned for Windsor Chapel by Queen Victoria, following the death of Prince Albert in December 1861. The original is kept in the Frogmore Mausoleum at Windsor whilst a plaster cast can be seen at the National Portrait Gallery in London. Queen Victoria noted in her diary that it had been prompted by a suggestion from her daughter Victoria, the Crown Princess of Prussia. The descriptive label next to the copy in the National Portrait Gallery states that, 'this sculpture is thought to symbolise the ties between the German and English peoples from Anglo-Saxon times to the marriage of the Royal couple'. In this full-length portrait Prince Albert is dressed as an Anglo-Saxon warrior and stands with his right arm raised, pointing upwards. He is wearing a belted tunic and has a long cloak gathered on his right shoulder. The oval base of the sculpture is decorated with images of shells, sea-animals and waves and is believed to represent Prince Albert standing at the shore of eternity. His sword lies between his feet and has been set down, following his good fight of Faith in his mortal life. It is a scene that is intended to show the sorrowful parting of Prince Albert and Queen Victoria after his death. It also features a hexagonal pedestal which was made from an antique African marble taken from Rome which has the inscription, 'Allured to brighter worlds, and led the way', carved on to it. This line is taken from the poem *The Deserted Village*, written by Oliver Goldsmith and published in 1770. The death of Queen Victoria in 1901 also coincided, by chance, with the millennial celebrations of the death of King Alfred, held in Winchester and attended by leading dignitaries from around the world. These celebrations culminated with the unveiling of the famous statue of King Alfred by Hamo Thornycroft in Winchester where it can still be seen today.

Sutton Hoo

Public interest in the early Anglo-Saxon period was to reach new heights in the first half of the twentieth century with the spectacular discovery of a ship burial at Sutton Hoo near Woodbridge in Suffolk in 1939. The ship burial was excavated in one of two sixth- and early seventh-century barrow cemeteries located on the edge of an escarpment that overlooks the River Deben. The barrow cemeteries lie not far away from the Suffolk coast and the North Sea. The discovery of the ship burial at Sutton Hoo was so important because so little material remains had otherwise survived from this Dark Age period. The excavation of 1939 found the outlines of a ship in the sandy soil of the area that measured 90 feet in length.

The burial ship had been loaded with a range of treasures and military items that appeared to have belonged to an important warrior. The richness of the items was such that it seemed most likely that the person buried within the ship must have been of extremely high social status, even a king. Although there is evidence that the site was settled and in use from the Neolithic period, circa 3000 BC, and continued to be occupied and used during the Bronze Age and the Iron Age, it was during the Anglo-Saxon period that the significance and use of Sutton Hoo reached its peak. It is now widely argued that the apogee of Sutton Hoo's use as a burial site was during the reign of King Raedwald who was ruler of the Anglo-Saxon Kingdom of East Anglia from 599 to 624 and that he is the most likely candidate to be the occupant of the ship burial itself. Raedwald held a royal vill or residence at Rendlesham which is very close to the site of the Sutton Hoo burial.

The most recognisable and iconic find from the ship burial is probably the ceremonial helmet that for many people has come to symbolise the Anglo-Saxon age. The highly decorated helmet was first made from iron and then patterned sheets of tinned bronze were attached to it. Perhaps the most recognisable feature of the helmet is the face mask along with its cheek guards which would have been mounted on hinges to allow the wearer to pull them close to the face when worn. The helmet features three dragon heads which appear at either end of the iron crest running along the top of the helmet and between the eyebrows. It has also been decorated with gilded boar heads close to the temples of the headgear. The central burial chamber within the ship also included a range of richly decorated items such as a pattern-welded sword and an ornate shield, spear tips, a lyre, a set of ten silver bowls, silver spoons and bronze cauldrons. The spoons are thought to have come from the city of Constantinople in the eastern Mediterranean and the bowls are also thought to have been made somewhere in the eastern Byzantine Empire during the sixth century. In a fascinating recent development, it was discovered in 2016 that a substance previously thought to be pine tar found in the burial was actually bitumen from Syria. Pine tar was believed to have been used for boat maintenance. Staff from the British Museum and Aberdeen University worked on the analysis of the bitumen which was found as small black organic fragments scattered amongst the burial finds. The tests were part of an EU-funded research project that studied the preservation of tars associated with ancient boats. The study suggested that the fragments should actually be considered as valuable grave goods themselves and be viewed as treasures. Bitumen which is also known as asphalt is a form of oil deposit and its discovery in the Sutton Hoo burial suggests that petrochemical products were being traded on an international level at least as long ago as the seventh century. It provides further evidence, together with the Byzantine materials found in the burial, that the Anglo-Saxons had a wide-ranging trade network and had contact with cultures in the Middle East. It is not known whether the organic fragments were part of a larger object or are what remains of a collection of smaller objects.

Many people drew immediate parallels between the ship burial and its contents and the society and culture described in the Old English poem *Beowulf*. *Beowulf* is set in the south of Sweden and archaeologists have found that similar ship burials were made there that contained comparable goods to the Sutton Hoo grave. There are many passages from *Beowulf* that have striking echoes of the Sutton Hoo burial site and its setting. For example, after the body of Beowulf has been burned on a great pyre at the end of the poem:

'Then the Geat people began to construct
A mound on a headland, high and imposing,
a marker that sailors could see from afar...
And they buried torques in the barrow, and
   jewels

and a trove of such things as trespassing men
had once dared to drag from the hoard.
They let the ground keep that ancestral treasure,
gold under gravel, gone to earth,
as useless to men now as it ever was.'

(Seamus Heaney, *Beowulf*, p.99)

JRR Tolkien

The bestselling author and Oxford don JRR Tolkien
had both a personal and professional interest in
Anglo-Saxon language, literature and history. He
made a close study of *Beowulf* and produced a
translation of the poem in 1926. Ten years later, he
gave a lecture entitled *Beowulf: The Monster and the
Critics* based on his previous work on the subject.
In his lecture, Tolkien argued that the poem's
meaning and its central themes concerning death
and defeat were becoming increasingly eclipsed by
academic disputes over archaeological and linguistic
issues. When Tolkien wrote his fantasy adventure
story *The Hobbit*, which was published in 1937, he
drew directly on the narrative of *Beowulf* and he

acknowledged that it had been a major influence on him.

Seamus Heaney

One of the most acclaimed and widely read translations of *Beowulf* in recent times was produced by the Irish poet Seamus Heaney and was published in 1999. During interviews he gave at the time of the publication of his translation, Heaney drew parallels between the events described in the poem and the Irish Troubles. In a *New York Times* review of Seamus Heaney's translation of *Beowulf* from 27 February 2000, James Shapiro wrote that, 'Though he never says so, it will be obvious to anyone with the sketchiest knowledge of recent Irish history that the Troubles have also given Heaney access into the *Beowulf* poet's profound understanding of internecine strife. A striking example occurs when Beowulf predicts what will happen at a wedding feast intended to reconcile two peoples locked in an unyielding cycle of violence…'

In the introduction to his translation of the

Anglo-Saxon epic, Heaney also identified further parallels between the Anglo-Saxon age and the modern world in the poem's account of the hero's funeral: 'The Geat woman who cries out in dread as the flames consume the body of her dead lord could come straight from a late-twentieth-century news report, from Rwanda or Kosovo; her keen is a nightmare glimpse into the minds of people who have survived traumatic, even monstrous events and who are now being exposed to a comfortless future.' (Seamus Heaney, *Beowulf*, p.21). Heaney also used the term 'bawn' in order to refer to Hrothgar's hall, 'which in Elizabethan English referred to the fortified dwellings that the English planters built in Ireland to keep the dispossessed natives at bay, so it seemed the proper term to apply to the embattled keep where Hrothgar waits and watches'. (Seamus Heaney, *Beowulf*, p.30). Heaney's translation of *Beowulf* helps to celebrate the achievement of the unknown Anglo-Saxon poet who wrote it and demonstrates its timeless qualities as a work of world literature, and its ability to resonate with audiences and remain relevant during any historical period.

Game of Thrones

One of the most popular television series of recent years has been the award-winning *Game of Thrones*. Based on the bestselling fantasy book series *A Song of Fire and Ice* by the American author George RR Martin, the television show draws heavily on medieval and Anglo-Saxon history and culture. *A Game of Thrones* is the first book in the series and is based in a fictional world that features two continents called Westeros and Essos. Its epic and sprawling narrative centres on the dynastic disputes of the noble houses of Westeros and their seemingly endless struggles for control of the Iron Throne, the seat of the ruler of the Seven Kingdoms. In Martin's story, the inhabitants of the Seven Kingdoms are the linear descendants of the Andals, a people who had invaded Westeros six thousand years previously. The Seven Kingdoms of the fictional fantasy world of *Game of Thrones* have many clear parallels with the story of the Anglo-Saxon invasion of Britain and the seven major kingdoms they created which, in the past, were often referred to by writers and historians as the Anglo-Saxon Heptarchy.

Chapter Eight

Recent Discoveries
from the Anglo-Saxon World

The Staffordshire Hoard

The most sensational archaeological find from the Anglo-Saxon period in recent years is the Staffordshire Hoard. On 5 July 2009, amateur metal detectorist Terry Herbert discovered a number of gold artefacts whilst searching farmland near to Hammerwich, close to Lichfield in Staffordshire. The area in which he was searching had been ploughed and, in the course of the following five days, yielded a huge array of gold objects from the Anglo-Saxon period. After filling 244 bags with finds, Herbert contacted local authorities to notify them about what was clearly a very important discovery. The Staffordshire Hoard is the largest hoard of Anglo-

Saxon gold and silver artefacts that has ever been found. In total over 3,500 items of gold and silver objects have so far been discovered. The finds also included garnet jewellery and it is thought that the hoard was buried in the field during the late seventh or early eighth century. They are predominantly martial in nature and include fittings from helmets and swords. A total of 86 sword pommels have been found some of which are thought to have been made during the middle of the sixth century. Three crosses were also discovered along with a corner fitting, probably from a bible, made from gold and garnet. When the hoard was deposited the area was part of the Anglo-Saxon kingdom of Mercia.

Amongst many discoveries found during the excavation, a small strip of gold measuring 179mm by 15.8mm by 2.1mm has proved to be of particular interest. It had been folded up and, when straightened out and examined more closely, was found to have a biblical quotation written in Latin cut into both sides of its surface. The quotation is taken from Numbers 10:35 and reads, 'Surge Domine et dissipentur inimici tui et fugiant qui oderant te a facie tua'. This translates as, 'Rise up,

LORD, and let thine enemies be scattered; and let them that hate thee flee before thee'. The inscription is thought to date to the eighth century although it is possible that it was made during the late seventh century or the early ninth century. There are a number of theories about its original purpose. It has been argued that it may have been part of the arm of a cross or it could have been attached to either a sword belt or a shield.

Interest has focussed on the location of the hoard which was found just south of the old Roman road, Watling Street. Many of the items are of an extremely high quality and have been deliberately stripped from war gear such as shields and swords. It has been observed that the practice of stripping the sword pommels of defeated warriors is recorded in *Beowulf* and this offers an interesting insight into the practices of the Anglo-Saxon world. However, it was also the custom in late Anglo-Saxon England for noblemen to pay a death duty known as 'heriot' to their king which often consisted of swords, shields and helmets, and other martial items. It is possible, therefore, that the hoard was assembled in this way. Some interesting theories have begun to emerge about why the Staffordshire Hoard was buried in this area. In his 2016 book *The Hoard and its History*, author Robert Sharp has suggested that the hoard is linked to a Viking attack on Lichfield and its Cathedral in 875 and that the Lichfield Gospels were removed to Wales for safekeeping at this time. Martin Wall argued in his book *The Anglo-Saxon Age* (2015) that the hoard is linked to the reign of King Peada of Mercia. Peada was the son of King Penda and he ruled Mercia briefly from 655 until his death in 656. However, there is still no widespread agreement about why the Staffordshire Hoard was buried where it was or about the exact origin of the artefacts it contains.

Lichfield Angel

During the summer of 2003, an excavation in the nave of Lichfield Cathedral led to a fascinating discovery. Part of the floor of the nave was being dug up prior to the installation of a retractable platform, intended for recitals and concerts. The nave had never been excavated before but it was believed that the Anglo-Saxon cathedral was located west of the Church of St Mary. Previously, evidence of the location of the Church of St Mary had been found located under the choir. The archaeological excavation preceding the new building project was overseen by Dr Warwick Rodwell, the Cathedral Archaeologist. The excavation found evidence for the Anglo-Saxon cathedral along with the north and south lines of the Norman cathedral. This was the second of three cathedrals to have been built on the site. At the east end of the excavation site an intriguing sunken chamber was discovered. The nature of the chamber led the excavators to believe that they had found a grave or shrine of some importance. Its position matched Bede's written description of the shrine of St Chad that was built early in the eighth century by Hedda.

However, the most exciting find of all was a sculpted panel of the Archangel Gabriel that also dated to the eighth century. It is thought that the complete carving would originally have shown the Archangel Gabriel delivering the news to the Virgin Mary that she was to give birth to Jesus as described in the New Testament. The scene of the

Annunciation is, of course, an important one in Christian iconography but it is particularly relevant to Lichfield Cathedral because it is dedicated to both St Chad and St Mary. The carved limestone panel which is 600mm tall was discovered in three pieces and may have formed the corner of a shrine chest that housed the remains of St Chad. Although the panel had been broken into three pieces, it was in remarkably good condition and even still had visible traces of red pigment on the carved figure. The Archangel Gabriel had been painted in red and his wings were also red with white tips. It was also found that the pigments were a close match to those used on the *Lichfield Gospels* which have been dated to around 730. Because the *Lichfield Gospels* contain marginal inscriptions written in some of the earliest examples of Old Welsh, it is thought that they may have spent time in Wales, possibly for safe-keeping, as mentioned earlier in this chapter. It may be the case that the limestone chest containing the relics of St Chad, of which the panel of the Archangel Gabriel was a part, was smashed into pieces during a Viking raid on Lichfield. The Revd Dr Pete Wilcox observes that 'the destruction of the Angel may be witness to the same disaster as that which drove the Gospel book west into Wales: that is to say, late eighth-century Viking raids may have cost Lichfield both treasures'. (Revd Dr Pete Wilcox, *The Gold, The Angel and the Gospel Book*, p.16).

Lenborough Hoard

Another even more recent archaeological discovery from the Anglo-Saxon period has been that of the Lenborough Hoard. This hoard consisted of over 5,000 Anglo-Saxon silver coins that were found in the hamlet of Lenborough in Buckinghamshire. The coins date from the first half of the eleventh century. A large number of the coins were minted during the reigns of King Ethelred the Unready who ruled from 978 to 1013 and 1014 to 1016 and King Canute who ruled from 1016 to 1035. The value of the Lenborough Hoard in today's terms is £1.35 million.

Little Carlton Anglo-Saxon Island

In 2011, amateur metal detectorist Graham Vickers discovered an unusual silver writing tool that dated from the Anglo-Saxon period in a ploughed field at Little Carlton, close to Louth in Lincolnshire. He reported the find to the Portable Antiquities Scheme and subsequent investigations of the site led to an announcement in early 2016 that a wide range of Anglo-Saxon artefacts had been unearthed at what is believed to have been an important trading site. During the Anglo-Saxon period, that site was an island in a channel of the River Lud and was located five miles from the coast. However, centuries of work to drain the area mean that it is now dry land.

Great Ryburgh

Another intriguing and potentially illuminating find from the Anglo-Saxon period was the discovery in Norfolk in early 2016 of the burial ground of a Christian community dating from the seventh and ninth centuries. Archaeologists working at Great

Ryburgh discovered six plank-lined Anglo-Saxon graves as well as 81 coffins that had been created by hollowing out oak tree trunks. The planks in the pits had been crafted with some skill, with the pits being lined first to receive the bodies, then roofed with further planks. Log coffins dating from much earlier periods such as the Bronze Age have also previously been found. Historic England had been excavating the site after local archaeologist Matthew Champion spotted high-status Anglo-Saxon pottery alongside Roman Samian ware in the ground whilst preparatory work was taking place to create a fishing lake. A team from the Museum of London was called in to assess the site, leading to the unusual discovery. They also found evidence of a wooden structure there that may have been a church.

The excavation site is located close to the edge of the River Wensum and it is thought that the river has changed course over the centuries and may have obscured other surface evidence that could have pointed to this being a settled area in the Anglo-Saxon period. It is thought that the graves are those of early Christians because they were dug along an east-west alignment and had been marked with timber posts. Significantly, no grave goods have been found within the burials as was common amongst prehistoric or Roman burials or indeed pagan Saxon sites. The main reason for the well-preserved state of the graves appears to be that the area is waterlogged. Interestingly, Matthew Champion views the site as representing an example of an Anglo-Saxon 'monasteria'. This would have been an early type of monastic settlement that also contained a civic community. During the seventh and ninth centuries, when the Anglo-Saxon kingdom of East Anglia was at its peak, the site was located next to an important river crossing. However, no written documents are known to exist that describe the site. Interestingly, archaeologists do not currently believe that the different forms of burial indicate differences in social status.

The Bones of Alfred the Great

There has been considerable interest in recent years in discovering the fate of the bones of Alfred the

Great. Following his death in 899, his body was originally buried in the Old Minster in Winchester. However, in the centuries that followed his remains were seemingly never allowed to rest undisturbed for very long and were moved and interfered with on numerous occasions. Interestingly, William of Malmesbury, writing in the twelfth century, reported that the canons of the Old Minster were convinced that Alfred's spirit had 'resumed his corpse' and he was believed to be haunting the building. Whether these observations were the result of superstitious belief or not, the image of Alfred's ghost wandering restlessly after death would seem to provide a suitable metaphor for the fate of his mortal remains. In 903, four years after his death and burial in the Old Minster at Winchester, Alfred's body was transferred to a chapel within the New Minster by his son Edward the Elder. The New Minster was a Benedictine Abbey built by Edward perhaps specifically for the purpose of housing his father's remains. Alfred had bought the land at the end of his life with the intention of building on it himself. Edward appointed St Grimbald or Grimwald, a Benedictine monk from St Omer in France, to be the abbot of the New Minster but he died before its completion in 901. Grimbald had been invited to England by Alfred the Great because he was a scholar and the king wanted his assistance in his translations and literary interests. St Grimbald was buried in the New Minster along with the Breton St Judoc. Edward was also to bury his mother Ealhswith in the New Minster, following her death in December 902. The New Minster was also the site of the burial of Edward's brother Aethelweard in 920. When Edward the Elder died in 924, he was also interred there, together with one of his sons, also called Aethelweard, who died only days after his father. The Old Minster and the New Minster were located so close together that it was said that the two different choirs could hear each other singing and that also the ground around the Minsters became waterlogged and swampy causing difficulties for the monks.

In 1109, Henry I ordered that the monks of New Minster build a new monastery on land that he had gifted to them outside the northern gate of the medieval city of Winchester at Hyde Mead. Hyde Abbey was consecrated in 1110 and the bodies of

Alfred, Eahlswith and other members of the Wessex royal family were moved there. Other relics that were transferred at the time included the body of St Grimbald and the head of St Valentine which had been donated to the New Minster by Queen Emma or Aelfgifu, the widow of King Canute, in 1041. In 1538, during the reign of Henry VIII, Hyde Abbey was dissolved. The body of the church above ground was then demolished by Henry's men. The sixteenth-century antiquarian John Leland wrote that the bodies of Alfred the Great and his son Edward the Elder had been translated from the New Minster to Hyde Abbey and placed in a tomb before the high altar but he makes no reference to Ealhswith or any of the other members of the Wessex royal family. Leland also recorded that the graves of Alfred and Edward had been opened around the time of the dissolution of Hyde Abbey and that lead tablets naming Alfred and Edward had been found inside. It is known that in 1524 Dr Richard Fox, then Bishop of Winchester, had gathered together the bones of a number of early Anglo-Saxon kings and bishops, including King Canute, from a position behind the high altar of

Winchester Cathedral. He had rehoused them in a number of 'mortuary chests' that can still be seen today in Winchester Cathedral but it is not believed that the burials at Hyde Abbey were included in this work.

It then seems as if the graves of Alfred and his family at Hyde Abbey were rediscovered by accident in 1788 when the land where the Abbey had stood was sold in order to build a prison. Convicts who were working at the site dug across the area of the altar and appear to have found the graves. The coffins that were found were stripped of lead and broken up. The bones that they contained were treated with disregard and scattered in the ground, and presumably carelessly reburied during the building of the prison. However, the prison itself was demolished between 1846 and 1850. In 1866, an amateur antiquarian called John Mellor undertook his own investigation of the Hyde Abbey site, searching for the remains of King Alfred. He claimed to have found the bones of the king and also those of his son Edward, together with some accompanying items, including a sceptre, and some gilt cloth. Mellor then appears to have passed the bones that he had discovered during his excavations to Hugh Wyeth, one of the churchwardens of the nearby Hyde parish church, St Bartholomew's, who was acting on behalf of the church vicar, William Williams. The bones were then placed into two separate boxes and were eventually reburied in an unmarked grave at St Bartholomew's Church graveyard. The bones were photographed at the time and show five skulls, not all of which were complete. According to Mellor, they were placed in a brick vault which was then covered with a plain slab made of stone. During the 1990s, new excavation work was conducted by the Winchester Museums Service at the site of Hyde Abbey. This was carried out in 1999 and unearthed the pit that John Mellor is thought to have dug in 1886 and the foundations of Hyde Abbey along with more bones. Amongst other remains, they discovered part of an adult female pelvis that was found to date from the post-medieval period. Although more human remains were found, enough to fill two boxes, they were not dated because of a lack of funds.

In 2010, which marked the 900th anniversary of the founding of Hyde Abbey, a community group called Hyde 900 instigated the decision to open the unmarked vault at St Bartholomew's church believed to hold the remains of Alfred the Great. Although they received support from Winchester University and St Bartholomew's Church, it took a further three years for permission to be granted to open the grave. The project was to gain major impetus following the discovery of the grave of Richard III in February 2013. Fearing that the grave might be tampered with around this time, an emergency petition was granted to allow the grave to be excavated in March that year. The excavation was led by Dr Katie Tucker and colleagues from the University of Winchester. They began by lifting the slab that covered the grave and found a small vault made of red bricks that appeared to match the descriptions of John Mellor. The vault was full of soil but, after digging down a short distance, it was discovered that there were two more slabs covering another sealed area. After lifting one of the slabs, it was found that the small brick chamber contained five skulls, long bones, ribs and other skeletal remains.

The skulls in particular appeared to match the

photographs taken during the nineteenth century and the excavation raised hopes that the bones of Alfred, Edward and Eahlswith had finally been rediscovered. The remains were taken to the University of Winchester to be stored and it was discovered that there were six individual skeletons within the grave as well as a number of separate bones not associated with them. However, it was not until August 2013, when further permission was granted to analyse and date the remains, that the bone samples were sent for radiocarbon dating. The results showed that the oldest skeleton present dated from around 1030-1150 whilst the latest remains dated to around 1415-1460. Therefore, none of the skeletons were old enough to be the remains of Alfred or his family who had all died earlier than this time period and before the foundation of Hyde Abbey in 1110.

However, the story did not end there. Dr Katie Tucker contacted the University of Winchester about the excavations undertaken at Hyde Abbey in the 1990s. Dr Tucker requested permission to examine and analyse the bones unearthed during that period and was presented with two boxes of material that had not been radiocarbon dated before because of a lack of funds. After they were sent for radiocarbon dating it was discovered that the majority of the bones were from a similar date range as the bones excavated from the unmarked grave at St Bartholomew's Church. However, one sample which had been taken from the pelvis of an adult male was discovered to date from the much earlier period of 895-1017. This predated the foundation of Hyde Abbey and it was also noted that there was no evidence to suggest that the land upon which the Abbey had been built had previously been used as a burial site. This seems to suggest that the bone may have belonged to one of the bodies moved from the New Minster in 1110. The date range of the pelvic bone also encompassed the death dates of Alfred and his family as well as that of St Grimbald.

It was also discovered that the sample taken from an adult male pelvic bone belonged to an individual who was in their mid-twenties to mid-forties. It was therefore unlikely to have belonged to Edward's son Aethelweard who died at the age of 20 or 21 or to Eadwig who died at a similar age. St Grimbald can also be discounted because he is recorded as having died when he was in his eighties. It is possible then that the bone could have come from the bodies of Alfred, his son Edward or his brother Aethelweard. Dr Katie Tucker has argued that, although Alfred and Edward were in their late forties or early fifties, 'the osteological methods used to determine an age from the pelvis tend to underage older individuals, meaning an upper limit of mid-forties for the piece of bone is only to be taken as a guide.' (Edoardo Albert & Katie Tucker, *In Search of Alfred the Great*, p.227) Whilst the circumstantial evidence and the carbon dating raise the tantalising possibility that the bone may have belonged to Alfred or his son Edward, it currently remains an unproven hypothesis. However, Dr Tucker has also argued that DNA analysis of bone held in the mortuary chests at Winchester Cathedral and which are said to include the remains of Alfred's father, Aethelwulf, and comparison with the bone from Hyde Abbey could potentially yield new and important information. With so many new sources continuing to throw light on the world of the Anglo-Saxons, it seems highly likely that their history will continue to be revealed to us and that their voices will continue to speak across the centuries to future generations about their culture and lives.

Bibliography

Albert, Edoardo & Tucker, Katie, *In Search of Alfred The Great*, Stroud: Amberley, 2015

Bullen, Annie, *Sutton Hoo*, Suffolk: National Trust, 2014

Farmer, David & Sherly-Price, Leo, *Bede: Ecclesiastical History of the English Language*, London: Penguin, 1990

Farmer, David, *Oxford Dictionary of Saints*, Oxford: Oxford University Press, 2004

Fern, Chris, *Beasts, Birds and Gods: Interpreting the Staffordshire Hoard*, West Midlands History Limited, 2014

Garmonsway, GN, *The Anglo-Saxon Chronicle*, London: Everyman, 1972

Heaney, Seamus, *Beowulf*, London: Faber and

Faber, 1999

Hindley, Geoffrey, *A Brief History of the Anglo-Saxons*, London: Robinson, 2006

Lawson, MK, *Cnut: England's Viking King 1016-35*, Stroud: The History Press, 2011

Morris, John, *Nennius: British History and The Welsh Annals*, London & Chichester: Phillimore, 1980

Niles, John D, *The Idea of Anglo-Saxon England*, Chichester: Wiley-Blackwell, 2015

Pollard, Justin, *Alfred the Great*, London: John Murray, 2005

Sharp, Robert, *The Hoard and its History: Staffordshire's Secrets Revealed*, Warwick: Brewin Books, 2016

Smyth, Alfred P, *King Alfred the Great*, Oxford: Oxford University Press, 1995

Symonds, Dr David, *The Staffordshire Hoard*, Birmingham: Birmingham Museums Trust, 2014

Wall, Martin, *The Anglo-Saxon Age*, Stroud: Amberley Publishing, 2015

Whittock, Martyn & Whittock, Hannah, *The Viking Blitzkrieg*, Stroud: The History Press, 2013

Wood, Michael, *Domesday: A Search for the Roots*

of England, London: Book Club Associates, 1987

Wood, Michael, *In Search of the Dark Ages*, London: BBC Books, 1981

Zaluckyj, Sarah, *Mercia: The Anglo-Saxon Kingdom of Central England*, Logaston: Logaston Press, 2013

Web Pages

http://www.bl.uk/learning/timeline/item126532.
html

https://www.bl.uk/collection-items/beowulf

http://www.britishmuseum.org/visiting/galleries/
europe/room_41_europe_ad_300-1100.aspx

http://www.bl.uk/onlinegallery/sacredtexts/
lindisfarne.html

http://www.english-heritage.org.uk/visit/places/
1066-battle-of-hastings-abbey-and-battlefield/

https://www.lichfield-cathedral.org/

https://www.lichfield-cathedral.org/downloads/
lichfield-angel.pdf

http://offasdyke.org.uk/

http://www.staffordshirehoard.org.uk/

http://www.visitstoke.co.uk/see-do/
Staffordshirehoard.aspx

Index

THE PROBLEM WAS ME

THOMAS GAGLIANO
With Abraham J. Twerski, MD

THE PROBLEM
WAS ME

A Guide to Self-Awareness, Compassion, and Awareness

THOMAS GAGLIANO

With Abraham J. Twerski, MD

Gentle Path
P R E S S

Carefree, Arizona

Gentle Path Press
P.O. Box 3172
Carefree, Arizona 85377
www.gentlepath.com

First Edition: 2011

For more information regarding our publications, please contact-
Gentle Path Press at 1-800-708-1796 (toll-free U.S. only).

Book edited by Rebecca Post, Marianne Harkin
Book designed by Serena Castillo
Typesetting by Kinne Design

ISBN: 978-0-9826505-7-8

Contents

Acknowledgments

I am grateful to and proud of my wife and children for their willingness and courage in allowing this book to come to fruition. Their faith that this book could help others was a vital source of strength for me. A special thanks to Tony, who has always been there to cheer me on, especially when I felt this book would never become a reality. Tony, along with Robert and Joe, supplied me with the support I needed to keep going, especially when my warden was telling me I would never be able to follow this through. Thanks to everyone in my support system who have journeyed along with me as we have silenced our wardens' commands together. These people have always been an important part of my life, and they are important contributors to this book.

Preface

By Abraham J. Twerski, M.D.

When I was in psychiatric training and assigned to report on Thomas Mann's *The Magic Mountain,* I was deeply impressed by Mann's insights. I recall asking my professor if Thomas Mann was a physician. His response, "Don't be silly. No doctor could be that sensitive."

There is truth to the professor's statement. Scientific medical training so saturates the left brain that the right brain, the part that receives and develops feelings, is overwhelmed. The occupational hazard of being a physician is that we may lose some measure of sensitivity. Tom Gagliano is neither a psychiatrist nor a psychologist, but he is a sensitive human being who holds valuable psychological insights gained from life experiences rather than from books and lectures. Tom's words are laden with emotion.

In one of my earlier books, *Addictive Thinking,* I described the unique thought processes of an addict. These same processes occur in non-addicts but are exaggerated in addicts. Tom Gagliano speaks from the vantage point of a recovering addict, but everyone can identify with the emotions he describes. He points out the destructive impact that early experiences can have on a person's life, but if you are aware of these early obstacles then you can take proper steps to free yourself from their stranglehold. *The Problem Was Me* is not only a self-help book, but a valuable textbook for mental health professionals.

Introduction

By Thomas Gagliano

*Not until I stopped denying my own past and began sharing
my wounds, did I allow myself to be loved by other people.*

ℰℭ

You do not have to be addicted to drugs or alcohol to benefit
from this book. This book can help you with whatever distraction you
are using to avoid whatever it is you should be doing. Before the rapid
proliferation of computers, video games, satellite TV, and cell phones,
we had fewer choices for acting out our compulsions. Now with the
explosive growth of digital devices, we can gamble, shop, play video
games, and view pornography with a click of a mouse or by pressing a
button on a remote.

While I am not a licensed therapist, I have gained great insight
through my own process of healing from the destructive behaviors
in my life. In addition, I have coached many people who have been
crippled by their own internal demons. Having faced my own demons,
I know how it feels to be overwhelmed, hopeless, and completely
paralyzed with fear.

With the help of Twelve Step programs, group sessions, organized retreats, workshops, and sponsors, I discovered the way to a better
life and how to help others find their own paths. It was not until I
opened myself to change that I began to transform from the person
who once isolated himself from others to a man who has become rich
with the wonders of life and the love of family and friends. I found
peace and my own spirituality.

Healing is an ongoing process of self-determination and self-
discipline. While the rewards are not always immediate, beautiful gifts
await if you are patient and can take direction. As I healed internally,

a need emerged to share how I did it with others. I began to help people from all walks of life, including rabbis, priests, doctors, plumbers, housewives, computer technicians, CEOs, therapists, sales people, and engineers. Because we could identify with each other's struggles, the people I coached opened a part of their lives to me that had been off limits to others and even to themselves. As I helped them face their biggest fears, I was encouraged to face my own shortcomings and the obstacles I needed to overcome in shaking off my personal demons. Not until I stopped denying my own past and began sharing my wounds did I allow myself to be loved by other people.

Some of the people I have helped have shared my philosophies with their therapists. After sharing my insight with some of the professionals I met with, they began to adopt my methods in treating their own patients. This book is filled with nuggets of wisdom that are invaluable and affirming. It explores the underlying reasons why we behave the way we do. The book is designed to be a reference tool. You could turn to any chapter and find helpful information on ways to deal with life on life's terms.

The encouragement from the people who allowed me to help them has inspired me to write this book. *The Problem Was Me* contains the tools gained from my personal struggle with compulsions and applies a methodology as exemplified by Abraham Twerski. Through the experiences, insights, and the wisdom I have gained in my journey in life, combined with Dr. Twerski's professional wisdom, this book can help those with destructive behaviors as well as supply others with a blueprint to give their children the love denied to many of them. So many people feel they were denied of loving behaviors from their parents. This book will also bring an understanding to family and friends who seek to prevent themselves or their loved ones from continuing on a path of self-destruction.

The common problems we face are from unhealed childhood wounds that have remained buried and have haunted us. Only when we permit the window into our past to be opened, exposing the core of our adult difficulties, can we begin the healing process. Today, I am aware of how deeply I was imprisoned by childhood wounds and how negative voices from the past disturb me today.

Throughout *The Problem Was Me*, I refer to the warden, an imaginary person with a bat, who sat on my shoulder. Whenever someone made me feel defective, he would come out swinging. The warden instilled in me a peculiar definition of intimacy. Intimacy meant pain, and should be avoided. The warden was trying to protect me from getting too close to anyone. This imaginary guy on my shoulder has been with me a long time, as far back as I can remember. His motive for using the bat was to take a swing at me if I ever got the idea that I deserved to be happy or if I stumbled and made a mistake. He permitted me no margin for error.

The warden becomes the little voice inside our heads that won't go away. The little voice keeps us imprisoned by reminding us of the intrusive messages we received in childhood over and over again. Childhood wounds are reopened, isolating us from others. In many ways, we play roles in our lives that can bring harmful consequences to others and to ourselves. We wear masks to hide who we really are. The little voice makes us feel ashamed and unworthy. We become self-centered causing us to feel that we have the right to something regardless of the harm it causes others. We call this destructive entitlement.

The warden's voice inside our head repeats that we do not deserve to be happy. His voice leads us to sabotage happiness when it comes our way. He is so powerful that even though he imprisons us to destructive roles in our lives, we listen to him.

What roles in your life did your warden command you to play?

1. *Caretaking Role*—Taking care of the world can be tiring, yet the warden will not allow you to let go of taking care of others.

2. *Victim Role*—The warden's voice exempts you from taking responsibility in your life. All your problems are caused by your spouse, employer, children, parents, or others.

3. *Transparent Role*—The warden warns against sharing feelings; no one wants to hear how you feel.

4. *Defiant Role*—The warden creates a voice that directs you to disagree with everyone, especially those of authority.

5. *Compliant Role*—The warden creates a voice that directs you to agree with everyone. How they feel about you matters more than you feel about yourself.

6. *Angry Role*—The warden forbids against admitting to mistakes, so you use your anger to always prove you are right. How you hurt others reflects your inner pain.

7. *Underachieving Role*—The warden warns that failing is so painful that it is not worth even trying.

8. *Controlling Role*—The warden warns us that any process we cannot control will not end positively; therefore, everyone must act and think the way we want them to.

The warden keeps us emotionally shackled and orders us to keep our doors locked, so no one can enter. This book provides the key to unlocking the locked door and allowing happiness into our lives.

There are three essential strategies to healing that will free us from the chains of our childhood wounds. These include awareness, action, and maintenance. First, we must become aware of what is broken inside so we know what to fix. Second, positive actions allow us to see our true responsibility in each situation and help to stop the voice inside of us from directing our behavior in negative ways. We discover that if we do what we always did, then we'll get what we always got. As we start to act in healthier ways, the distorted view we have of others and ourselves begins to melt away. Eventually, through positive actions, our perceptions and dynamics change, bringing more peace into our lives. Third, maintaining positive actions in an environment where there is group support will stop the destructive inner voice from coming back to take charge of our behavior again.

If you do not have *awareness*, you cannot take *action*.
If you cannot take *action*, there is nothing to *maintain*.

One of my most rewarding feelings is the gratitude I receive from a spouse or family member of someone I have coached. Once the healing begins, the love returns to their marriage and is passed down to their children. This miracle, which is reflected in my own marriage, fills me with overwhelming joy.

Sometimes we act in ways that do not always make sense as we hurt ourselves and others. We feel compelled to listen to the destructive inner voice in our heads. Making sense of our actions is like figuring out a jigsaw puzzle. This book will allow you to put the puzzle pieces together. If you are still unsure if this book could help you, take a few minutes to ask yourself the following questions.

- Do you tend to focus on the shortcomings of others to avoid looking at yourself?

- Do you say yes to people because saying no is too painful?

- Do you feel like you are carrying the burden of the world on your shoulders and are powerless to let it go?

- Do you feel victimized by people or circumstances in your life?

- Do you have problems trusting any process that you are not in control of?

- When you make a mistake, do you feel shame so strong it overwhelms you?

- Do you take the time to celebrate the victories (successes) in your life, or do you beat yourself up over your failures?

- Do you feel comfortable being intimate, or do you avoid intimacy?

- Are you most comfortable being isolated from others even though you realize that avoiding social contact keeps you locked in depression and self-pity?

- When you get angry, do you terrify the people around you, or do you suppress, ignore, or stuff anger?

- Do you feel invisible in your relationships?

- In social settings, do you feel either superior or inferior to others, rather than feeling like you belong?

- Do you always have to be right, even if you push people away?

- Do you have destructive behaviors that hurt you or others, but still feel entitled to continue your addictive behavior?

- Do you give away your power to others by letting them determine how you feel about yourself?

- Do you make up stories in your mind about the way others feel about you, but don't have the courage to tell them how you feel?

- Are there tasks you must do, but are paralyzed to start?

- Do you want help, but aren't able to take that first step and don't know why?

If you answered yes to any of the questions, this book is for you. Each of us can benefit from a better understanding of how childhood wounds mold the person we are today. Some addicts who have been sober for a long time may continue to lead tormented, angry lives. This book will explore why and how to make positive changes. The intention of this book is not to bash our caregivers or parents. Rather, it is to understand the effects of these messages given to us in childhood that impact our lives at this moment. Today I can fail at times, but it does not mean I am a failure. I can make mistakes, but it does not mean I am a mistake. The words expressed throughout this book are from my heart. It is my fervent wish to bring hope to those imprisoned by a wounded past.

Chapter One: Damaged Goods

Something had to be wrong with me or my parents
wouldn't act the way they did.

ഇൻൽ

As a child in a family filled with dysfunction, my belief system told me that I was the cause of the insanity within my home. When my needs were not satisfied as a child, rather than acknowledging that something might be wrong with my parents, I believed that something must be wrong with me. My father was often away from home while I was growing up. My mother was always trying to locate him. As the oldest child, I became a caretaker for my mother. One night she threatened suicide. She told me to find my father or she was going to carry out her threat. She held a long, sharp knife used by my father to cut meat. She pointed the sharp end at her stomach, threatening to stab herself if I did not phone my father immediately and get him home. I was about ten years old. The first phone call I made was to my grandmother. She told me where I could find my father. My hands trembled as I dialed the number. When I heard his voice I started to sob, pleading with him to come quickly.

When my father arrived home, I noticed that even he was scared that my mother was about to do something crazy. I kept my eyes glued to the knife in my mother's hands, saying to myself, *Please put the knife down.* Instead of yelling or screaming like he often did, my father tried to calm her down. As he tried to talk her out of committing suicide, I heard him saying, "What about the children? Who will take care of them?" My mother replied, "I don't care about the kids. I only want you." Eventually, my mother put down the knife. It would take me another twenty-five years to acknowledge that on that night I also become a victim. Something inside me died when I heard those hurtful me from the pain. When alone, the negative voice would dominate my thinking. As much as I tried to ignore the pain from early childhood, I could not. I had a void deep within me, preventing me from experiencing any true sense of fulfillment. Eventually, I realized that my insanity would continue until I accepted the truth about my life.

I had to start at the beginning to fully understand the origin of my pain that had a stranglehold on my life. Once I acknowledged my difficult childhood, I began to see myself as a discouraged person who needed help, not the evil man who deserved to be punished. When I took off my mask, I discovered that most of my fears were of my own making.

The Resulting Destructive Behavior

At this point, I realized I wasn't gambling to win; instead, I was gambling to fill a void inside. The most significant part was finally realizing I would never be able to control my gambling addiction again. I could never gamble casually. Gambling had beaten me into submission. I surrendered and accepted defeat. I was soon back with my therapist who suggested I go to Twelve Step recovery programs and join a therapy group where he was a co-facilitator. This was the first time I realized I had to do the actions I was told to do, not necessarily what I wanted to do. Going to my first Twelve Step meeting was terrifying. I sat in the back of the room with an imaginary wall built around me, covered by layers of fear and shame. I permitted no one to get close.

I didn't know then that these people saw right through this wall. They knew what my problem was long before I did. They knew me because they knew themselves. I was suffering from an illness called "uniqueness." I truly believed that no one could ever understand how I felt inside. When I heard others expressing joy and laughter it was ridiculous to me. I asked myself, How could they be happy when their lives were so screwed up? When they hugged each other at the end of a meeting I felt uncomfortable. For months I could not shake a hand, let alone give someone a hug.

Not surprisingly, I made no connections with any of the people at the meetings. Nonetheless, I kept going. After a few months of going to meetings my wife asked why I never received phone calls from other people in group; she knew that this support was an important healing aspect of Twelve Step fellowships. "They were all ass kissers!" I responded. Beneath the exterior mask of false pride I was a shattered person who eventually realized that these people weren't ass kissers at all. We were joined together because of our common feeling of profound pain. Eventually, I realized they loved and accepted me long before I loved or accepted myself. Once I understood this, I began to embrace the program. I finally allowed help into my life.

I discovered the hard way that complete abstinence from my destructive behaviors was essential for my healing. Without it, my self-hate would become overwhelming. I learned that I can't be in the ring all day boxing with my addiction and expect to work on improving my relationships at the same time.

I continued to go to Twelve Step meetings, individual therapy, and group therapy. In meetings, the compulsive gamblers spoke about the huge amounts of money they lost. One elderly man said he lost more than everyone put together. He lost fifty years of his life to his constant working and gambling. He wasn't around for his children as they grew up. He noticed he was absent in all of his children's pictures. His comment stuck with me. While I realized the ways I was hurting others and myself through my actions, I never considered the experiences I missed with my family, experiences I could never get back.

Between group meetings, I began to make phone calls to other group members to encourage them. While doing this therapeutic activity, that inner voice was telling me this was a waste of time. As a result, it became increasingly difficult to pick up the phone to call people. I wrestled between the benefits of being in group and going back to my old habits and ways of thinking. I was actually grieving the loss of my compulsions as if I were grieving the loss of a loved one.

I never did go back to gambling, and I cut down on the hours I worked. On the surface, things appeared better. On the inside it was a different story. I was still ignoring the reasons why I felt so wounded and defective. While I was no longer medicating my feelings with work or gambling, I soon chose another destructive alternative to ease my pain.

Womanizing and Attempting to Fix the Emptiness Inside

One evening after working late, I had a sexual encounter with a married woman who worked for me. After the encounter, I felt ashamed and disgusted over what I had done. I went home that night and scrubbed my body until my skin was raw. How could I do this? I looked in the mirror and said, "I'm my father's son." No matter how hard I tried, I was doing the same thing to my family that my father did to his. I attempted to justify my actions by telling myself that I was different from my father, but my guilt was unbearable. I coached my kids' teams, always did homework with them, and was there when they needed someone to talk to, yet I betrayed them and my wife in the worst way a man can betray his family. The warden was beating me up with his bat, which made me feel even more worthless.

I was setting up my kids to repeat the same dysfunction passed down to me by my father and by his father before him. Despite the shame, I wasn't ready to work on my brokenness, and I had sex again with this same woman. Throughout this madness, there was a miracle occurring with my father. I started to see a change in him. My parents came to our house just to be with their grandchildren. The special attention he gave them was something that I had never witnessed before with him. He had such patience with them. Both my parents watched the same movies with the children over and over again. Their favorite was *The Land Before Time*. I don't know how many sequels were made, but my children wore out the VHS tapes, watching them with my parents.

In addition to his time, my father gave my children encouragement. The longer he remained sober, the more his goodness came out. Watching the love grow between my children and him was amazing. My father was learning to give and accept unconditional love. The only words my father ever uttered to our children were words of encouragement and love.

Years later, following a checkup at the clinic, his blood work came back abnormal. After a battery of tests, they found a malignant tumor in his stomach. Within just six months, the cancer spread throughout his body. I never felt so helpless. I was so self-sufficient that I felt I could fix anything in life if I worked hard enough at it. With my father's condition, I was so powerless. All I could do is watch him wilt away. My father said he had one favor to ask me. He did not want to see his grandchildren to see him after he became extremely ill and near death. As much as I disagreed with him, I honored his request. Before he died, he said his biggest regret was not being able to see his grandchildren grow up.

One night at the hospital, a priest came to give him some spiritual support. As the priest left the room he told my mother that my father was more spiritual than anyone he had ever met. I found this amazing because when I was in second grade, he ridiculed me when I told him about Noah's Ark. He said, "What, are you stupid, how you could believe that stuff?" After hearing the priest's comment, I discovered that he had found spiritual peace after he stopped drinking. That surprised me as I remember this man as somebody who once only worshiped money.

My parents had been divorced and remarried so many times that nobody knew for sure if they were married at this point in time or not. My father's will was dependent on them being married. It turned out that they were not married at the time. We held a somber wedding ceremony in the hospital, while my father was on his deathbed. My father was hooked up to a morphine drip as he held my mother's hands and repeated their vows. All of my brothers and their wives were there.

I visited my father in the hospital every night. One evening he asked me how his dog was doing. We were watching his dog during this time. Every night when the dog went out to do his business, our three-year-old daughter would greet the dog at the door with a wipe in her hand and clean the dog's bottom. My father laughed so hard that he told me to stop because it was starting to hurt inside.

One particular night in the hospital he felt very weak, and he knew he did not have much time left. Although I felt sadness I didn't know how to express my feelings to him. As I was about ready to leave, he said with a weak, tired voice, "Son, about twenty years ago my father was in the hospital dying of lung cancer. I was sitting right beside him as you are seated beside me, and I could never find the courage to tell him I loved him." I was amazed that even in the midst of my father's physical pain, he was able to recognize my pain. As he tried to reach out to me, the warden would not allow me to let my guard down and hug my father and say, "I love you." I was paralyzed by fear and was silent.

My father was riddled with cancer, and he was frail and weak, yet he still had the power of a ten-foot giant. The warden told me, "Run out of this room as fast as you can. Don't be vulnerable in front of him!" I grasped my father's hand. He pulled me closer and began to weep. The only time I saw my father cry was when he was drunk and seeking forgiveness for being abusive. On the outside, I showed no emotion as he wept. I silently left the room with a horrible lump in my throat. At the time, I didn't have the strength to say "no" to the warden and tell my father that I loved him.

As I approached the hospital elevator, the door opened and out came a friend from one of the meetings I attended. He was visiting someone else in the hospital that night. I gave him a big hug. I needed to hold someone I could trust, and this guy miraculously appeared. In time, as I grew spiritually, I recognized that divine intervention had taken place that day in my life. That guy in the elevator was sent to comfort me because I didn't know how to comfort myself. Without him, I might have chosen a very destructive solution to ease my pain. Within the next few days, I told my father that I loved him.

One week later, my father suffered a stroke, and the doctors induced a coma. My mother asked me to come to the hospital as the doctors did not think my father would make it through the night. He took his final breath the instant my brother and I walked into his room. My mother explained to us that he didn't want to die until all his kids were there.

The wake was two days later. At the funeral home, I recognized more than thirty men and women from the groups and Twelve Step meetings I attended. Once they heard about my father's death from my wife, word spread quickly to the other group members. I was touched by their kindness. For the first time I had a sense of belonging and connection that I had been searching for my entire life. The message I received from their presence told me I was important, that I mattered. No amount of money, expensive cars, or houses gave me the feeling of warmth I felt that day from these people.

I was beginning to grow. I had the willingness to seek help, but now I acquired a willingness to *take direction* and do what others suggested I do. I was ready to trust others enough to let my guard down and let them see the parts of me that I had covered up for so long because of my shame. I realized that I subconsciously chose to be unhappy because that was familiar to me, especially when faced with frightening changes. I didn't like to own my character defects, especially when I was exposed to challenges. Eventually I learned that when I own my defects, I can respond to challenges in a much healthier way.

I became willing to take direction and do what I was told to do, regardless of how I felt. I began to surrender control which resulted in huge changes in my life. I began to practice humility and swallow my pride. My priorities changed. My businesses were not as important anymore. I eventually sold the businesses that required me to be there and helped the long-time employees who were faithful to me find employment in the industry. I kept my real estate business enterprises that were run by others. I had the luxury of retiring young.

I needed to learn why I kept going from one false solution to the next. To accomplish this, I spent years going to retreats, workshops, groups, meetings, and therapy. During this time, I stayed away from all of my destructive behaviors and did what I was told to do. I listened to the healers in my life that consisted of my therapist, sponsors in the Twelve Step fellowships, and many of the people I met in groups and meetings. I also listened to the stories of other recovering people who were trying to find hope and peace in their lives.

As I began to better understand myself, I started helping others with similar destructive behaviors. Eventually, I held support groups in my home for a diverse group of people, including rabbis, priests, doctors, lawyers, plumbers, and the unemployed. These groups helped people work directly on healing and growth. Some group members spun off to create their own sub-groups. Over time, the group itself became a valuable tool in the healing process for all. These were not just people with addictions, but others who wanted to explore the reasons they acted in ways that sabotaged their happiness. Some of the group members were mystified why they kept choosing relationships that only brought destruction to their lives.

I learned I would never recover until I accepted and embraced the emotional scars of the past. I needed to face the real problem, instead of smashing someone in the mouth whenever provoked. I was only able to realize the real problem when I finally confessed to feeling broken inside. My problems were never gambling, working, or womanizing. These were poor solutions to my real problem. My real problem was my victim thinking. My childhood wounds created a distorted view of life. The warden's voice kept giving me the faulty information that was fed to me as a child. I finally discovered I could not afford to be imprisoned by the warden for the rest of my life. I became more comfortable trusting other people. As my self-esteem improved, I no longer needed the validation from others to feel worthy. I started to *listen* to the people who directed my growth, rather than *fight* them.

If I managed my business like I managed my life, I would have gone bankrupt. I may even have fired myself. When I stepped down from the position of managing my life and took direction from others, my growth accelerated.

As my father found peace during the last ten years of his life, baking became his hobby. He taught my young children how to bake. His specialty was cream puffs, which were so heavy they required a shovel rather than a spoon. He compiled a cookbook consisting of his best calorie-laden desserts.

My mother gave the cookbook to my wife after my father died. One afternoon as I began to look through the cookbook, I discovered that it included more than just recipes. In fact, every other page contained my father's journaling. He wrote down all of his fears, pains, and feelings each day. Since I was struggling with my feelings at the time, I was overcome with emotion. I always viewed my father as a ten-foot giant who could handle anything. I never saw him show fear. He took charge of every situation. For the first time, my father appeared the same size as others. He was not the indestructible and heartless person I knew as a child, but rather someone in pain and in need of help. He was just a flawed human being like all the rest of us. My father reminded me of myself. His journal and mine were similar in that we both disclosed the pain that we hid behind a mask. Like father, like son. We lived with shame and the fear of God and others. Like me, my father had learned to trust others, and this helped heal his pain.

After I read the journal entries, I made an appointment with my therapist. When I arrived, I uncharacteristically burst into tears. What I read in those journal entries had touched something deep inside of me. For the first time, I saw my father with no mask, no toughness, and no perfection. He had stripped himself down to bare skin and bones. He was human, after all. Only then, when reading my father's innermost thoughts and feelings, did I permit myself to find a deeper forgiveness for myself and for him.

The Power of an Inner Voice

That inner voice, the warden, knew my vulnerability. Through my written inventories I discovered one of the many false messages he told me was that asking for help was a sign of weakness. He kept me away from the help I needed to heal. I struggled so long to find forgiveness and a spiritual connection. When I got down on my knees to pray, I felt paralyzed with shame and fear. The warden made it clear that I didn't deserve the love of anyone, including God.

My mother was imprisoned by her warden as well. She regrets her actions just as I did mine. My father's insanity created some of the insanity within my mother. Raising four children while dealing with my father's behaviors was not easy. My mother lived in constant fear, never knowing my father's whereabouts or when the next bomb would go off. Even with this chaos, my mother tried to hold things together as best as she could. She also made holidays and birthdays as special as possible. These are the memories that bring warmth to me, memories I'm happy to share with my children. My mother was nineteen when I was born, so in many ways she was a child herself. She, too, was hurting inside and looked for me to give her what she could not get from my father. Her fear of losing him sent her into self-survival. She was like a drowning person who would pull anyone down in her need to get air.

My mother's father was a very kind and gentle man, but he was also an alcoholic, and alcoholism leaves emotional scars on loved ones. All of us from discouraged childhoods have our own warden, just as my mother did. If my mother could have found a support group, she might have allowed others to carry her through those difficult times when she felt so alone. She didn't understand how her actions affected others. I also find it difficult, at times, to believe I was capable of doing what I did to those I loved the most. Today my mother is still a wonderful source of love and support for our children.

I Am My Father's Son

I remember the night I looked in the mirror, with rage, and said, "I am my father's son." All of the hatred I felt spewed out toward my father. I also recall hating myself for bringing the same wreckage into my home that my father brought into his. Today, my feelings for my father emanate from the loving messages he gave my children and the love he received from people he helped. I am proud to be my father's son. Today when I watch a movie or television show about a father and son relationship, it brings up deep feelings of emotion. As a boy, I so desperately wanted to feel loved and special.

By the time my father found peace, I was still dealing with my own demons. Because he died at age fifty-seven, we missed having quality time together. His death motivated me to make certain that my own children know how much I love them. With my self-acceptance came empathy and compassion for my father. None of this would have been possible had I not taken the steps to heal my internal wounds first.

Complete forgiveness is an ongoing process, beginning with the willingness to take the action of forgiveness rather than choosing the path of victimhood. My father did not hurt me because of something I did. Instead, his actions were a result of his internal demons. He never meant to hurt me, just as I never intended to hurt the people who mattered most to me.

Gratitude and Acceptance

I feel the most grateful at the end of the day when I crawl into bed. There was a time when I dreaded waking up because of how shameful I felt. Today, I finally have peace and appreciate the gift of life. My wife and I enjoy newfound intimacy and I revel in the joys of family life. I feel great joy listening to my youngest son tell me and my wife stories about the world from a perspective of a nine-year-old child. My children share stories about their lives with my wife and I that neither of us could imagine sharing with our parents. This brings us comfort in the knowledge that they trust us this much. Life has its imperfections just as people have their flaws. Most of the time my faith outweighs my fears, but every now and then I slip up and allow the warden's voice to get a little too loud. Usually this happens when I feel entitled or expect the entire world to revolve around me. This is exemplified in my overbearing moments when I tell my wife what she should or should not do, even though she just needs me to be there for her and to listen.

Today, when I hear the warden's voice, I thank him for sharing his opinion, then I redirect my thinking toward healthy actions. These actions may only consist of making a phone call and sharing my thoughts and feelings with those whom I most trust. They continue to hold my hand until I accept myself and remove the mask that shields me from the outside world. Today, I proudly stand as a man without a mask, allowing the world to view me as I am—imperfect, with all my strengths and weaknesses. By removing the mask, I could reach out to others and help them find their way along the journey of life. The ability to help others is a wonderful gift, both for the giver and the recipient.

I found inspiration in Rick Warren's book, *The Purpose Driven Life.* Warren postulates that God will lead you to your true calling in life through the people you trust the most. This gave me pause to reflect. My true calling was in helping others. People began to suggest that I write a book about my life and the healing process that helped me and helped others. My internal voice told me this was too big a task, so I thought I would get more advice. As in the past, I gained courage through the support of others. They gave me the strength to do things I could not have accomplished alone. An example is this book.

After writing an early draft of *The Problem Was Me,* I found myself in uncharted waters. I was wondering how to write it. That is when my path crossed with Abraham Twerski, M.D. A mutual friend introduced us. The idea of asking for help made me uncomfortable. Dr. Twerski put me immediately at ease. He believes that in the core of every human being there is a nucleus of self-respect and dignity.

As I sat in Dr. Twerski's living room, he told me in a gentle, soft-spoken voice about an ex-convict named Avi. He shared, "Some years ago, I began a modest rehabilitation program in Israel for ex-convicts incarcerated for drug-related crimes. During a session with the first group of clients, I illustrated the power of man's natural resistance in the avoidance of damaging some object of beauty. Since everyone knows that drugs are damaging, greater resistance should have been self-enforced before the addiction took hold. But, their lack of resistance was the result of a poor sense of self-worth and the inability to find beauty within their being. Long-term recovery depends on the development of self-esteem, and when healing begins the urge to inflict self pain is diminished."

Avi, one of the ex-convicts, asked, "How can you expect me to have self-esteem? I am thirty-four years old, and sixteen of those thirty-four years have been spent in prison. When I'm released from the penitentiary, who will hire me? When the social worker tells my family that I'll be released in ninety days, nobody is happy. I am a burden and an embarrassment to everyone in the family, and I'm sure they would rather I stay locked up forever until the day I die. How am I supposed to get self-esteem?"

Dr. Twerski's response was, "Avi, have you ever seen a display of diamonds in a jewelry store window? Those diamonds are scintillatingly beautiful and worth hundreds of thousands of dollars. Do you know what they looked like when they first were brought out from the diamond mine? They were ugly, dirty pieces of glass that anyone would think worthless.

"At the diamond mine, there is an expert called a maven who scrutinizes the ore. He may pick up a dirty piece of glass while marveling at the precious gem that lies within. After he sends it to the processing plant, it emerges as the magnificent and brilliantly shining diamond that you view at the jeweler.

"No one can place anything of beauty into a dirty piece of glass. The beauty of the diamond was always present, but it was concealed by layers of material that had long camouflaged its original exquisiteness. The processing plant only removed these layers of grime to reveal its natural beauty; it did not create the beautiful stone.

"I may not be a maven on diamonds, but I am a maven on people. You have a beautiful soul that has been covered with layers of ugly behavior. Therapy will help to rid yourself of all those years of ugliness and reveal the natural beauty of your human soul."

Avi remained in the program for several months before being

transferred to a transitional facility for another eight months. When he finally was released, he obtained a job and remained drug free.

One day Annette, the administrator of the AA program, received a call from a family whose elderly mother had died, leaving an apartment full of useless furniture. They offered to donate the furniture to the rehabilitation program. Annette telephoned Avi and asked him to help move the furniture. Avi reassured her that he would get a truck to move the furniture.

Two days later, Avi phoned Annette back to inform her that he was at the apartment, but there is no point in moving the furniture as it was old and dilapidated. Annette, who did not want to disappoint the family, asked that the furniture be brought to the office in hopes that perhaps someone could restore some of it.

Avi loaded the truck and delivered the furniture to the facility, located on the second floor of the building. As he dragged the old sofa up the stairs, an envelope fell out from beneath the cushions. That envelope contained five-hundred shekels ($1,800 in American currency). This was found money that nobody knew existed, and the rule of "finders-keepers" could easily have been applied, especially by someone like Avi who used to break into houses for a mere ten shekels.

Instead, Avi called Annette and told her about the money. "That's the family's money," she said. "Call them and tell them." When the family heard the story, they donated the five-hundred shekels to the rehabilitation program.

When Annette relayed the story to Dr. Twerski, he turned to Avi and said, "Do you remember our first meeting when you did not know how you could ever obtain self-esteem? It was then that I told you about your inner soul, that beautiful diamond that was buried within you. Many people who never stole a penny in their life may simply have pocketed that money. Not you. What you did was exceptional and revealed the true beauty of the diamond that is your soul."

Some months later, Avi affixed a bronze plaque on the door of the Rehabilitation Center that read: "DIAMOND PROCESSING CENTER." This is why I began to help others because of my love of exposing beautiful diamonds.

As I left Dr. Twerski, I thought about my father. Both of us were dirty pieces of glass with precious gems inside, deeply hidden from view. Once the dirt was washed away, we were freed from fear. Our goodness, the diamonds inside, could finally be revealed. During our conversation, Dr. Twerski agreed to help with my book. As I share my life story, he shares what he's learned as a psychiatrist in the field of addiction. Together, we aspire to help free you and other people from the destructive roles we play in our lives.

Chapter Three: Enter the Warden

*If the messages given by the child's caregiver
do not match the actions they show, then distrust, fear,
and confusion permeate the child's belief system.*

ॐ

I self-medicated with work, gambling, and womanizing to ease the pain of my perceived failures. Whether gambling, drinking, overeating, pornography, over-spending, or compulsive cleaning, the culprit is usually a flawed belief system that propels people from one harmful behavior to another, or from one bad relationship to another.

Dr. Twerski explained to me how early life experiences affect our lives. Dr. Twerski says, "We walk in the same way we did when we took our first steps. Much of our automatic behavior is derived from early life lessons. When we attempt to change these behaviors, we meet strong resistance. We enter the world as helpless creatures and are totally dependent on our parents for our very survival. As children grow and develop into mature adults it is normal for them to gradually wean themselves from their lifeline of support, the parents who nurtured them from birth. But, the child who grew in body, but whose spirit remains scarred from childhood, will not be able to successfully shed his apron strings. These children have difficulty adjusting to reality and lapse into some form of addictive behavior. Until, of course, they seek help for their problems.

"When a group of psychologists jointly constructed an experimental house for adults, proportioned according to the size that a normal house would feel like to a small child, the ceilings were thirty feet high and the adults were forced to stand on their toes to reach the chairs and tables. All doorknobs were out of their reach. When a control group of normal adults inhabited the house, they began to exhibit neurotic symptoms within only two days. But, this is reality for our small children who feel dwarfed by the large world in which we live. Without parents to serve as intermediaries, life for our children would be intolerable."

Messages that Drive Our Behavior

A core belief system is the network of messages that tell us what to do to survive. It also forms the basis of our attitudes and perceptions so we know who and what to fear and trust, and what we should expect from others. It is based on the early influences of family, teachers, and peers. A faulty belief system makes it difficult to perceive the world in realistic terms and keeps our fears at bay. Healthy information from outside sources helps provide stability and comfort in the face of helplessness, hopelessness, and despair.

Children have a distorted perception of the world. If their father removes a splinter from their mother's finger and she says, "Ouch," they may think their father is harming their mother by inflicting pain. If a sibling is ill and their parents spend extra time caring for their sick child, the brother or sister may come to the conclusion, "They love him more than me."

My biggest misconception was the way I perceived how others saw me. Since I viewed myself as defective, my assumption was that others saw me that way. This is why I shielded myself from vulnerable situations. When I was a child, being vulnerable brought pain and misery. I chose to avoid intimacy, believing if I let down my guard, even with my wife, I might be wounded in the same way my parents hurt me. The consequences of not being intimate were staggering. In addition to being a victim, I was filled with profound loneliness. I believed that I was entitled to harmful behaviors because they ultimately brought me comfort. This resulted in me being angry with myself and everyone else. It was as if everyone was out to get me. I blamed everybody . . . except myself.

I believed I was the center of the universe and the world owed me everything I didn't receive as a child. The real problem was my fear of vulnerability and my tendency to not allow anyone close enough to be intimate. I created unrealistic expectations of people when they didn't give me what I wanted. I was, after all, "the victim."

My behavior in many ways mirrored that of an adolescent, which is where my emotional growth stopped. My sense of entitlement created the basis for my distorted thinking. I turned my attention to the shortcomings of others as a way to focus away from myself and to escape my own pain and misery. To feel better, I relied on my addictions.

Vicious Cycle of Pain

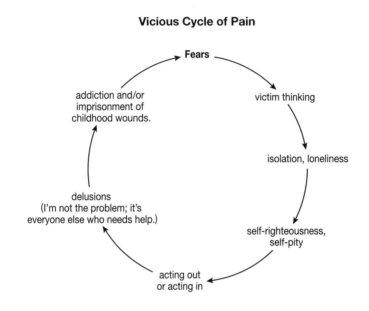

If you do not reprogram your belief system, you will continue to choose one bad solution after another. Although people may be aware of their own destructive belief systems, it is hard to break old patterns and shut off old voices. The longer these messages have been playing in your life, the more difficult it is to turn them off. To make changes, you need to be aware of your faulty belief system. It will help you heal and grow. Then, you need to take action. This won't be easy. Old voices can loudly tell us that we can't trust anything we can't control. Finding a support group where you feel comfortable will help you deal with old wounds that resurface.

Dr. Twerski believes that we live and act according to our sense of perceptions. According to Dr. Twerski, "When we see something, we generally do not think we are viewing some optical illusion. Travelers in the desert are known to observe the occasional mirage, such as an optical illusion of water ahead. On close inspection, the water does not exist. In our daily lives, mirages do not exist. On the other hand, our eyes may not fail us, but the information we receive through our senses is processed by our mind and may undergo distortion. For example, it is not unusual for an adult to panic at the sight of a small, harmless puppy. This may stem from some fear experienced in childhood when the child was frightened by a dog that barked and jumped on him. Our subconscious mind may not mature with time. From the vantage point of an adult, our subconscious views the harmless puppy as a huge, ferocious dog. As anyone who has dealt with dog phobias knows, the logical explanation that this is a harmless puppy is to no avail. Panic supersedes reason. Impressions that reside in the subconscious mind may overwhelm logical thought and cause us to respond according to our subconscious impression rather than to any factual reality."

When my life became unmanageable, I tried anything and everything to bring about change. No matter what I did, I felt broken inside. Although I intended to seek help, I did nothing until I made the conscious decision to do so. I had good intentions, but, ultimately, actions are all that count. I needed something to give me the necessary catalyst to change. Weekly therapy sessions and workshops helped me understand what had happened during my childhood to cause me to seek such harmful solutions. In addition to that, I also needed daily disciplines to transform my attitudes about life and people. These disciplines came in the form of daily connections with the people in my therapy groups and meetings. These were the people I trusted most.

To help heal my wounds, I needed to take two different kinds of inventories. One inventory showed how my parents and teachers influenced my concept of what an authority figure represented to me as an adult. If I did not trust my parents to care for me as a child, it's not surprising that I found it difficult to trust others. My early relationship with my father also affected many of the relationships I had with authority figures, including supervisors, sponsors, spouses, and even spiritual leaders. It took some time to develop new positive inner voices to substitute negative messages I received as a child. Today, I am grateful for the many people who have helped to reinforce the positive messages while providing support when my thinking goes haywire.

The second inventory dealt with childhood wounds. I began to realize how thoughts of worthlessness and defectiveness affected my relationships with other people. I learned how easily childhood wounds could be reopened when I became agitated or someone struck a raw nerve. When I felt pain, I either shut down in shame or lashed out in anger. Through therapy, I discovered it's not my choice that painful events occur, but I do have a choice in how I handle those events. I can either seek help from my support group or permit myself to become a victim. Written inventories are discussed in more detail in Chapter Eight. Pages 99 and 111 have useful examples of how to do inventories. Appendix A on pages 151 and 152 also contains blank inventories for readers to photocopy and use for pesonal use.

My belief system has changed for the better. Instead of misery and turmoil, I am more serene, accepting, and self-forgiving. Whatever overwhelmed me in the past now lacks the same power. During this journey, I discovered a new voice that told me that I no longer had to carry the load of others. This does not mean that my old beliefs went away. I still hear echoes from the past and need to be mindful at all times.

The diagram on the following page, shows how our belief system can be corrupted by childhood wounds, leading to self-destructive behaviors. This allows your inner voice to take control of your actions. Note that the diagram does not take into account other factors, including mental health disorders or compromised social environments. Living in poverty or other oppressive situations affects shame levels and self-esteem.

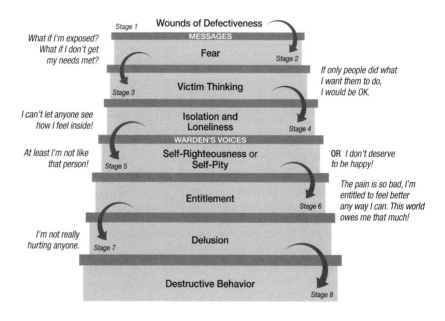

The Old Belief System

Guided by Wounds and Destructive Messages

Stage One: Wounds of Defectiveness

Defectiveness begins from the earliest messages we receive as children from parents and guardians. Healthy messages tell children that they are loved unconditionally. Unhealthy messages tell them that something is wrong with them. When authority figures don't feel good about themselves, it becomes difficult for them to model self-esteem to children. Since children don't have the ability to understand these complicated dynamics, they blame themselves for the defects and shortcoming of their guardians. Over time, they develop coping mechanisms and begin to adopt the faulty belief system as their reality. When they mature, their inner voice tells them to hide their true self from the world.

Stage Two: Fear

Healthy fears protect us from harm. On the other hand, manufactured fears can be harmful and insulate us from experiencing joy.
The stories I create in my head initiate a process I refer to as *awfulization*.
This is a process where my belief system plays out the end of the story
to an awful conclusion. People with untreated emotional wounds have
greater fears than those who grew up in healthy environments. Since
they have often experienced disappointment in the past, they expect
and fear not having their needs met in the future. Past emotional depra-
vation prepares them to expect the same in the future.

Stage Three: Victim Thinking

When children are victimized, they carry victim thinking into
their adult lives. They expect others to fill their existing emptiness. For
example, if a child grew up hungry, the fear of hunger may perpetuate
well into adulthood, even if the person has plenty of food available.
The same occurs if a child grew up without enough nurturing. The
child seeks more nurturing in her adult life and expects more from
those around her. When someone needs more than others can give, it
is a prescription for disaster.

Stage Four: Isolation and Loneliness

Inner voices tell us to isolate ourselves to deal with a world
that will not accept us. As a result, we don't share our thoughts
with others, increasing the likelihood that our thinking will become
distorted. We believe that trusting others will only be harmful and
we'll be harshly judged. Instead, we connect with our inner voice.

Stage Five: Self-righteousness or Self-pity

Looking at ourselves eventually becomes so painful that we
focus on the shortcoming of others instead. We make a decision to be
either self-righteous or wallow in self-pity. We don't like to connect
with others, unless it's with the wrong people. The warden justifies our
distortions.

Stage Six: Entitlement

When the pain inside becomes more intense, the person either acts inward, outward, or both. Acting in can occur when we internally berate ourselves for the mistakes we make. Acting out can occur when we engage in destructive behaviors that are obvious to others, as with addictions. The self-righteous person feels entitled to behave destructively, regardless of the harm he or she causes. Essentially, they give themselves permission to act out in destructive ways.

Stage Seven: Delusion

Eventually, the combination of manufactured fears and victim thinking makes all thoughts and stories real. Isolation convinces us that we are right as we settle into our comfort zone as victims. Focusing on the shortcomings of others becomes more natural than looking within. This faulty belief system supports our position that the world is the problem, not us. As time goes on, the pain intensifies.

Stage Eight: Destructive Behaviors

All belief system stages are built on the foundation of negative core beliefs, which were developed from childhood wounds. The cycle starts over again in stage one, when the person is triggered by someone or something that recreates the feeling of defectiveness.

Chapter Four: Intrusive Messages

Eventually we learn it is all right to say "no," and
we recognize how we had empowered fears to control our life.
The more we do this, the more we learn that our fears
are more imagined than real.

ℰ)ℭ

Reaching back to the messages we heard in childhood will help us discover what needs to be healed. Only by admitting that our best thinking is not working can we work toward finding a cure. Some people need to experience something catastrophic before attempting to improve their situation. Many of us continue through life until we fall off a cliff, arriving at a state of complete hopelessness and despair.

Earlier, Dr. Twerski told the story of Avi, an ex-convict, who was nearing the end of his incarceration only to be told by family members that they were unhappy about his impending freedom. They gave him the message that he was a burden and an embarrassment. It was their right to feel this way. Unfortunately for him, not only was he physically incarcerated most of his life, but mentally imprisoned by his feelings of total worthlessness. His sentence began long before he was locked up. He remained powerless to change until he became aware of how the intrusive messages from early childhood led him to a lifetime of ugly behavior. Before he could find peace, he had to control his addictive behavior. Only then could he begin a journey back in time where he would discover the meaning of those early messages that held him hostage.

Why do we turn to actions that will only create more problems for ourselves and others when we are in despair? Why do we allow ourselves to be deceived into thinking these actions will make us feel better, even though they cause nothing but grief, guilt, and self-loathing? It is insane to believe the lie that, "Next time will be different." If someone lied to you repeatedly, you would stop trusting that person. Yet, those of us with intrusive childhood messages continue to believe the lies. We are delusional, incapable of important decision making, and crippled by our dysfunctional state of mind. Figuring all of this out is like putting together pieces of a puzzle.

Puzzling Behavior

The first piece of the puzzle is to discover how we became the person we are today. We are all products of messages handed down from parents, teachers, friends—even the media. Nobody is born a bad person. We are the product of our experiences and our environment. If we can accept the reality of our situation, we can rid ourselves of self-loathing. The second piece of the puzzle is to understand how early intrusive messages may have formed the basis of our belief system. Negative internal voices can unleash a tsunami of destructive thinking that interferes with our ability to think clearly and enjoy healthy relationships.

In attempting to understand more about our belief system, old information and new information are significant. New information is the healthy set of messages we receive from our therapists and support groups. Conversely, old information is the messages we received in childhood that formed the basis of our dysfunctional families.

The Power of Authority Figures

One of the most powerful messages I ever received came from my nine-year-old son. While watching a baseball game on television, my son asked me why the kids in the stands were so excited. I said some baseball players are heroes to those kids. I suggested that some day one of those players might be his hero. My son paused and said to me, "They may be my hero someday, but you will always be my first hero." I was so touched, I could not reply. As parents we are our children's first heroes, whether we want the responsibility or not.

As children, our parents or adult caregivers were the dominant authority figures. The messages they communicated to us, healthy or otherwise, influence our thinking and behavior for the rest of our lives. These messages, which are deeply rooted, tell us how us how others in the world view us. Changing one's belief system requires a willingness to be open minded. People need the equivalent of an anti-virus program for computers to filter out unhealthy, intrusive messages that threaten our lives. If these intrusive messages are not processed by a healthy support system, they can create destructive actions. The greater the pain, the more intense the fear and the louder the demands of the warden's voice.

Normal and Irrational Fear

Fear is normal and often necessary to protect us from danger. Healthy fear alerts us to danger. For example, with healthy fear we look twice before crossing the street. On the other hand, irrational fear paralyzes us, and we become incapable of taking that first step toward freedom. If we become too afraid to even cross the street, we may never know the joys that wait on the other side. Other people have no fears at all. They carelessly dash into dangerous situations. The solution is to find a healthy, balanced perspective toward our fears. A therapist or support group can serve as your guiding force to help you face these situations and arrive safely at your destination. As we discover more about ourselves, we may find that many of our fears originate from within and have no basis in reality. When I finally found the courage to face my fears, to tune out my inner voice, and to ask for help, I began my journey toward acceptance and understanding. Otherwise, I might never have been able to experience the joy and serenity of a balanced and fruitful life.

When a child lives in constant fear, the child's view of the world becomes distorted. Fear is a great motivator to succeed, but it also can be deceiving if what's really driving us is the fear of failure. We feel defective inside, and one of the ways we protect this secret is by hiding behind a mask. The fear of never being good enough can drive a person toward achieving financial success under the faulty assumption that it will fix the defective feeling inside. If the pursuit of success is merely to cover up feelings of inadequacy, then only the symptoms are treated and not the actual wound that caused the insecurity. It took me some time before I recognized that this was exactly what I was doing to hide my low self-esteem.

Toxic Shame

If we do not feel good about ourselves, we don't want others to get too close. Toxic shame, along with fear, separates us from our family and the rest of the human race. Toxic shame informs us that we are to blame for the problems of our parents and for everything else that goes wrong in our lives. The burden of carrying all this shame damages our self-esteem. Excessive shame takes our rights away. We give up the right to say how we feel, the right to express anger, and even the right to be loved. It distorts our processing and causes us to overreact because we take everything as a deliberate act of disrespect toward us. Whenever I was criticized I took it as a personal indictment. I allowed the criticism and the resulting shame to define me as a person. If my wife brought up any of my shortcomings, I would overreact and immediately become defensive. Also, when people's behavior does not match their values it creates a tremendous amount of shame. I never wanted to behave the way my father did. When I began acting like him, the shame this created was unbearable.

Shame is also the toxic fuel that drives destructive behaviors. It brings us to the doorstep of addiction and invites us in so we forget who we are and how hopeless we have become. We are deluded into thinking that certain actions will make us happy and ease our pain. When my wife brought up the impact of my indiscretions on her and our children, it touched the deepest core of my shame. The feeling of worthlessness and pain brought me to a new level of hopelessness. I would either shut down emotionally or fly into a rage. The anger was directed at my wife, but caused by shame I felt deep inside.

Lack of Trust

It is normal for young children to think only of themselves. When my son was five years old he asked me what present I was going to get him for Father's Day. We enter this world dependent on the nurturing and unconditional love of our parents or guardians. We expect them to take care of us and speak the truth. Trust breaks down as we begin to notice the differences between what they say and what they do. For me, as a child, I received the message that I was an object to be used for the benefit of fulfilling the needs of my parents. My mother said that she loved us kids more than anything or anyone in this world, yet her actions elicited a different impression.

Sometimes as children we may have felt invisible, as if our feelings did not matter. Sometimes the messages we received about love did not reflect the actions we witnessed. This discrepancy can create a destructive inner voice that warns us about the pain we will receive if we trust others later in life. Our inability to trust directly influences our ability to experience intimacy. In the end, all of our relationships are negatively affected.

Perfectionism as a Way of Life

Perfectionism is doomed to failure because no one is perfect. To err is human, and we all are members of the same flawed human race. But, when we focus on our shortcomings rather than celebrating the things we do right, it creates unrealistic expectations for ourselves and for others. It also sets us up to be the victim because we believe others judge us the way we judge ourselves. A perfectionist must have everything just right or life is viewed as a failure. There is no gray area. Perfectionism also blocks us from trying new things because we don't want to fail or be considered a failure. We become hard on ourselves and judge others. We ask, "Why should I have tolerance for people if they have none for me?" I never viewed mistakes as a normal part of life. Instead, I saw failure as an unforgivable and unbearably shameful thing.

Perfectionism makes it difficult to accept opinions from others. Our inner voice tells us we are defective if someone disagrees with us. My wife once said that she could not discuss certain issues with me because I always needed to be right. My mask of perfection hid my shame. For me being wrong was too much to bear. What never occurred to me was that others accepted me for myself although I could not. Pete's story demonstrates the pitfalls of perfectionism.

Pete

Pete is a married man in his forties. He is a successful professional who is highly respected in his field. According to Pete, "As a child growing up in a household where both parents were active alcoholics, trauma was a daily event. One such event occurred when my father, amidst one of his drunken rages, told me I was a mistake and should have never been born. I was devastated. As a result, I spent a lot of time trying to prove this wasn't so. I decided to excel in all aspects of my life to prove to them that I was no mistake. Long after my friends went home from school to be with their families, I often stayed in the schoolyard. I fantasized about making the winning basket while shooting hoops, pitching the last inning of the World Series as I threw a ball against a brick wall, or scoring the winning touchdown during the Super Bowl while kicking a ball in the air.

"In this fantasy world, I was the star and not the mistake. When I finally got into organized sports, I wanted to show others that I mattered. I played Pop Warner football at age seven. The father of one of my friends was the head coach and probably knew the story of my home life. As a result, he bought me spikes and helped pay for my uniform so I could play. I was the smallest player on the team, but with a no-quit attitude, I became the starting running back. Since the first game was to take place a block from my house, I was excited knowing that my parents could easily walk over to watch. The first time that I carried the ball I ran for a thirty-yard touchdown. I floated on air for the last five yards because I felt so happy. When I reached the end zone, I looked for my parents on the sidelines but could not find them. Later in the game, I ran for a seventy-yard touchdown. By that time, most of the euphoria had worn off when I realized that my parents were not there. Even though everyone was cheering, I felt crushed.

"When I went home I found both of them passed out drunk. I guess I was really a mistake after all. After this, I became even more determined to succeed. I thought, when they discover how great I am, they definitely will come watch me. To make sure that I could continue playing, I worked especially hard during the team fundraising drive. My friend and I would stand at the local Shop Rite for hours each Saturday and Sunday to collect donations. We raised the most money of anyone on the team. When I got home, I put the container in a kitchen cabinet so I wouldn't lose it. The week before I needed to turn in my money, I went to look for the container but it was gone. I could not find it anywhere. My parents told me that the coach would understand if I told him I lost the container full of money. I was frustrated because I didn't lose it. I didn't realize until later that my parents had taken the money to buy booze. When it was time for the meeting, my parents forced me to go and admit to losing the money. The coach was very angry and told me that unless I came up with some money, I couldn't play the next season. My mother told me I couldn't play because they couldn't afford to pay for spikes or the uniform.

"I continue to tell myself that failure is not an option for me and still have the need to prove that I am not a mistake. However, it's impossible to hold myself to such unrealistic expectations. Therefore, whenever anyone, especially my wife, says or insinuates anything that implies weakness or failure, I get extremely angry because it reinforces my childhood feelings of rejection. I had to continue to be perfect because I mattered. This perfectionist attitude has never allowed me to be real or vulnerable with anyone. I hid my feelings by working all the time."

Pete wanted to be perfect so he could be accepted. Rejection by his parents, his shame, and his fear of abandonment created this intense need for him to be perfect. However, he is finally beginning to realize the insanity of the unrealistic expectations that he placed upon himself. If he wasn't perfect in everything he did, his inner voice called him a failure, took over his belief system, and eventually crushed his self-esteem. Whenever Pete felt challenged by someone, his anger would flair up to protect his inner childhood wounds. Psychological scars from the past can only be healed by sharing the sadness with others in a safe, supporting environment. Over time, Pete has begun to feel safe enough to allow his support group to enter a part of his life that had been sealed off. He is now able to share what was once too painful to expose to the outside world. As Pete continued to work on his written inventories, he began to realize that many of his fears were of his own making.

Control Was Part of Survival

Some of us correctly believed that if we were not in control we were in danger because in families like ours, violence was the norm, not the exception. As a young boy, seated at the top of the stairs, I kept a nightly vigil to protect my mother in the event my father came home drunk. This control was, in my belief system, essential because I believed there could be harsh consequences. Control and survival went hand in hand. My inner voice told me that to survive childhood, I needed to take control of the situation. If my father was drunk, I had to be there to protect my mother so she did not get hurt. I also tried to find ways to get my father to come home at night so my mother would be happy. But control, like perfectionism, is a no-win situation and everything eventually spirals out of control. Although an unrealistic way to cope, the need to take charge of everyone is a comfortable role for some of us to play. Controlling impulses are not conducive to maintaining healthy adult relationships. Nobody wants someone else telling them what to do. As long as we expect people to act and think the way we want them to, we are setting ourselves up for major disappointment.

We also have inner controls that stop us from expressing feelings toward others since we *feel* we don't have the right to be heard. Expressing feelings in a healthy way, even in conflict, is an important part of the healing and growth process.

Caretaking

Caretakers put the needs of others before their own. My inner voice tried to reinforce my belief that a good son takes care of his mother's needs before his own. Whenever I put my needs ahead of others, I felt ashamed. The consequences of being my mother's caretaker as a child had harmful effects later in my life. Children who become caretakers find it difficult to ask for help and have an even harder time saying no or being intimate. Caretakers can give the impression of being able to care for everyone and everything, but eventually if they don't ask for help, they break down. Letting go is difficult. They may be self-reliant and dependable, but the irony is, the role they play inhibits them from getting what they really need. As a child and later as an adult, I longed to have someone care for me, but as a caretaker it was more natural to place the needs of others first. Not until I found the courage to invite others into my life and to ask for help was I able to change my attitude and tell the little voice in my head to shut up.

Sara

Sara is a classic caretaker. She blamed herself for all of her family's problems. Sara's fear of confrontation made it impossible for her to let go. Her fear pushed her further into shame and isolation.

According to Sara, "My parents gave me all the material things I needed. There was never physical abuse. On the outside everything appeared fine. My mother never complained. Since she believed that good people don't complain, I wanted to be considered a good person and didn't complain. As a child, I felt our neighbors took advantage of my parents. They came over uninvited and stayed for dinner but never reciprocated. They borrowed items and never returned them. But, my mother never complained and seemed to always keep everything bottled up inside.

"My father was a kind man, but lacked self-esteem and seemed disappointed in me whenever anything went wrong. If a problem developed between me and someone else, my father faulted me, no matter what the circumstances were.

"As an adult, I felt responsible for anything negative that happened in the lives of my husband and children. It was always my fault. When a problem occurred in our household, I was blamed and I'd convince myself that they were right. One evening I received a phone call from my son. He was screaming at me because his car broke down. It was my fault, he implied, so I should immediately pick him up. When my husband learned about my son's car, he shouted at me, too. I don't recall the exact words, but the message was clear. Had I gotten the car fixed this would never have happened. As always, I accepted the blame.

"Resentment for my family and myself was growing, but I didn't realize it until it was brought to my attention during a therapy session. Once I started to express my feelings all that pent up anger spewed out from inside of me. I found myself talking faster and faster until I realized that all this baggage had piled up inside of me after years of carrying everyone else's burdens.

"After realizing this lesson, I took the giant step of dealing with my family. I needed to confront them and tell them that I would not put up with their nonsense any longer. In the past, my husband blamed me for everything. I accepted the blame. I apologized when I should not have since I believed that good people didn't complain. Now things are different. Through my support group, I have found the courage to confront my family. I am no longer responsible for everything around the house. As I draw strength from others, I feel a greater sense of self-respect as well as the respect I notice from others. My life today is so much freer than ever before."

With the help of her support group, Sara has begun to realize that she can neither right a wrong, nor can she continue to help those people closest to her without inflicting further harm on herself. Only when she was willing to accept the aid of her support group, could she stand up for herself and ignore the faulty messages generated by her old belief system. Now she realizes that even though she may disagree and argue with a family member, she would never lose their love. By helping herself, Sara also became a better role model for her husband and children.

Alex

Alex, a psychologist, married with two children, has always had problems with intimacy. Alex views women as mere sexual objects. Alex spends a lot of time surfing the Internet and viewing pornography.

According to Alex, "I grew up in a small apartment in a middle-class Jewish neighborhood in New York. I can honestly say that there is nothing my parents wouldn't have done for me, but my brothers and sister always came first. My parents both worked full-time. There were no great traumas, no abuse, and no addictions. I had a simple, safe, loving, and happy childhood. My parents always told me to be a good boy. The message was to be kind and respectful to others, compassionate, thoughtful, patient, and wait your turn. Don't be mean or angry, selfish, boastful, arrogant, or hurt anyone's feelings. See the good in people and accept them for who they are. It also meant work hard in school, be successful, and make us proud. Growing up, I felt that my needs and feelings were not as important as others. I could not be myself if that upset or hurt you. I could not express myself or do what I wanted, if it caused you discomfort. So, I learned to keep my opinions to myself and to be submissive. I paid close attention to nuances in facial expressions and voices to determine if anyone was upset with me, as if my very survival depended on their approval.

"At a young age, I felt that if I was bad I would hurt my mother. Later in life I transferred those feelings to others. When I hurt anyone it would cause me terrible shame and guilt. Throughout my life, I felt as if I was walking on eggshells. I was saying and doing things only to win approval from my mother or others. I kept my true feelings to myself so others did not have the opportunity to know the real me. The only comfort I found was in continuing to project the safe, people pleasing, neutered 'good boy' identity, whose genuine, deeper, and more conflicted self lay hidden in fear. So many times I wanted to break out of my shell, but I was too afraid to surrender. And, as much as that made me feel safe, I felt lonely, shameful, and weak.

"Through therapy I have learned that my mother's love was conditional, and if I didn't please her then I would risk being emotionally abandoned. Now I realize that I was not afraid of losing her love, but rather of causing her pain or making her suffer. The shame was almost unbearable. As an adult, I no longer want to make that sacrifice. I want to be who I am, to be authentic, and to let the world see the real me.

"My parents were also very smothering and wanted to do everything for me. But, there were times when I needed to do things for myself, to solve my own problems. Because my parents would always come to the rescue, I got the message that I could not take care of myself. So, I stopped asking them for help and kept my problems and concerns to myself. If I didn't talk about my problems, then they couldn't take it away, fix it, critique it, or tell me what to do. As a teenager, others would always come to me for advice, but rarely would

I share my own problems. I wanted them to believe that I had it all together. My parents never talked to me about their problems. I was so over protected that I believed having problems was unusual.

"Today I feel overly anxious when my wife becomes upset with me. There's a voice inside me that insists that it can't be my fault because I'm a 'good boy' who doesn't hurt someone else. Therefore, I wind up blaming her for the problems. But I realize now that I'm wrong to believe she will walk out on me, then leave me alone to face my loneliness if I make a mistake. Maybe people pleasing is a way to avoid my loneliness. Instead, I focus on the feelings of others and how I can please them, rather than concentrating on my own sense of helplessness at not being able to fill up the empty, lonely place inside of me."

Alex's wounds were not as visible as most, but on closer examination, he somehow received the message that his role in life was to be a people pleaser. All of his messages and inner voices suggested that he had to act in a certain way regardless of how he felt. His feelings were dismissed unless they fell into the category of being a good son, a good husband, or a good father. His happiness could only be achieved through the happiness of others. Alex also learned to avoid conflict. He thought he would lose the love of his family if he disagreed with them. So, he accepted full responsibility regardless of whether he owned the problems or not.

Whenever a problem arose with a loved one, the imaginary guy on his shoulder would hit him over the head with a bat, blaming him for everything that happened. His clarity improved as he became more willing to open up to his support group. He recognized the personal harm from his distorted sense of family loyalty. He asked his support group to help him overcome that fear. For instance, he would agree to call me if he had an argument with a family member and was fearful that the conflict would cause separation, abandonment, or rejection. The fear of abandonment can be so terrifying that it can cause some people to say or do anything to make the fear go away. This fear distorted Alex's thinking. As the honest and caring person that he was, Alex frequently made promises he couldn't keep because he didn't want to disappoint or hurt anyone's feelings. This negatively affected his credibility until he could finally accept the truth and look at himself honestly for the first time.

Eventually, Alex would learn that it was OK to say no and that his family would not abandon him for turning them down. Having an addiction to pornography was safe for Alex because he did not have to deal with the expectations that occur in a real life relationship. There are no confrontations or expectations with pornography. Earlier in his life when Alex had relationships with other women they would quickly dissolve before any commitments were made.

Dr. Twerski suggests that problems may arise even without abusive parenting. According to Dr. Twerski, "Children must be disciplined and limitations must be set. A five-year-old child may want ice cream before dinner and is not capable of understanding why he should not have it. All he knows is that someone is refusing something he wants, and he may react with, "I hate you, Mommy." Although most children are not adversely affected by proper discipline, instances may arise when even good discipline elicits a strong negative feeling toward a parent. This can put the child in conflict if he or she feels that hostility directed toward a parent jeopardizes his or her security. The juvenile mind may deal with this conflict in a variety of ways. Realize that some thoughts and feelings that enter children's minds may linger for years and affect their adult behavior.

Distorted Anger

When the support of healthy role models is absent in a child's life, the child who received mixed signals is at a tremendous disadvantage when required to respond to anger. He may either react in rage or shut down altogether. Either way, the child's anger is not processed in a healthy way. Like Alex, if a child is informed that a good boy does not complain and does as he is told, chances are that his internal messages will direct him to stuff the feeling and avoid conflict since he is angry. Eventually, this won't work because a volcano forms inside until it eventually explodes. As a child, I took my anger out on my brothers even though they did nothing to deserve my wrath.

We try to control our sadness by not allowing ourselves to cry. The message is that big boys don't cry because it is a sign of weakness. My father tried to challenge this old belief in the hospital before he passed away. I couldn't cry in front of my father under any circumstance. This message was so ingrained that I couldn't let it go even though he was dying. My inner voice told me to hide my anger in front of my wife and kids because I would remember how angry my parents were with each other, and how I suffered as a result. So fearful was I of bringing anger into my own home that I never asserted myself. As a result, I created a sense of isolation and I would react in anger when something unexpected happened. Anger is controlling and leads to self-righteousness. The feeling of superiority is transient. By focusing on the shortcomings of others rather than our own failures, the result will be feelings of resentment and a victim mentality.

Selfishness

Selfishness, like isolation, is inherent in dysfunctional families. If the child of alcoholic parents can only rely on himself, then selfishness becomes a coping mechanism or survival skill. He quickly learns that nobody can do for him what he can do for himself. Eventually, the child becomes his own higher authority and can never accept trust or guidance from others. This selfish thinking, which was once needed for survival, is carried into our adult life, but naturally it is not popular with others.

Selfishness leads to a very serious character defect known as destructive entitlement. Destructive entitlement and self-pity become a great tag team and when combined can produce destructive actions. Unfortunately, destructive thinking can be very delusional. When the inner voice tells us we can do certain things, it neglects to inform us of the terrible consequences.

I recall the first time I sought outside help. One evening I received a call from my father, who by then had been in recovery for nearly ten years. With a sad voice he said, "Maybe now we can stop the insane thinking before it hits your children." I did not understand the impact of his statement until years later. I also did not want to hand down to my children the negative messages that I grew up with from childhood. I realized that I had to change my belief system so I would not transfer those same sick messages to my children.

Be aware of the ways that belief systems are formed and how childhood wounds affect our perception of life. We cannot change our emotional wounds unless we first find out what is broken. If we never learn what intrusive messages we received in childhood, we cannot pass down healthy messages to our children. These wounds, if untreated, will block any chance of recovery or intimacy, and we will be destined to listen to the commands of our inner voice for the rest of our lives.

Chapter Five: Childhood Wounds

If others were to look beyond our masks,
would they ever accept what is buried deep inside?

ℰℭ

Imagine if you had an open wound. Next, think about your wound being poked at constantly as you go through your day. As you were enduring this, you would most likely find ways to hide this wound to protect yourself from the pain of other people's actions. While emotional wounds aren't as obvious as the physical kind, they can be just as painful.

While driving, when another driver cuts you off, how do you react? Why do we get so angry, even if there was no harm or accident? The amount of negative energy we burn is not proportional to the incident. Where does all this anger come from? Most likely, the other driver doesn't know us, yet we give him or her tremendous power over our emotions because our wound was reopened. The deeper that wound, the greater the control it has over us, and the greater the lengths we go to hide and protect it.

In my experience of helping others, it becomes apparent that for many, everyday experiences such as driving shake up a sense of being dismissed, invisible, inadequate, or worthless. These feelings often stem from untreated childhood events or trauma.

Dr. Twerski refers to a psychological maneuver known as *transference*. According to Dr. Twerski, "A person may transfer feelings that were appropriate toward person A to person B. To the conscious mind, which operates logically, a wheel is just a wheel, not a car, and a sleeve is just a sleeve, not a suit. The subconscious mind operates according to different rules: the part equals the whole. A wheel can be a car, and a sleeve can be a suit."

Have you ever met someone who, at first sight and before

exchanging a single word, you immediately dislike? Conversely, do you recall meeting a person who, upon first sight, you decide, "This is a nice person." Why would you have negative or positive feelings toward someone you've never met before? It is not logical. However, the subconscious mind is not logical.

According to Dr. Twerski, you may have had a grade school teacher (like I did), who was downright mean. Thirty years later I entered an office, and when I first met the secretary I disliked her, although I didn't know why. She reminded me of my fifth grade teacher. Although there was just one small similarity to my teacher, the subconscious mind equated the secretary with my teacher. This is what is meant by transference. One transfers the feeling from one person to another or from one object to another.

In situations of transference, our wound may be exposed. As we start to feel diminished or inadequate, our anger swells to cover the pain of the wound. When this happens, the guy on our shoulder with a bat thinks only about protecting our tender emotional wound and not about the other person's point of view. Meanwhile, we create distance from others. Over time this becomes a major problem with relationships.

I never accepted criticism well. Whenever someone disagreed with me, I'd get defensive. I felt like I was being ridiculed. I still am dealing with childhood wounds and insecurity. Although my wife loved me very much, I did not love myself. By failing to accept my own weaknesses, I could not allow myself to be loved by anyone. I felt undeserving of that love. The imaginary guy with the bat on my shoulder would push away anyone attempting to show me love. My role as a victim set me up for isolation. I dreaded a close relationship with others, including my wife, because I was afraid of being exposed as defective.

To relinquish the power these internal wounds had over me, I began a treatment plan to heal my wounds and mend my broken relationships. I had to find a way to feel safe when I was around other people. Intimacy was not possible until I understood the root of my feelings of defectiveness and inadequacy and stopped listening to the destructive voice inside my head.

Dr. Twerski explains how children feel dependent on their parents for survival and their adjustment to reality. According to Dr. Twerski, "Children must feel that their parents know what they are doing. To think that one's parents are incompetent or wrong would cause a child intolerable anxiety. If a parent abuses a child, it is easier for that child to feel he deserves the abuse than to think the parent is crazy. If a parent punishes a child for something he did not do, the child will feel, I didn't do anything wrong, but if I am punished I must somehow be bad. If a parent says something like, 'You are stupid,' the child must accept this as true. By the time the child is old enough to think for himself, his mind has already been primed and the impressions that he developed cannot be undone or disproved by logical reasoning."

One of the best ways to evaluate your childhood is to explore the feelings you had when you made a mistake. Were you allowed to blunder and learn from your mistakes or were mistakes unacceptable? When you made an error, were you able to see it as such, or did you identify yourself as defective? Since the consequence of making a mistake is unbearable pain, many of us have the need to prove we are right at all costs. If we make a mistake, we inflict inner punishment and self-hate. We then learn to conceal our feelings of defectiveness by playing roles that allow us to mask our shame, thereby losing a part of our humanity.

One of my children had a bed-wetting problem that caused him shame every time he had an accident. Once when dining out with my family years ago, I had an experience that most men can relate to. After a trip to the men's room, I zipped up my fly but not before a few drops dripped onto my pants. When I returned to the table, I quietly pointed out the spot to my son and said, "See, even Dad has accidents." He thought this was great. He believed I urinated in my pants. You could read his mind and see the way this made him feel more human for his mistakes. The downside was that he proceeded to tell the world about my experience! I did not count on this, but I did give him the message that it's OK to make mistakes. Unfortunately this was not the case with Morris.

Morris

Morris is a computer consultant in his forties, married with two children. He grew up in a household where he felt terrified about admitting to mistakes. As a result, Morris developed a distorted sense of reality that caused him and his family great heartache.

According to Morris, "The message I got as a child was that I was safe if I made myself invisible. If I rocked the boat, there was a good chance I would be physically abused by my father. My father had a terrible temper, and if I made some mistake I was terrified that he would hurt me. This created an atmosphere that told me to never admit my mistakes because the outcome had terrible consequences. On one occasion my father was driving over the Brooklyn Bridge and another driver cut him off. He gave my father the finger. My father got him to pull over, and when my father shouted at him the man rolled up his window. In a burst of anger my father actually broke the window, and the man drove away in fear for his life. I believe there also were times I feared for my own life when I felt his anger. If I made a mistake, I had the choice of admitting what I did wrong or lying. I chose to lie. My mother was supportive in many ways, but when it came to my father, she sided with him. She, too, was afraid to challenge his authority.

"My inner voice always told me I wasn't good enough, and being invisible reinforced this belief. This created the need to feel validated by others. It was as if I had a hole in my stomach and was trying to have others fill it up. It just didn't work. The same happened when my wife questioned my ability as a husband or father. I immediately flew into a rage because she touched on my defectiveness. I dreaded that my wife might leave me. To cope, I disguised myself with ego and false pride. Underneath this huge ego was a terrified little boy who protected himself by raging and bullying. Eventually my wife kicked me out of the house and told me not to return until I grew up."

Although Morris makes a good living as a computer consultant, he continues to feel inferior. Morris grew up in a family that did not tolerate mistakes. As a result, he learned it was better to lie than to admit he slipped up. Morris has begun to recognize how he projects that same intolerance onto his wife and kids. While he did not physically abuse his wife and kids, he created a family environment similar to his original family where little, if any, tolerance for mistakes is acceptable. Morris's wife threw Morris out of his house for one year. During this time, he worked on his written inventories. This situation allowed him to see how he was pushing his loved ones away.

Morris realizes how his intolerance and his obsession for being right is what pushes others away. Morris still suffers the pain of his childhood wounds, but his new willingness to surrender his impulsive anger has helped him get closer to others. The anger that once comforted him can be found in his written inventories. Over time, Morris has realized that mistakes are part of being human. As he finds compassion for himself, he finds it for others as well.

The Mask We Wear

The different masks that we hide behind are as varied as the people who wear them. They depend on our unique childhood experiences. Some people who want others to see that they have everything together wear the mask of responsibility. On the outside, these individuals appear to be highly functional and successful. On the inside, they are engaged in self-destructive behaviors designed to ease their inner turmoil.

Hank

Hank is a successful businessman with three children. According to Hank, "Some of the messages that I received from my parents during childhood were, 'You're not safe, you don't matter, you're a burden, don't tell anyone what goes on in our house.' By the time I was four years old, I had spent half my life in foster homes. I went into my first foster home when I was two years old after my mother's nervous breakdown. My father could not take care of me and my older brother because he worked full time, so the state put both of us into the foster care system. The only thing I remember about foster care was getting beaten for wetting the bed and having my face rubbed into the wet mattress like a dog. When I returned home, I had no idea when or if I would be sent to another foster home, which would be determined by my mother's mental stability. I did not feel safe in foster care, nor did I feel safe at home, because I didn't know how long I would be there. I just wanted to be left alone.

"My parents argued a lot. Once, my father hit my mother and she called the police. It was absolute chaos. My parents decided they were going to get a divorce. My father told me that if I told the truth in court about him hitting my mother, I wouldn't get to see him anymore. Tell the truth and don't get to see my father again, or lie and get to see him. What a choice! I decided to lie, but never had to go to court. My parents did not divorce, as I was told, 'for the sake of the children.' What a bunch of crap. My parents didn't do us any favors by staying married. My father slept downstairs on a foldaway couch, and my mother slept upstairs in the master bedroom. My brother and I were threatened never to tell anyone that my parents didn't sleep together. Again, my father was reinforcing the message that the truth was bad and that I should lie. I was just five years old and had spent two of those years in abusive foster homes. I would carry his message with me into all aspects of my life through adulthood. I felt shame for wanting to tell the truth, and I felt shame for lying. My life was all about shame."

Hank continues, "I continued to believe, I'd be safe if I was alone. The truth was shameful. More specifically, my true self was shameful. I always found ways to perceive myself as different. But I was different in a shaming way, always feeling 'less than' and 'not good enough.' These feelings were repeated when I continued to wet the bed until eleven years old. I lied about wetting the bed. On reflection, I'm certain that some people must have known. I always had brown teeth from taking tetracycline as an infant. Brown teeth, bed wetting, mentally unstable mother—I held onto anything to make me feel less than. I didn't know another way. I couldn't and didn't trust anybody. I only could rely on myself. I would tell myself that childhood would be the worst part of my life. When I don't need anybody I would be fine and safe. I wasn't a loner, but I didn't fit in. I always felt different. I would create excuses not to go birthday parties. I feared trusting anybody and the truth. I missed 210 days of high school. I stayed home and watched television. I pretended to be sick a lot. I just felt safer being alone."

Hank's loneliness led to many compulsive and isolating activities later in his life. He says, "I became a compulsive gambler. I was a workaholic. I was a food addict. I became addicted to pornography and masturbation. I didn't need drugs or alcohol. I could create a soothing medication for my fears with my own thoughts and actions. When I did drink alcohol, I would drink excessively to get drunk. These behaviors reinforced my shame. I believed that nobody else did these things. I had such low self-esteem on the inside, but I was so egotistical on the outside. I was driven by fears and engaged in such isolating, addictive behavior. I lived in my own world to escape and survive my childhood traumas and to keep myself or anyone from knowing the real me."

Hank put himself through college, stopped gambling with the help of Gamblers Anonymous, and became a certified accountant. He says, "I met my wife, got married, and had children. On the outside, everything looked great. On the inside, there was emptiness. I didn't think that I was worthy of having a wife. I didn't think that I was worthy of being a CPA. Eventually, I got my MBA and became the CFO of a company. I was still consumed with shame and fear. I felt like a fraud. My obsession for pornography grew. I was on the Internet for hours at a time. My wife knew nothing of this, but she did know that we weren't having sex that often. Most nights I fell asleep watching television downstairs and came to bed much later, while she fell asleep alone upstairs. I felt like a fraud. Nobody knew the real me. My childhood was something I never wanted to relive. Yet I was still driven by my fears and shame from childhood.

"Eventually, my wife saw that I had been on the Internet, looking at other women. She was devastated. I had hurt the only person who accepted me for me. I was sad and angry at myself. I feared she would divorce me. If I ever wanted true intimacy, I needed to be truthful and vulnerable and had to trust the process. This went against everything I had learned about coping with life. I did not want to be truthful and reveal who I am, nor did I want to trust another person. But, my wife was too important, so I tried to be open and honest. The fear of losing her was more powerful than the fear of letting her see the true me. I didn't want to trust my sponsor, but I needed to trust him and did so because he had walked in my shoes. He seemed happy and serene. I needed that. "

Hank's inner voice told him to avoid intimacy and being vulnerable in front of others. Hank erected huge barriers to keep others away. Although kind and generous, he was consumed with shame, inadequacy, and his overarching fear of being vulnerable, which prevented him from letting down his guard. He was a prisoner to all of the messages inside his head, which included, *people weren't safe, he didn't matter to anyone, he was a burden, and never tell anyone how you feel.* Not until faced with the devastation that occurred after his wife learned of his secret addiction to Internet pornography was he able to admit his problem and begin the journey to freedom.

Hank continually wrestled to keep his secret fears from surfacing. As he opened up to his support group, he began to feel more comfortable with himself and others. He came to realize that he did not have to be perfect to be accepted. The more he was willing to accept himself, the more he was able to see the corrupt nature of his old beliefs. He began to recognize and surrender his fears. As this happened, he began to rely less on the mask he used to wear to protect himself.

Mask of Victimhood

There are people who wear the mask of victimhood. They have a hard time functioning and their problems are more obvious to the world. Jobs are lost, home utilities are turned off, and marriages are ruined. Yet, it is always someone else's fault.

Murray

Murray is in his forties, married, and has one child. According to Murray, "My parents worked all day, so when school was over, I went straight to my grandparents' home. When I eventually got home, it was late at night and time to go to sleep. When I saw my parents, they spent most of their time yelling at each other. I remember feeling I had to live up to my father's expectations or risk making him unhappy. As a child, I attended a musical school for gifted children. I had to prepare a program that was graded twice a year. It was very important for me to get excellent grades. When I received anything less, I felt like a failure.

"I loved being with my grandparents. I used to read with my grandfather and felt that he paid attention to me. When my grandparents passed away I was devastated. But, when my mother died, I really didn't feel a great loss. I started hitchhiking because I wanted to travel to new places. One day I returned home and thought I would surprise my father. As he opened the door to let me in, he appeared disappointed. He said he answered the door because he thought it was my sister. He then turned and walked away. To help cope with the feelings of rejection, I started to drink and take drugs. I always hated alcohol, but used it to medicate the pain I was feeling inside."

Murray says he realized that whenever anyone ignored him, he would initially shut down inside, but later rage out at whoever touched this wound. He says, "When my boss or wife ignored me, I felt like a victim. I realized I was angry, but I didn't realize where this anger came from. I blamed them. In the past, I held a job for many years without getting a raise. I was always making excuses for why I stayed with this job. Every time I thought about leaving, my fear would tell me that things would get better. My bosses took advantage of me. I felt like a victim, but instead of taking responsibility for my actions, I just got angry with them. I would vent my anger with my sponsor. When he suggested I find another job, I didn't want to consider it. I also wanted to start my own photography business, but was so paralyzed by fear I couldn't move. My support group kept pushing me to do a few jobs for free as a way of getting my work out to the public. I had enough trust in them to do as I was told."

When Murray started to look for a job, his inner voice of fear spoke. He told himself that he would never find a better job. He had visions of eventually becoming unemployed and his family starving to death. Though he hated his present job, he was afraid of looking elsewhere. His inner voice kept telling him the old job was not so bad, but the facts proved otherwise. Murray pointed the finger at everyone but himself. He promised to keep going on interviews whether he wanted to or not. Through persistence, eventually he did find a better job.

His need to be right was destroying him. The more willing Murray was to complete the written inventories of Twelve Step work, the more he became aware of the disruption in his life caused by his negative inner voice. He realized how much of his fear was manufactured by his warden, who never really wanted him to find happiness in a better job. His courage to take direction would eventually allow him to say no to the imaginary fears the warden created.

Mask of Superiority

Some people wear the mask of superiority. These know-it-alls have little empathy for others and harshly judge others. This disguises the self-recrimination these people feel inside. The following story about Paul shows how he underwent the greatest devastation a father could have and how it ultimately removed his mask of superiority. After life threw a devastating curve, he finally asked for help.

Paul

Paul is a successful businessman in his early fifties. He has been married twice with a child from his first marriage and two from his second. According to Paul, "I grew up in a very religious family with a lot of discipline. I guess my family loved me but I felt very controlled by them. I was always defiant of authority. If they wanted me to do A, I would do B. This defiant voice permeated every one of my relationships. Even as a child, I never wanted to conform to anything. I could have gotten A's in school, but I had to do things my way. I married very young and had one daughter. The marriage did not last long. I remarried and had two more children. Most of my life was plagued by one addiction after another. I would go to Twelve Step programs, but they never helped. I had to do things my way.

"Eventually, my drug of choice turned to prostitutes. One night I was cruising for a prostitute and saw my daughter, age twenty, on the streets. I knew she had problems with drugs, but I never thought it would bring her to prostitution. I was devastated. I took her to an inpatient rehabilitation center for help. She tested positive for HIV. This was at a time when HIV was a death sentence. A second and third test came back negative. I learned that I couldn't give her what I didn't have myself. Every time I got the urge to become defiant, I instead chose to obey. Listening to others for guidance and support lifted a tremendous weight from my shoulders. I surrendered. It's a wonderful feeling to know there are people in this world who are there for me, no matter what. I thank God for my support system because I don't know what I would have done without them."

The devastating reality of seeing his daughter on the streets paved the way for a miracle. This miracle caused a transformation in Paul that enabled him to willingly give up control. His willingness to listen to others instead of resisting them has allowed him to enjoy a newfound serenity. Life has not been easy for Paul, but he is happier today than he has been in all the years I have known him. While he attempts to give his daughter all the love and acceptance that he was never able to give her as a child, he understands that some things are beyond his control. He still prays and asks God to watch over her. He knows now that he does not have to face his pain alone.

Mask of Uniqueness

The mask of uniqueness proclaims to the world, "I am unique; no one is like me, nor can anyone possibly understand me." People wear this mask as a way of keeping others at a distance. Consequently, they remain isolated from other people. The warden's message is very clear: *Do not trust anyone, ever.*

Jimmy

Jimmy is a single man in his forties. According to Jimmy, "I grew up in a poor household and felt ashamed as a child. I believed that people saw my family as trash because of our poverty and our filth. I received mixed signals from my father. He was warm at times, but when drunk, he was verbally abusive. I would confide in him about things that were going on in my life, but as soon as he drank, he would use anything I told him against me. My mother was very needy and I felt that it was my responsibility to take care of her. She seldom interacted with my father, so in many ways I was closer to her then he was. The message was clear, my needs could only be met if I took care of her needs first.

"As I grew older, I started to realize I was attracted to men. This created tremendous self-hatred. I loathed myself for being a homosexual and despised God for allowing this to happen. Eventually, life became so unbearable I contemplated suicide. When I finally asked for help, I was lucky to find someone who guided me toward self-acceptance. I did written inventories on my childhood wounds. I discovered that I not only hated men who were proud to be gay, but I also hated gay men who were angry for being gay. I also hated heterosexual men because they weren't gay. I set myself up to dislike everyone, because I really hated myself. I believed the world saw me in the same negative way. My feeling of uniqueness toward the world ensured me that I could remain a victim. My uniqueness also created a fear of people. Even as I started to join groups and fellowships, I would always find a way to make myself feel different from everyone else."

Jimmy found it hard to believe that others would accept him. He says, "I tried my best to convince people that I wasn't worthy of their friendship. When I isolated myself from everyone in the support network, I still got phone calls telling me I was loved and missed. These people saw through my mask and realized the pain I was in. Eventually, I would ask, 'Why are you always there for me?' The answer was always the same, 'Because I don't see you the way you see yourself.'

"I made up stories about the ways I was different or unique from others. Through the help of my support group, I began to feel connected to the human race. Although this feeling of connection was short lived, I was told to be patient with my progress. As time has passed, I have become more aware of the ways my destructive thinking has pulled me away from all types of people. I see that whenever I was in a social setting, I always focused on the person or situation that made me feel unique and different. I would concentrate on the way people have disappointed me. Self-acceptance has come slowly for me, but I have increased my trust in others. Although I hate to admit this to others, the more I allow people to accept me, the easier it is to accept myself. I keep moving forward while pursuing the necessary steps in finding self-acceptance, especially when my fear of people pulls me back."

Jimmy still fights the voices of self-loathing, but he demonstrates courage by fighting his biggest demon, the fear of other people. When he is making up a negative story in his head about someone, he calls that person to find out if the story is true or distorted. That takes courage to make those phone calls. The more he attempts to connect with others, the more he sees that people are not there to hurt him. The reality is, they do not see him the way he feels inside. He can only conclude this by finding courage to confront his demons and challenge his fears.

These stories show the different ways that people choose to wear masks. Some people may wear one or more masks, depending on the roles they think they need to play in front of certain people. Still, beneath the surface of these masks lie the same wounds of inferiority and defectiveness. The masks help shield them from a world in which they feel inadequate and unable to participate.

No matter what mask we wear, the feelings of defectiveness and inferiority are similar. People who wear a mask of responsibility may have a tougher time asking for help, because they are convinced that they are solely accountable for their success.

I can relate to the person who wears the mask of responsibility. For me, success in business gave me false confidence. I thought I needed no one to succeed, not even God. Individual achievement may work when it comes to obtaining material things, but it will not help to fill that empty void that resides deep within you.

Emotional Wounds Beneath the Masks

Childhood wounds are acerbated especially when dealing with any form of rejection, abandonment, or criticism. Those wounds are rooted in the violation of basic trust that we had placed in our parents and other loved ones. To protect myself from pain, my inner voice supplied me with a barrier to keep others outside while limiting my chances of being exposed to potential harm and criticism. Intimacy, vulnerability, trust, and pain were to be avoided at all cost.

In group therapy, I met a man who had an abusive, alcoholic father. As a child, he would confide in his father when he was sober. He shared both weaknesses and disappointments with him. In the beginning, the sober dad would listen to his son's story and would be occasionally supportive. However, during an alcoholic rage his father would turn against him. He would yell and put down his son for being weak. The message he sent to his son was loud and clear: Do not be emotionally vulnerable with other men by sharing your weaknesses; they will only betray and hurt you badly by using your weaknesses against you." I encouraged him to speak up at group and share his story, but he was terrified to do so. He would never speak up or share, and frequently dashed out of the group as soon as it ended.

Another man in group struck back verbally to keep people from getting too close. Knowing his short fuse for anger, nobody dared to challenge or confront him. The reopening of old internal wounds was so painful that he would go to any length to protect these wounds from exposure.

Healthy Treatment for Wounds

I never believed that others would accept me for who I was, yet over time I learned to let go of those fears as I developed closer relationships to people. By finding a group willing to accept me with all my shortcomings, I grew in self-acceptance and found the courage to say no to the voice inside my head. I learned to expose my wounds and to feel part of a fellowship for the first time in my life. *Self-disclosure which leads to intimacy and greater self-acceptance is vital to healing.* That is why releasing secrets, shame, and guilt is so important. The wounds can be treated by acknowledging your past, how you were hurt, and how you may have hurt others. Only then can the process of healing begin. I began by first sharing my wounds with others. As I grew in humility, I grew in self-acceptance. If I can accept myself then I am capable of accepting others. I humbly ask, "How can I support or help you?" Rather than fix other people's problems, I let them know I'm there for them, no matter what.

Before my recovery and healing began, I had far less empathy for others. When my emotional wounds were triggered, it was hard for me to feel the pain of others. However, as I begin to heal, I noticed how much easier it was to identify with the pain of others. This is why it is so vital to first address your own internal wounds before helping others. Until then, it will be difficult to think beyond yourself.

Gratitude is another indicator of healing. I always wanted to be grateful for the things I had, but gratitude never came easy. I was always amazed how some people with so little could be grateful, while others with so much took everything for granted. As I began to heal, I realized how little material things really mattered. Pain is an internal problem and cannot be eased by external objects. Gratitude does not happen overnight. It takes time. I was so impatient with the entire healing process. I expected instant gratification, but it doesn't work that way. I needed to follow the recommendations of others. As I heeded their advice, my feeling of gratitude came naturally. I felt thankful for what I had, and less resentful and victimized for what I did not have. My support group gave me strength.

Not Giving Away My Power to Others

In the past it was easy to predict that if anyone pushed my buttons, I would lash out in anger. But, as I began to heal I no longer permitted anyone that power over me. Anger is a natural emotion, but now I have healthier ways to cope. I reach out to others and ask for help or guidance when I need it. I am no longer the victim. I no longer try to control my wife. Now I am comfortable surrendering control and thinking only about being present in the moment so I can more fully empathize with my wife's feelings and needs.

The most challenging test for me is when my wife brings up my past compulsions. I would rather focus on her shortcomings than mine. But, there is no denying that I hurt her profoundly, and that I need to confront the issues with her without lapsing into self-pity or self-victimization. To be a better husband and father, I had to get past the notion of being like a defective person. I had to avoid listening to the little voice inside my head and learn to accept myself, both the good and the bad, and to understand that I am not perfect. People with deep childhood wounds tend to be selfish in nature, not because they are bad but because selfishness develops as a survival instinct. When I accept my imperfections instead of berating myself, I find the willingness to work on my character defects. In addition, with acceptance comes the ability to find empathy and compassion for my wife and others. Although I never will know the full extent of the pain I caused her, I can show her my sincere regret. We cannot undo the past. But, we have the power to transform our future by learning from past mistakes. Today, we still have our disagreements, but we've learned how to declare a truce and bring our issues to our individual support groups. We no longer focus on trying to fix each other. In looking at our own character defects and wounds, we pray for strength and for each of us to find our individual paths.

Chapter Six: Silencing the Negative Inner Voices

The inner voices, created from the childhood emotional wounds,
can distract us from the work of healing.

ᏚᎧᏣᎡ

My own childhood wounds created such an inner void that I tried to fill the emptiness with one harmful solution after another. When the consequences of one became too much, I would replace it with another. I believe that my destructive behaviors were never the real problem. My problem was my victim thinking, led by the little voice inside my head. Both guided me toward harmful behaviors. These negative messages not only distorted my perception of reality, but also my ability to do the right thing. This warped sense of reality led me to engage in destructive behaviors, often hurting the people I loved most in order to ease the internal pain. I was living in a state of victimhood and had developed an attitude of "me versus the world."

For this reason, I needed to find people who I could trust to be there for me. These people could point out my victim thinking and that destructive inner voice. Without them, my false beliefs about life and myself would lead me toward isolation. That inner voice would try to control my thinking, and my thinking, in turn, would control my actions. Consequently, my shame would become so great that I would never allow anyone to get close to me. The guy on my shoulder would be swinging away constantly, reminding me of my faults and causing me to spiral out of control into even greater self-loathing and shame. My victim thinking convinced me that in order to feel good about myself, I always had to be right.

A Good Person Doesn't Make Mistakes

For me, mistakes were inexcusable and had to be hidden at all costs. I couldn't imagine exposing my shortcomings because that would only reinforce my feelings of inadequacy. A healthy, compassionate voice would have told me that mistakes were a part of life. But that voice did not exist for me. I felt that I needed to hide my failings, which made it difficult to listen to anyone, especially when I was criticized. My inability to listen also contributed to my victim mentality. Eventually, I came to understand that I needed to find the courage to admit my wrongdoings and ask for help. The asking-for-help option was tough for me. My victim thinking, so deeply embedded, was more difficult to surrender than even my destructive behaviors. While my destructive behaviors took a huge toll on my life, my victim thinking fueled the flames of self-righteousness. Victim thinking was the root of the problem, even though the destructive behaviors needed to be isolated before I could begin treatment.

A Good Person Does Not Get Angry with His Parents

Dr. Twerski talks about a psychological maneuver known as *displacement.* According to Dr. Twerski, "The subconscious mind diverts or redirects ideas and feelings. It is as if a guided missile went off course, aiming for the wrong target. People at the control center can change its course, so it lands in an uninhabited area where it can do no harm."

Dr. Twerski further explains, "Suppose that a child develops angry feelings toward a parent. The guilt from such feelings may be very intense. To protect the child from the distress of feeling guilty, the subconscious mind represses this anger. That is, it takes it out of the person's conscious mind so he no longer is aware of his anger. But the subconscious mind cannot eradicate this angry feeling and stores it away, deep in the subbasement where it can hibernate for years."

The voice that tells us we have no right to get angry at our parents is responsible for a lot of inner turmoil. When we do things for our parents out of guilt or manipulation, eventually we turn the anger on ourselves and them. It's not easy to go to your parents and say, "This is your baggage, not mine." But, that may be necessary. The fear of saying no to our parents is carried into our adult life through our relationship with spouses, children, other family members, and friends.

Rory

Rory is single and in his forties. According to Rory, "I grew up in rural South Carolina, the first of three sons born to very young parents. My father worked double shifts leaving my mother and me alone at night. To protect our family and ease my mother's mind, my father kept a pistol in the attic that could be fired by pulling a string to scare away intruders. I remember long nights being as scared as my mother. The difference was, when my father got home she was relieved, but I was not. I was close to my mother then, but the man who was my father I saw mostly on Sundays. He seemed as frightening to me as the burglars and psychos in my mother's mind.

"Both my parents were strict disciplinarians with little tolerance for disobedience or sassing. My father's reaction was usually swift and direct. A flash of anger led to a painful and humiliating spanking. My mother used manipulation to discipline me. In addition to warning me of my father's reaction when he got home, she'd often use guilt to manipulate me. She would say, 'After all your daddy and I do for you, this is how you act?'"

Rory says he was a mama's boy from the start and wanted to please her. He continues, "But early on, I also began to distrust her. When I was very young I told my mother that I wished my father would die so I could marry her. The next day she told me never to say that again. She said that when she told my father he replied, 'If he ever says that again I will castrate him.'

"I learned two things from this experience. First, my father was dangerous and my mother could not be trusted. Therefore, I needed to keep my thoughts and feelings to myself. No matter what I felt, it was easiest to say, 'Yes, I'll do it,' even if I had no idea how I could and had no intention to follow through. At times, my mother would forget what she'd told me to do, and occasionally my father would be in a lighthearted mood and let it go. I found that saying 'Yes' had its rewards. Being the good little boy brought my mother great pride. I savored the pats on the back from grandparents and other relatives when I excelled at school or was in a church performance."

Rory says his only real escape in childhood was his imagination. "I became a chronic daydreamer. In my dreams I could be myself and do as I pleased, unlike in the real world. Gradually the imaginary world became preferable to reality. When the real world became too much, I took refuge in my fantasies. My escape into the fantasy world increased as the fantasies became sexual.

"In day-to-day life, I became a natural born follower. I felt like a stow-away on a passenger train speeding off to some unknown destination. Everyone but me seemed to know where they were going and acted as if it was their right to be there. My goal was to fake it, to play along, hoping that I wouldn't be thrown off at the next station. This is how I went through life, until I sought help.

"As I let others in I have experienced many changes and received many gifts. For the first time in my life, I feel at ease in social situations. I recognize many of the distorted thoughts and beliefs I have for what they are. I still believe that if I say 'No' to someone that I'll disappoint them and they'll end up rejecting me, making my life unbearable. The feeling is so strong that I often have trouble identifying what it is that I want or need. With the help of others I am learning to challenge this fear. I'm learning that it's OK to say 'No' and often better than the pain of selling myself out and hating myself for doing it."

Rory has been a caretaker his whole life. He is afraid to say no and is worried about being criticized if he does so. His inner voice tells him a good son never disappoints his parents by saying no. It was a setup for resentment since caretakers often assume more than they can handle and become overwhelmed. Sometimes they may even feel they deserve payback for their efforts, which furthers resentment. I shared my own struggles with Rory about my difficulty of saying no to others. I now would rather someone dislike me for telling the truth, than for believing I'm someone I'm not. Saying no may be hard at first, but in time it gets easier. Our inner voice has the power to dominate our thinking and keep us from reaching our true potential. It tells us that people would never accept us as we truly are. We begin to believe that the world owes us big time, which can lead to destructive entitlement, hopelessness, and despair.

Inner Voices of Failure

Many of us are completely overwhelmed because our inner voice tells us we are failures. I worked with a woman who felt ashamed because of her messy house. It symbolized how she felt about herself. By keeping it messy, she continued to isolate and keep people away. Each time she envisioned the overwhelming task of cleaning she began to feel worthless. She said she could commit to doing housework for one hour a day. I suggested she break the job down into manageable tasks, doing one small portion at a time over that hour. I would call her at the beginning of the hour and at the end of the hour to make sure she kept her commitment. It worked. Having a support group persuaded her to take the necessary action.

I Don't Deserve Happiness

Dr. Twerski says the most damaging misconception is the development of unwarranted feelings of self-negativity. According to Dr. Twerski, "The person who, in reality, is quite capable but thinks of herself as inferior in one or more ways will have a difficult time adjusting in life. A person can adjust optimally to reality only with a valid perception of realism, whereas a deluded person will not adjust. If a destitute person fancies herself wealthy and makes unrealistic purchases, she is certain to get into trouble. If a person is bright, handsome, and personable but thinks of himself as dull, unattractive, and unlikable, this person is destined to a lifetime of problems unless he can recognize his dilemma and get the proper help."

Dr. Twerski explains that we generally assume that other people see things just as we see them. He says, "If we see a garbage dump, we will assume that everyone looking at it will also see a garbage dump and not a bed of beautiful roses. Similarly, if we perceive ourselves as negative, we will assume it is how others see us and we will relate to them accordingly."

Children who receive negative messages grow up sabotaging happiness. They are attracted to people who will treat them poorly and push away people who treat them kindly. Many religious people struggle the most before their holy days. In times of worship, we may find ourselves alone with our own thoughts, when the reality of our consequences becomes clearer. During my destructive years, my self-hate increased on Sundays and holidays, because I didn't go to work. Sunday was the day I had nothing to do but think of who I was. During holidays, all I could feel was emptiness inside. I would shut down emotionally and could not understand how I could feel so alone in the company of the people I loved most. My wife would notice my sadness. She tried to gently cheer me up, but nothing she did would ease my pain. In time, as I continued to work my recovery program, my gratitude increased and I felt more deserving of happiness.

Feelings of hopelessness can pass from generation to generation. Many times these inner voices are so subtle that the person is unaware that he or she is setting himself up for pain. One such person is Mario. Mario rarely felt that deep sense of security that most children take for granted. He grew up in a dysfunctional home where chaos was the norm. The battle zone made it easy for him to avoid his feelings. He felt that he did not deserve to be happy, so he played out that role by sabotaging everything good that came his way.

Mario

Mario is married with two children. According to Mario, "Everyone in my family led a secret life. My parents divorced because of my father's infidelity. My mother was unfaithful to her new husband after she remarried. Whenever I told my sister something in confidence, she betrayed me. Believing that nobody would be there for me, I felt frightened and alone. I tried to live up to my stepfather's expectations by playing sports even though I wasn't interested. A voice told me that I had to be who he wanted me to be. As I grew older, I could never stick to anything for too long, especially if things started to get tough. I had become a very angry person. While I never physically hurt anyone, I was prone to overreact. For example, I would get very angry at my wife when the house was messy. I would become paranoid when she would go out with her sister, believing that she was having an affair with another man. Then I'd have to apologize for not trusting her.

"I did this with my boss too. I was a good money earner, but when he gave jobs to other employees, I thought he was telling me I was no good. All of these things brought out a very deep feeling of dread. I felt so let down and angry that I started gambling to ease the pain."

When Mario could no longer live with the anger and the constant need to apologize, he decided to get help by joining a support group and asking the group leader for help. He says, "I felt ashamed even asking for help. My stepfather's voice was in my head telling me I would be judged if I shared my weaknesses with other people. I learned a lot about myself. When my wife didn't listen to me or my boss overlooked me, I realized how humiliated I felt and wanted them to feel the same way. I needed more than awareness, however. I needed to start making changes in order to deal with my anger and resentment. My sponsor was my savior. I was told to call him as soon as I got angry and take my anger out on him instead of others. He also wanted to hear all of my thoughts, no matter how horrible they were. Today, I can't say my anger is completely gone, but as I stay away from my addictions and keep talking about my difficulties, I definitely have found more peace in my life."

As comfortable as Mario was with me, he still believed I saw him as he viewed himself. His warden led him to this destructive way of thinking, making him believe he needed to act the way others expected or they wouldn't accept him. Over time and with help, Mario was able to guard against such harmful thinking. He learned that the stories he was making up about others were untrue. When he was convinced of this, good things started to happen. He started up his own company and called me for guidance whenever he felt discouraged. Even though his business was doing well, the good times were not enough to keep him from going astray. In his business, he needed to make forty calls a day, but at times he had no strength for even one. I asked him how many calls he could make in an hour, and he said eight to ten. I suggested he make the calls and get back to me one hour later. We did this on an hourly basis until he ultimately attained his goal. With each passing hour, his attitude improved. Today, he continues to call me when he uncovers something too troubling to process alone. He takes comfort from his newly adopted voices that tell him he no longer needs to face his difficulties alone.

Like Mario, I also had to examine how my childhood messages affect the role I play as an adult. I now know that I can choose to listen and share my own experience, but I do not need to attempt to resolve the problems of others. Learning how to let go of the expectations of others takes time, patience, and practice. Accepting people for where they are in life rather than where I *think* they should be can be difficult. I still slip up and get angry at times when people aren't acting and thinking the way I feel they should. When this happens, I pause and try to examine what my role was in the incident, rather than focusing blame on the other person who I thought triggered my anger.

Destructive Voices

Dr. Twerski explains the ways that intrusive messages of childhood can direct our thinking as adults. According to Dr. Twerski, "When confronted with challenge, there are only two possible ways to react: we can either cope or escape. The decision is made based on how we view the challenge. If we think we're capable of coping then we're likely to try. But if we view the challenge as overwhelming, then we probably will choose to escape. It follows that if a person has unwarranted feelings of inferiority and inadequacy, he or she will seek escape even if that challenge may be within his or her ability to cope."

According to Dr. Twerski, "Addictions of all types are escapes from what we perceive to be unmanageable realities. In reality, addictive behavior is too often the result of our misguided thinking that we are inadequate or unworthy and must therefore take the easy way out."

Jerry's story demonstrates how difficult it is to trust. When I first met him, he was so fearful of trusting me that he wouldn't tell me his real name for several months.

Jerry

Jerry is a thirty-year-old married man who grew up in a religious household. According to Jerry, "I was always expected to be a good boy, which in my family translated into doing everything perfect. The opposite also held true. If I wasn't perfect, then I was bad. When

I graduated from elementary school my father said to my mother in front of me, "Why can't my son get honors like everyone else?" I was taught that people have to recognize you and respect you, and if they don't then you're worthless. Based upon on this faulty value system, I attempted to build my own self-worth by chasing down compliments and lying about my accomplishments.

"In my mind it was better to project a false image than to be honest about how I felt. I believed that if I'm not going to succeed then there is no sense in trying, because it's what you achieve that's important, not who you are. And since you're going to fail anyway, why bother trying? I used to study and learn the Holy Torah and felt somewhat accomplished. As time went on, negative voices convinced me that I was hopeless and I gave it up. I felt so unworthy and afraid that I couldn't accomplish that perfect status or image, so why even try?"

Jerry says he had a poor self-image and did not feel accepted by others. He says, "It seemed like others were always judging me, and I wasn't sure if this was a distortion or reality. I finally became so sick of myself that I joined a support group. Because I didn't trust anyone, I gave them a false name. Eventually, I began to reveal more of myself to the group. They never judged me or made me feel I wasn't good enough for them. They allowed me to share my difficulties at work and even helped me look for a new job. I was ashamed to disclose my real name to them until months later. I was very surprised to find out that they forgave me and accepted my action because they understood my fear in trusting others. They also helped me deal with the relationship with my wife. Whenever I was afraid to talk to her about my painful feelings, they reminded me that my wife would never judge me the way my parents did when I was a child. In time, I learned to put my trust in others."

As I spoke to Jerry about my own difficulties, including my struggle with trust, he became more comfortable with me. Jerry eventually became more willing to open up to our group. Unlike his family, the support group provides a safe haven for him to share his feelings. The more trusting he becomes, the more he can recognize that he is no different than anyone else.

Before we can heal, we need to process our personal struggle. At the heart of the struggle is the person who must place his or her faith and trust in the support group. The voice of destructive entitlement wants us to see our behavior as the primary solution to our problems. Our inner voice may drown out all reasonable thoughts, causing us to be like spoiled children who constantly demand attention and instant gratification.

There are certain themes that can be found in the destructive inner voice that drives our pain. These unhealthy message are

- You do not need others.
- You can behave as you please.
- Nobody will ever be there for you.
- You are different from others.
- You are a victim.
- Your false pride is acceptable.

You Do Not Need Others

The little voice inside our head becomes very angry when we refuse to listen. In turn, our healthy relationships are sabotaged. The closer we get to those who can help us, the more this voice tries to push them away. There are kind and loving people who would gladly help us if we asked for it. The fear of asking for help can be terrifying for some of us. If we ask for help and are rejected, we are bombarded with shame and unworthiness. We need these compassionate, supportive voices to overcome the voice that guides us toward harmful behaviors.

You Can Behave as You Please

The voice of destructive entitlement tells us we have the right to act the way we want to, but fails to inform us of the resulting consequences. This is distorted thinking at its best. Whenever I slip back into old habits, the only thing that remains is shame and self-hatred. My inner voice preys on my fears and insecurities and reinforces the belief that something is wrong with me, that I am undeserving of love, and will eventually end up alone and hopeless.

Mel's story illustrates what can happen when these voices are out of control.

Mel

Mel is single and in his late twenties. According to Mel, "When I was three years old my mother died. I believed she died because I wasn't important to her. As an adolescent, I knew how silly this was but I still felt abandoned. My father had a volatile temper and was having a difficult time coping without my mother. He would take out his anger on me. He would yell at me when I didn't take out the garbage or clean my room, or when I failed to wash the dishes and do the laundry. I started to believe that I couldn't do anything right or that I didn't matter. Once when a young man babysat me when I was eight and my brother was five, he started to masturbate in front of us. When my father got home my brother told him about it. My father beat this kid to a pulp. I actually thought he killed him. Whether my father was right or wrong, his display of anger scared me to death.

"As I got older, I avoided intimate relationships, because I dreaded being hurt or abandoned. Even though I hated being alone, I never allowed myself to get close to anyone. Instead, I would go to strip clubs or masturbate to pornography online. Whether things were going good or bad, I felt entitled. Shame kept me inside my head and I never let anyone into the horrible world in which I lived. The insanity of my thoughts and actions were overwhelming. I felt completely hopeless and thought about suicide."

Mel says he didn't fully understand his situation until he found a support group and began sharing his troubles with others. He says, "In group I learned about acceptance, unconditional love, and everything else that I missed in childhood. My leader explained that when I get angry with someone, it is because that person has touched some deep painful wound, which creates a voice that tells me I'm worthless. Without this guidance, I would continue to react in the same destructive manner that had isolated me from the world. I know I need help and can't do it on my own. In the beginning, phone calls with supportive group members were difficult, but I was encouraged to continue. I have also learned that isolation, manufactured fear, and false pride are liabilities, and that by sabotaging everything good in my life I was setting myself up to be a victim. I now know my fears were out of whack because of my abandonment issues, although it was me who always found a way to push others away. When things were going well with my girlfriend, I found some excuse to get angry which resulted in her distancing herself from me. My group and written inventories have allowed me to recover from my wounds and discover my true identity. I no longer feel the emptiness inside that I always lived with."

Mel feared intimacy because of his abandonment issues. He continued to search for love in places where intimacy could never be found. His fear of women was precipitated by the death of his mother at a very young age. These fears played out a story which always ended with loneliness. His fear of being alone was so profound that he created enough mental evidence that it became real to him. Besides the abandonment issues Mel had with his mother, he also had a father guided by anger and victim thinking. His parents' relationship was built on avoidance and shame. Mel never had a chance to say no to the journey he was on. He considered prostitutes and massage parlors his only true relationships. To Mel they were safe, certainly free from any emotional attachment. All this came out in his written inventories.

Today, Mel is involved in a healthy relationship in which he feels safe. He still doesn't feel that he deserves happiness. He fears that he will be abandoned, but as long as he stays connected to his support group he will be OK.

Nobody Will Ever Be There for You

The voice of entitlement is cunning. Repeatedly it declares, "Nobody will ever be there for you but me." It tells us we must listen to our inner voice if we want to be happy and ignore the needs of the people we care about most. It says, "If your spouse really loved you, he or she would show it more," or, "If your friends really cared, they would treat you better." It compels us to be overly judgmental while being a victim. This voice makes us distrustful of others so we are unable to distinguish healthy boundaries between right and wrong.

You Are Different from Others

The voice inside our head uses any difference with others to drive a wedge between us and them. These differences may be age, ethnic background, religion, or sexual orientation. No matter how we look on the outside, on the inside we share countless similarities. Moreover, we all want peace and happiness despite our addictions to alcohol, drugs, excessive working, eating, gambling, or sex. The question that must be asked is, "When I am in discomfort do I *depend* on my support group for help or do I run to my addictions instead?" If one is an addict their addictive voice will always try to take them back to their addiction as their solution.

You Are a Victim

Our inner voice informs us that the world will always disappoint us. People won't do what we expect of them. In turn, this creates self-pity and sets us up as the victim. This leads to the feeling of self-righteousness, which suggests our problems stem from the shortcomings of others. Sometimes the voice will team up with self-hate to make us feel worthless inside and once again separate us from others. Many of us are so comfortable with this message that we end up wearing the mask of victimhood for our entire lives.

Your False Pride Is Acceptable

Even though our inner voice will congratulate us on a job well done, we need to be careful. It may be an opportunity created simply to gain back control of our old behavior. As we grow, we learn that we don't need to listen to the destructive messages from the past. As we begin to embrace our support group, we begin to notice, in time, that our inner voice becomes quieter. The destructive messages from our past gradually are replaced with the new, more compassionate thoughts we have learned. I accept my destructive inner voice as being a part of who I am. Rather than empowering the voice, I now say "Thank you for sharing," then reach out to my support system for guidance.

Chapter Seven: Trusting Others

Please help me, but don't get too close.

There is no program of recovery or growth that is painless. All of us will find reasons to avoid this kind of inner pain. Before I could place my trust in others, I needed to take three steps. First, I had to discover the nature of my problem. Second, I had to find a solution. Third, I had to work out a plan of action. Only by trusting other people could I successfully process new information into my belief system. In so doing, I was able to purge myself of some of those negative beliefs.

The Problem

During my years of acting-out behavior, I often repeated the words, "Please God, protect me from myself." I felt disconnected from any type of environment that promised healing or recovery. I felt superior *and* inferior. Although I knew I needed help, I dreaded the vulnerability of sharing my innermost feelings. Intimacy was too painful. The abandonment I felt in childhood left deep scars. I couldn't risk getting hurt again. This created a self-centered belief system that did not permit trust.

My inner voice told me that I could not survive without my habit, even though I understood this was insane. The addiction kept me in chains. A part of me hated myself so much I frequently thought about suicide. I couldn't look at myself in the mirror anymore. I wanted the pain of living to go away. What stopped me was thinking about my family and what the wounds of suicide would inflict on them.

Still, I needed to feel in control of my healing process. The more fearful I was, the more I felt the need to control the process. I wanted to heal, but I was neither ready nor willing to take the appropriate steps. Not only did I need the willingness to *ask for help*, but also I needed the willingness to *accept direction* when help was offered.

The Solution

My first task was to find a therapist or a support group that satisfied my needs even if I felt it was a waste of my time. When I realized that I was no different from others seeking help, I became more willing to remove my mask in order to heal. As I attended more groups, I gradually shed the outer layers of shame that had isolated me from the world.

Because of a continuing power struggle between the new voice of hope and the old voice of intrusion, I needed to attend these groups faithfully. Trusting others was difficult, but it was necessary for me to escape the pain of loneliness that I had lived with all my life. When I understood this, I stopped fighting.

Working the Solution

In high school, I had a physical education teacher who taught us the three requirements for obtaining a good grade. He was very clear: "First, do what you are told. Second, do what you are told. And third, do what you are told." To heal your wounds, you must do as you're told by your sponsor, therapist, or group. Don't listen to those destructive inner voices from the past. Healing requires the ultimate self-discipline.

My biggest obstacle was giving up control. This is the ultimate task for a control freak like me. My first assignment was to trust my therapist and support group. They decided I should disclose to my wife the details of my infidelity. This advice might not be appropriate for everyone, but it was the right advice for me. It would also become my most difficult and challenging test. I became defensive and was scared of my wife's reaction. I thought she would never forgive me. I reluctantly did what I was told while putting my faith in the power of the group and my therapist.

Disclosure

I had an appointment with my wife at her therapist's office. Her therapist was experienced with disclosure techniques. I kept telling myself that, in time, the truth would bring us closer and that she would eventually forgive me. With no more secrets we could begin a life of intimacy that up until now had been impossible because of my indiscretions. I didn't know whether my disclosure would to be more frightening for me or for her. I was terrified.

I prayed that she already knew everything that I was about to tell her. When I began to disclose, she started to scream. I was gripped with anguish but had no place to run. I could not rationalize my actions or deny the pain I caused the woman I loved. I broke down. It was the first time my wife had seen me cry. Years later, she told me that it was my tears that saved our marriage. I thank God for this special woman who was able to see my pain in the middle of her own agony. The therapist kept urging me to be as candid as possible. She told my wife that my disclosure was prompted by my love for her, which was why I wanted to turn my life around. In the upcoming sessions my wife told me, "Our marriage was a lie." Initially, I couldn't understand this. I knew I loved my family more than anything in my life. I would run in front of a bus for any of them and they knew this. However, in time, I understood exactly what she meant. If she had done to me what I had done to her, I would have felt the same way she did.

Her grief, at times, bordered on rage, and this would continue for more than a year. Telling her how profoundly sorry I was meant nothing. I had to back up my words with action. There were days she accused me of things that I did not do. There were also nights when her pain hit such a crescendo that she shut me out. Throughout this, I concluded that my place was to be there for her when she wanted to talk and to give her space when she needed to be alone. She was experiencing a roller coaster of emotions. One day her roller coaster would plummet to resentment and anger, and the next day it would lift toward forgiveness. It was a confusing and turbulent time. Her world was turned upside down and she needed someone to hold her up.

My faith that everything would work out for the best is what kept me going. During the most stressful times she pumped me with questions. On those occasions, I would call on my group for moral support and the strength to endure. Sometimes, my victim mentality would come back, causing me to wonder when she finally would get over this. On those occasions, I was forced to remind myself of the reality of what I had done—that she was the victim, not me. She told me how I had destroyed the image she had of me as her knight in shining armor. Other times, I sensed her turmoil as she tried to forgive me.

I was required to do a full disclosure. I was obliged to do as told. The worst times were when I heard her sobbing in the bathroom with the door locked. I was frightened, ashamed, and felt dirty. I also feared she might never again be happy. During these difficult times, my support group stood by my side and gave me hope. They insisted that I focus on my shortcomings and that in time our marriage would heal. They were right. Today our marriage is stronger than we had ever thought possible. I never would have been able to muster up the courage to come clean without the help and support of others.

Whether an addict or not, we all need people to do for us what we cannot accomplish for ourselves. When I finally reached the point in life where I felt comfortable trusting others with my decision-making process, I began to share in their strength and hope. Even when I started to isolate from my friends in the groups I attended, they knew me well enough to bring me out of it. Gradually, I began to make mental notes of new solutions to my problems.

I have helped many people in their recovery. The closer we get, the more they place their trust in me. This trust allows me to point out the blind spots they are unable to see on their own. Blind spots are usually created by the warden, that bully who berates us with destructive childhood messages of fear. Many of these fears are manufactured to inhibit growth and happiness.

Written inventories are excellent tools to bring our inner thoughts and fears to the surface. In group, these are our homework assignments. At our group meetings, we read what we've written to the group. We ask for feedback. These reports help identify our natural assets, liabilities, strengths, and weaknesses. In time, written inventories help to separate the manufactured fears of childhood from our healthy fears that are necessary for our survival. A healthy fear would tell us to say no to drugs or to stop and look both ways before dashing across a street. When people let imagined fears govern their lives, they lose their integrity and become angry and resentful. The combination of written inventories and fellowship support help us process our fears in a healthy way.

Being aware of manufactured fears is only the beginning. Awareness must be followed by action. Good intentions are not enough. Healing does not stem from intentions, but from a persevering attitude which can propel us to action despite discomfort.

Chapter Eight: ACTION!

Victim thinking gives us permission to
avoid taking responsibility.

ॐ

Healing involves much more than meets the eye. Before you can begin to heal, you need to overcome roadblocks, which are mostly of your own doing. As I became aware of the ways in which my childhood wounds and my inner voice affected my life, I began to understand that my victim thinking pushed people away. This thinking, compounded by my fear of trusting others, created a distorted view of life. As I gained clarity, I realized that I needed to assume responsibility for my own actions and that being a victim was not working. I also needed the guidance of others.

The Stakes Are Higher for People with Destructive Behaviors

People with very destructive behaviors have a more compelling need to rely on the power of the group. The actions they need to take are more critical, because the consequences of their actions are more life threatening to themselves and to those around them. I have discovered one of the best ways to help myself is to help other people. When I'm busy helping others, I put their needs first rather than focusing solely on myself. In giving to others, I receive more in return.

The deeper the childhood wounds, the greater the difficulty it will be to ask for help. Deeply wounded people tend to blame others without assuming any personal responsibility for their own problems. Their sense of personal responsibility is eclipsed by layers of self-loathing, false pride, and toxic shame. When newcomers first begin to attend our groups, it takes them time to fully understand the meaning of acceptance as it relates to their personal problems. As a group leader, I try to be the voice of acceptance for them. I urge them to keep coming back to group. In time, and after a lot of hard work, they can begin to free themselves from the fears and intrusive voices that have chained them to a life of isolation and regret.

One of the first things I do when a newcomer joins the group is to inquire why he or she needs help, and if they are willing to accept it when given. When trying to urge a newcomer to participate in group therapy, I begin by sharing the feelings and problems I had when I first came for help. I tell them about the warden, the guy who sits on my shoulder with a bat. I ask if they have a warden on their shoulder too, and what he tells them. When someone has a difficult childhood, they go through life with a feeling of defectiveness. When they experience failure, their past shame resurfaces in the present. Eventually, the failure takes on a bigger meaning and can represent how the person defines him- or herself. Of course, this message is encouraged by their warden.

I ask newcomers how they feel when someone disagrees with them. Do they shut down, believing they do not deserve to have their feelings heard? Or, do they rage at any opinion that doesn't agree with theirs? In the past, when I met with disagreement my feelings of defectiveness would resurface; I mistakenly thought that being right would make the pain go away. But, the only thing that went away was the people in my life. Whether a newcomer shuts down their emotions or lashes out in anger, neither way is healthy.

Learning to trust is a slow process, and it's OK to build it by taking tiny steps. Our darkest secrets are the most critical ones to expose. These secrets imprison a person to a life of toxic shame, adding fuel to our destructive thinking. My responsibility as a guide is to nurture sufficient trust so the newcomer to our group will allow me to be their new temporary decision maker. Dark secrets are like cancerous growths. If they are permitted to grow and metastasize, they will devastate a person's emotional well-being.

Positive feelings, on the other hand, are short-lived because the old voices return to haunt us. Our inner voice convinces us of our inadequacies; it becomes even more critical for me—as their guide—to stay close following any disclosure of secrets. Gary's story demonstrates the importance of disclosing our destructive secrets before healing can begin.

Gary

Gary is single and in his forties. According to Gary, "My childhood was shrouded in shame and secrecy. My father and I seldom spoke, and I was ashamed by his habit of walking around the house naked at times. I found this very humiliating. He was also so selfish that he would put a chain around the freezer so that no one would take any of his ice cream or desserts. My mother suffered from depression. As I got older I felt that even though she loved us, we were a bother to her more than anything else.

"At a very young age I became aware that I had an attraction to males. My mother caught me with someone and made me write a letter to my father explaining what I did. I had to read this letter aloud and the amount of shame was unbearable. I wanted to die. Ironically, my father, who was reading the paper at the time, said nothing. As I look back on it, I wish he would have gotten mad. At least it would have been a sign of emotion. In later years, I found out that my father was a cross-dresser and had many secrets of his own. As crazy as it sounds, I wanted his love anyway, but he never allowed this to happen. On occasion, I would ask him for money, but he always turned me down. I don't even think I needed the money. I just wanted something, anything, just a sign that I mattered. The strongest message I was given as a child was not to share your secrets—that the humiliation of doing so would be devastating. I turned to drugs and alcohol to kill the pain."

Gary tried Twelve Step meetings, but the fear of disclosing his sexuality kept him disconnected from the people in the group. Instead, he went to a therapist, who suggested Gary make a phone call to someone who he thought he could trust. Gary called me. Gary recalls, "I felt comfortable talking until I was asked about my childhood. When this happened, my anger would come to the surface. I eventually learned that my anger was the way I subconsciously tried to push people away. It was suggested I try to do some written inventories on my childhood wounds. I still got angry every time doing these inventories was suggested.

"I was told, 'You will never feel like doing them, so if you're waiting for that to happen, no progress will ever be made.' Eventually, I built enough faith and willingness to do what I was told. I hated to admit it, but I started to see how my fear of trusting others was manufactured from my childhood experiences. In time, I started to disclose stories about my past that I never thought I would share with anyone. Others were brought into my support system. I started to feel safer each time I had the courage to share my feelings with them."

It was difficult for Gary to open up about his fears and shame. But by bringing them to the surface, he was able to draw on the experience, strength, hope, and compassion of the group. He has slowly freed himself from those dark secrets of the past that had long kept him isolated in fear and desperation. This has also given him the willingness to go back to meetings, which in turn, have helped keep him from returning to his old destructive patterns.

The deeper the wounds, the greater our defenses that discourage us from hearing new information and insights about healing. New information requires us to look at our wounds instead of ignoring them. Old information is like an alarm system that sounds— *danger, danger, someone is trying to see who I am and I won't allow this under any circumstances.* Yet, there is a part of us that desperately wants to trust someone and feel protected and cared for. My cry was, *"Please help me. I'm in so much pain, but don't you dare come near me."* Building trust and closeness with someone who has never experienced intimacy can be the most beautiful experience to witness. If they have the willingness to keep reaching out, they will eventually expose a part of themselves that has always cried out for acceptance.

I helped a man who constantly tried to push me away by asking, "Why do you care about somebody like me?" He felt so worthless. Underneath his protective wall, he was begging for help and eventually found the courage to trust. There are times we can share our loving Higher Power with others who cannot find it on their own. One of the ways I share this gift is to let the person know they will never again be alone unless it is their choice to live a solitary life. What I cannot supply is the willingness to change. This they must find on their own.

The teacher of willingness is life itself, and we become willing students once we recognize that we can no longer live the way we had in the past. We must involve ourselves with others who are trying to improve their lives. The greater our participation, the more bonded we will feel with the group. These groups can be formed by a therapist, church, housewives, or any group of people who willing to adhere to the criteria and rules suggested here previously.

However, participation is mandatory. The decision to place phone calls to other members of the group is mandatory. Even if the person has nothing to talk about, he or she still is obligated to make phone calls. Gradually, the phone calls become easier as the comfort level increases in the members.

One common struggle we share as humans is our difficulty to admit defeat. This is because our society views defeat as weak. We were taught never to give up, but sometimes giving up allows us to seek help. At times, the sooner a person does this and admits defeat, the sooner he can begin to heal. By surrounding ourselves with the right people, we begin to stop some of the destructive habits and entitlements that have always hurt us.

I am grateful that on my journey I have established deep friendships with people of all faiths, sexual preferences, and walks of life. Some were brought up in an environment with a strong belief in a Higher Power. Yet they turned to addiction or other destructive actions to cope with life's problems. Defectiveness, unworthiness, shame, abandonment, and never feeling good enough are common threads. With these characteristics, it is easy to develop an inner voice that tells you how different you are from other people. If our care-givers manipulated or abused us in childhood in any way, we will carry this distrust into our adult lives. It affects all of our relationships with others.

The only reason I was able to trust others was because I realized that I could not stop my destructive actions on my own. What I found was even greater than merely staying sober. I discovered a freedom from my childhood wounds that was only possible when I became willing to permit others to do for me what I was incapable of doing for myself. One of the tools that I credit most for my growth is the written inventories included in this book on pages 99 and 111. These inventories allowed me to trust. The first written inventory focuses on the messages we receive as children. From these messages, we hear a voice that directs us toward inappropriate actions and destructive behaviors.

Displacement

According to Dr. Twerski's definition of displacement, "At any time, a person may come into contact with someone who occupies a position similar to that of a parent, perhaps an authority figure such as a teacher or boss. Since there is no guilt in feeling angry at one's teacher or boss, our subconscious mind allows our angry feelings to come out of storage and be directed at the teacher or boss. These feelings are *displaced* since neither the teacher nor the boss had done anything to warrant such feeling being directed toward them.

"Here we have a situation where this person feels angry at his teacher or boss with no justification. Although displaced anger at a boss is not as uncomfortable as anger directed toward a parent, it is nevertheless an uncomfortable feeling to be angry at someone for no good reason. The subconscious mind uses one of its other maneuvers, *rationalization,* to give the person logical-sounding reasons to justify his feelings. A person might say, 'Did you see how your teacher walked right by you, as if you didn't exist?' Or, 'Your teacher didn't show you adequate appreciation for the amount of work you did or the effort you made.' The subconscious mind is very clever in getting a person to believe what it wants him or her to believe."

The fact is, according to Dr. Twerski, you can go through life with distorted feelings about yourself and other people. These other people may be your spouse, parents, in-laws, siblings, children, employer, friends, and anyone else with whom you have a relationship. Dr. Twerski reminds us, "Your behavior toward them may be unpleasant, resulting in distress. You may think you know why you're behaving that way toward them, although your behavior is factually without foundation. They, in turn, may relate to you on the basis of your behavior. It is easy to see how many important relationships can be all messed up because of such misconceptions. If only we could free ourselves, think how much better life could be."

The following is an example of a written inventory. We complete inventories to make us aware of the ways our childhood caregivers have affected the relationships we now have as adults.

A Written Inventory

Who were your caregivers?	Messages received from those caregivers	Our inner voice created from the messages	The behaviors our inner voice commands us to do	What we need from our support system
1. Dad	From Dad: I wasn't good enough.	That I'm inadequate.	Isolation.	Help me renew trust in others.
2. Mom	From Mom: Her feelings mattered more than mine.	That I am not a good person unless I am pleasing others.	No one would like me if they discover who I really am.	
3. Priest	God's love was conditional.	Don't trust in others because they will unfairly judge you.		

Journaling is a way to explore thoughts and feeling while contemplating what action to take. As the person reveals what they have learned to others, he begins to connect the dots. For the first time he recognizes the fears he inherited from his childhood and how they led him to play a role in his adult life that helped him cope with his fears. As new, healthier voices take root, they rely less heavily on the old ones. The more we can challenge our old way of doing things, the more we can accept and strengthen our faith in ourselves and others.

When a person finishes his or her written inventories there will be enough evidence to demonstrate the reasons the person does not trust others in their life. I tell the person, "It is obvious why you would not want to trust the group, therapist, sponsor, or anyone else.

If trusting others resulted in such negative consequences, then why would you put any faith in a process you cannot control?" I ask each person what he or she needs from the group or me to help battle the destructive messages inside their heads. When members reveal those messages and inner voices to the group, they find they are not so unique. Others begin to share all the ways they can identify with the member. In time, the person will become aware of the ways these childhood inner voices are affecting relationships in the here and now.

One person who gained great insight from these written inventories was Ernie. Ernie never realized the damage caused by his resentment toward his father. He lost three jobs in two years and blamed it all on his bosses. In many ways, Ernie's written inventories brought him the self-awareness he needed to help him change.

Ernie

Ernie is thirty years old, married, and has three children. According to Ernie, "When I was young, my authority figure was my father. My dad's intended message was that his children were a status symbol and not worthy in their own rights. A successful person had lots of money, a big house, a nice car, children who listen, and community status. Dad had all these things, and my siblings and I were just part of his success.

"Dad worked long hours and rarely took time to spend with us. Much of his free time was devoted to community-related activities. Throughout my entire childhood, my dad took me to a total of one baseball game. He never taught me to play ball, nor did he just hang out with me. His other activities were more important.

"When Dad was around, he tended to be very strict and had a short fuse. At our Shabbat table, if I were to move around, speak too loudly, or do anything that my dad felt out of place, he would yell at me. He held us to a very high and probably impossible standard of behavior. Children were to be seen and not heard."

Ernie's father had an insult for every occasion. Ernie recalls, "His idea of interaction was to insult his kids. We learned to give as well as take, but God help us if we ever got the better of him in one of his tirades. If that happened, we were being insulting and disrespectful to our father, a major no-no, and subject to punishment. It seemed he didn't care about our feelings, and we were not allowed to fight back or defend ourselves against his authority.

"My dad did not have a problem expressing his disapproval, and he was always very blunt. 'You look like shit,' was the typical criticism referring to our state of dress. 'You're an idiot and have no idea what you're talking about, so shut up,' was the usual remark. He also used to say these things in front of other people, which made us feel worthless."

As an adult, Ernie realized how he used anger as a weapon, especially toward his wife. He says, "If I'm not acting out in anger, then I'm isolating. I also get angry at my kids for not behaving. I disconnect from those who can punish me, especially my wife. When I see my wife as an authoritative figure, I cut myself off from her. If I disconnect then she can't touch me. I'm so afraid of feeling worthless or ignored that when this feeling comes up I react with anger. This also creates a voice inside me that says I must be right all the time and when others disagree I become very defensive.

"Today, with the help of others, I've learned to take a step back from my old reactions of anger and rage and instead examine myself before the rage happens. I am learning how being gentle with myself and empathetic toward my wife can help me move away from rage. But in order to practice that gentleness and empathy, I need awareness and a course of action that I must take to short-circuit that process before it occurs. I also have learned to confront many issues that I have with my father, including repressed anger, sadness, fear, and my lack of self-worth."

Some people were so fearful of their childhood caregivers that they carried this fear into their adult life. This was the case with Ernie. Even therapists and guides can be targets of his anger. Ernie has a difficult time with change and accepting guidance, and he is frequently critical of new ideas. This created unmanageability in his life and stopped him from reaching out for help because he was so harshly judged in childhood.

In deeply wounded families, our mistakes are often used as weapons against each other. This was the case with Ernie. Ernie had the desire to punish himself for his mistakes by not permitting compassion into his belief system. As our relationship evolved, he began to make room in his life for kindness and tolerance, both for himself and for others. Inventories helped Ernie realize how he is passing on his distorted mindset to his offspring. They also helped him discover how much joy he gets from the role of victim, especially when it comes to his father. Anger toward his father is part of his natural fiber, but it also has served another purpose. First, anger protected him from the need to tell his father how he truly feels; anger also has allowed him to deny his own grief that was covered over with layer upon layer of anger. Eventually, Ernie found the courage to tell his father how it felt to be a little kid and face that ten-foot giant called Dad. By saying no to the voice inside his head, Ernie has slowly learned to share these fears and release himself from the wounds of the past.

Joining a Support Group

We have established the importance of trust and of learning how to rely less on ourselves and to rely more on others. In the beginning of my healing process, I had to have a Higher Power with "skin," such as a therapist or a support group.

A support group can be two or more individuals, which lend support to each other. A group can meet in a church, school, or in someone's house. A group must choose a leader to enforce the group guidelines. As the group evolves, it will take on a life of its own with its peaks and valleys. Start the meeting by discussing each member's goals and the obstacles that block these goals. Goals can range from increasing one's intimacy with family members to finding the courage to say no to parents or others. Goals can include asking your boss for a raise or finding a new job altogether.

Eventually, through the guidance of my support group, I found a spiritual power. It's hard to find a spiritual power when you feel like a victim. Victim thinking leaves little room for gratitude, and gratitude is needed to find a Higher Power. I must constantly remind myself that I could be alone, in jail, divorced, sick, or dead. Simply put, I am grateful for what I have rather than what I don't have. It could be worse.

Getting the Most from a Support Group

Through my own experience, I have found twelve ways to
help you get the most out of support groups and help free yourself
from victim thinking. The more willing you are to try helpful hints like
the ones listed below, the better chance you have to stay away from
being a victim and self-righteous. Destructive actions are deadly,
creating a spiritual death that separates the person from everyone else
in his life. Changing your behavior presents a day-to-day challenge.
To help you be more successful in your group therapy, consider the
following suggestions.

- *When anger strikes, take a time out.* Once anger takes control it
  becomes difficult to surrender. Seek guidance and strength
  from your support group, from friends, or from other
  sources that bring enjoyment to your life. The sooner you
  can do this, the easier it becomes to change old patterns
  of behavior. Be careful not to seek those that support the
  Warden's destructive messages.

- *Phone someone you trust in your support/accountability group
  when you are angry.* Make sure it is someone who will slowly
  guide the conversation to a healthy solution. The guide
  must direct you away from self-pity or entitlement.

- *Before approaching a person who angers you, discuss the problem
  first with your support group.* Group members can discuss a
  better way to communicate how you feel in a healthy way.

- *Talk to your group about your destructive inner voice.* Don't let
  your actions follow the voice. Your group will help you find
  healthy solutions for your problems.

- *Be direct.* Ask your group for courage and strength when
  your fears try to shut you down. Saying no to others can
  create unhealthy guilt. On the other hand, if you say "Yes"
  when you want to say "No," then the victim thinking starts
  to build again. The better choice is speaking with integrity.

- *Recite daily affirmations to increase self-esteem.* These affirmations are more powerful if they are done in front of a mirror. I had to say to myself that I deserved to be loved even if I didn't feel it inside. I did this every morning no matter how difficult or uncomfortable it was for me.

- *Tell your partner your struggles.* It may be uncomfortable, but this communication can increase intimacy between you and your partner. Learn to listen to your partner. To get the best results, couples should make the commitment to be honest with each other and to share their feelings in a safe way.

- *As parents, commit to sharing some of your challenges with your children.* By doing this, you can build a new belief system, one that enables your children to learn that it's all right to ask for help.

- *Keep your feet where they should be—not where they can get you into trouble.* This advice is especially important for recovering addicts.

- *Check in with your partner.* Share your feelings in scheduled get-togethers during the week. As you start to experience new feelings with your partner, you can share these feelings with your support group if needed. This enables everyone in the group to learn and grow from each others' experiences.

- *Admit when you are wrong as soon as possible.* If you aren't open about your mistakes, your thinking might naturally gravitate toward blaming the other person.

- *In addition to group, consider seeking the help from a qualified therapist.*

Doing the Next Right Thing

In healing, we talk about doing the next right thing. Unfortunately, the next right thing is not always the most comfortable thing to do. Often the right thing requires that you step out of your comfort zone. Making a connection with your support group is the right thing, but may not be comfortable because you have grown more at ease being isolated. When ruled by self-hatred and destructive behaviors, the only words a person is capable of absorbing are words that reinforce his worthlessness. If a person goes back to his destructive behaviors or is involved in relationships he is ashamed of, he will avoid the healthy people in his life. Being around healthy people causes his shame. He will only seek healthy people when he reaches utter despair.

Those who were judged in childhood will have a more difficult time feeling safe when expressing their shortcomings or mistakes to others. Sometimes the only option left is to leave a door open for them to call on when they decide to end their isolation. I can't help anyone battle their destructive inner voice unless they allow me to join the fight. When they are ready, I can guide them through the shame they are bound to feel upon coming back to their group. It does not matter how many times they come back, as long as they keep coming back.

People who are severely wounded do not have healthy boundaries. They either blame others for their troubles or make themselves responsible for everyone else's shortcomings. It is hard for them to see the gray area because victim thinking sees only black or white.

The Power of Personal Inventories

The first set of personal inventories helped us understand how early childhood messages created inner voices that affected our belief system as adults. The second inventory must be calculated regularly to help us cope with the daily occurrences of our lives and to recognize the distorted way we view ourselves. As our self-perception becomes less distorted, we become more accepting of others, which eventually decreases the victim thinking that has harmed us until now.

Personal inventories are an effective tool to gain valuable personal insight. When a flood of old information overwhelms you, it distorts your perceptions about yourself and the world around you. Taking a personal inventory at this stage helps to restore your balance by looking at your role in the incident, rather than viewing yourself as the victim. You begin to gain a better perspective on how your thinking has to change, rather than how others need to change. In one of my first inventories, I had so much denial that I could not see my responsibility in anything. I had a problem saying no to people, so I thought every problem I had was the other person's fault. I didn't realize that this was how I set myself up to be a victim. In reality I did not have the courage to say no because my inner voice made me feel like a bad person if I didn't make others happy. When this happened, I was angry that people took advantage of me. In reality, it was my fault for letting them take advantage of me. I also thought that I was a great husband, because I never complained. In reality, I was shutting down because I had no self-worth. These things became clear as I continued my written inventories.

Each member of the group must share his inventories with other members so we can discuss our experiences together. This is important because support groups can point out our blind spots. It allows us to recognize our victim thinking before we start to act on it. It also guides us toward a healthy solution and away from self-righteous thoughts. When we start to include inventories as part of our daily discipline, a healthy change in our thinking emerges. Instead of setting ourselves apart from the world and wallowing in self-pity, we start to examine our role in life. This allows us to become more accepting of others and to find forgiveness.

Celebrate Victories

People with troubled childhoods do not take the time to celebrate their victories in life. Rather than acknowledging progress, the person will immediately move to another dilemma. For example, when I did something constructive in my life or had a sense of gratitude, it was important to share these experiences with my support group. The accomplishment of one group member can bring hope to other members.

Beware of Complacency

Whenever I am introduced to something new, such as a self-help tool, my immediate reaction is to put up resistance, even if I know that it is the right thing to do. I have learned that if the suggestion is coming from a reliable source, it's best to do what I am told and guard against complacency. Many people who reach the point of taking a personal inventory develop a certain level of peace. They have started to feel better about themselves, and this feeling filters into their personal relationships. Then suddenly, false pride finds a crack in the armor and they feel they deserve a break from doing the things that have improved their lives. The cycle returns: first complacency, then isolation, then self-pity, and finally entitlement. Even those who have stayed away from their destructive ways for years underestimate the power of their inner voice and their victim thinking and eventual isolation. Isolation always provided a comfort zone for me.

Inventories serve as an important tool to keep you in the present, which increases the likelihood you will not go back to your old ways. There are no guarantees, but those who do inventories regularly will grow in self-awareness and acceptance of others. Inventories also help to form healthy boundaries in our relationships, so we can clearly see where our responsibility begins and ends. In the beginning, doing inventories is bothersome, but like other disciplines, once you are in the habit of doing them, you've won half the battle. The reward is the freedom that comes when other people can no longer control your life.

Another problem many people face is their own negative attitude. When I detect such a defeatist attitude, I tell them, "Your best thinking got you here." This is why I suggest they take their thinking out of the equation. I remind them that this takes time and patience. After all, they didn't get this way overnight. Whether it is praying, calling people, or taking an inventory, these processes take time before beliefs begin to change.

Before beginning your personal inventory, here are a few suggestions to get you started. All of these actions appear simple to do, but may be blocked by flawed thinking.

- *The habit of taking a personal inventory is like the habit of praying.* Do it on a consistent basis and not just when you are in trouble or when the spirit moves you. Do not wait until you feel like doing your inventories, as this feeling may never come. Just do it.

- *An inventory helps you find out more about the distorted thinking that creates the destructive behavior.* It also builds awareness about wounds that have influenced your life as an adult. Patterns eventually develop in these inventories so you can see how your victim thinking has affected your life.

- *Written inventories work more efficiently if completed for fifteen to thirty minutes a night, instead of three hours once a week.* It keeps the mind alert to the dynamics of daily thinking.

- *With time, inventories should bring acceptance and awareness of the ways our inner voice has influenced adult behaviors.* Eventually, the goal is to feel comfortable in our own skin, rather than carrying the shame-filled baggage of our childhood wounds.

Written Inventories

When I started my inventory, it was like a jigsaw puzzle. I could only conclude that I was on one end of the spectrum while everyone else was on the other. I placed the blame on everyone else for my problems. But after taking an inventory for a period of time, I began to better understand my role and how I allowed victim thinking and self-righteousness to influence my outlook on my relationships and the world.

Many people I have worked with, especially those with successful careers, are trapped in denial. They can recognize neither their victim mentality nor the warden sitting on their shoulders. Because they are successful, it is often difficult for them to accept the possibility that they can be engaged in victim thinking. The likelihood that they covered this up by becoming overachievers is a mystery to them. Even though they often struggle with hopelessness and sometimes despair, they still don't believe that something has gone awry. This is where the inventories come to the rescue. This is where they can discover that either directly or indirectly they can set up themselves or others for unrealistic expectations. This can trigger a downward spiral that often leads to drugs, alcohol, working compulsively, or some other form of destructive entitlement.

Taking an Inventory

An inventory is a personal self-examination where we record our thought process on paper. This enables us to see a clearer picture of the ways our thinking affects our relationships. As we do inventories, we begin to see patterns developing that make our part in the problem more distinguishable. By discussing these inventories with others, our wounds and defects are brought to the light, which brings healing and growth into our relationships. The first column of the inventory lists the names of persons or institutions that harmed us or did something to strike a raw nerve or open an old wound. The second column describes the nature of the incident. In this column, the individual must keep his writing to a minimum. It is tempting to be overly detailed in writing about the details of the situation. The goal here is to avoid self-righteousness—which keeps us from being in touch with our emotional wounds. The third column lists our initial reaction to the incident. The fourth column describes the old wound that has been reopened by the incident and the cause of our overreaction. It encompasses the character defects and wounds which influence our perceptions of the world. How have we let our childhood wounds set ourselves up to become victims, when the reality is that we are often the aggressors?

If the wounded person expects too much of another, then he will spend his life being victimized by that person. This makes acceptance of others impossible. Unless these wounds and voices are exposed, we will not find freedom from the power others have over us. Our feelings of defectiveness ultimately influence the way we respond to the incident. These childhood injuries make the person a prisoner to a defective belief system.

The wound must be named and the voice that comes from this injury must be brought into the inventory in column four. Were any unfair expectations set up that created predetermined resentments? Did the person judge herself or others too rigidly in the situation? Were there any feelings of defectiveness which might have been similar to those that were felt as children? Did the person feel invisible or ignored in any area, as in childhood? The person might have been too caught up in the right and wrong of the situation, which would feed into her belief that she had to be right in order to feel good inside. Maybe the person was too selfish in the demands she made of others. These people might not have been able to give the person what she needed at the time because they had their own needs or problems to deal with. Was the person caretaking to the point that she felt manipulated and used? Did she say how she felt and was she completely honest? All of these old beliefs and coping strategies, which were protecting the individual's wounds, had to affect the way the person viewed the story. This third column is where the individual brings in her support group, if needed, to find out where one's blind spots are. In the beginning, it is difficult to see the migration into victimhood and self-righteousness. This is why a support group is essential for directing the person away from negative thinking.

The fifth column shows us that we have a choice; we can be more accepting and forgiving than our initial reaction. We also played a role in the initial incident that triggered our anger, and we are not innocent victims deserving of pity. We are learning to give or to ask for forgiveness, which is what finally releases us from the pain of our childhood wounds. This starts to change our mode of thinking from self-centered to gratitude centered. We develop gratitude for the way things are rather than for the way we want them to be. Gratitude will always be the water that extinguishes the flames of victim thinking.

Instead of focusing on how others harm us, we begin to see the bigger picture—that everyone has problems and everyone is not out to get us. We no longer need to have their problems own us. After awhile, these written inventories lay the groundwork for building healthy boundaries. You will soon discover the insanity of doing the same things repeatedly and expecting different results. You will also discover the healing power of acceptance and forgiveness as the only way to release yourself from the grip that our inner voice and others have over us.

Review the sample inventory below. Then do your own inventory in the space provided. A blank example of this inventory is included in Appendix A on page 151. You may want to make photocopies of the inventories for your personal use.

The Aggressor	The incident	My initial reaction, aided by the Warden's voice	Old fears and wounds re-opened by event	A more mature & compassionate reaction that addresses my role in the incident
My wife	Criticized me for my past infidelity	Anger for dredging up the past	Abandonment, insecurity & inadequacy	Showing kindness empathy and compassion
My children	They don't help out around the house	Anger for not helping	That I'm a failure as a father	To establish boundaries and consequences
My mother	My difficulty in saying no	Anger and guilt	Fear of manipulation	No longer have to carry her shame
God	For letting my father die	I felt like a victim	Fear of abandonment	Your will, not mine, be done
Me	Making a mistake	Impatience & anger	Feeling inadequate	Feeling self-compassion

The Aggressor	The incident	My initial reaction, aided by the Warden's voice	Old fears and wounds re-opened by event	A more mature & compassionate reaction that addresses my role in the incident

After your written inventories are completed, read them to your support group or sponsor and talk about what happened to trigger your anger or other feelings. Explore if you felt *defective, unworthy, humiliated and invisible,* or *abandoned.*

The inventory can be a great problem-solving tool, especially regarding conflict resolution with family members. It has helped me resolve problems I have had with my mother and my brothers by allowing me to see how much emphasis I put on *being right* instead of *feeling connected* or close to them. Some parents unknowingly pit siblings against each other. All that a parent needs to do is imply that one child should act more like the other one to get positive attention. It isn't surprising when siblings give more compassion to strangers than they do to each other. When I get mad at my siblings, my victim thinking takes me right into self-righteousness. It is more comfortable to focus on their shortcomings than my own. The problem is, all of my energy is focused on being right, which leaves little room for compassion. Inventories have taught me that since I don't walk in other people's shoes, I have no right to judge them.

In my childhood, everyone wanted to be right, producing a climate where no one felt safe enough to admit his or her wrongs. The pain of exposing any failure to other members of the family would be catastrophic, so everyone wore a false mask. As I healed internally, I found myself praying for humility and the courage to allow my family members to see who I am and to surrender the outcome of what might happen afterward.

I was given a great opportunity two years ago. One of my brothers went into a treatment center for his addictions. I wanted so desperately to share my own experiences, strengths, and hopes with him, but the rehabilitation center did not allow visitors. I also wanted to ask him for forgiveness over how I treated him when we were younger. I had a lot of anger as a child, and, regrettably, I took some of my anger out on two of my three siblings. I asked him to let me know if I hurt him in ways I wasn't aware of. I also shared my own experiences, and how afraid I was as a child and as an adult. I was the oldest and always considered the strong, successful one. When he got out of treatment, we had several long, emotional conversations.

Because we had never shared such intimacy, I had never felt closer to him. Through our discussions, he began to share his childhood stories. He told me how he would come into my room at night and sleep at the end of my bed because he felt so afraid. He also told me that I was a source of protection for him, shielding him from the insecurity in our house. I was so caught up in my own survival that I never realized this, or had any empathy for my brother as a child. I felt sorry I could not be there, and told him how scary it must have been for him.

My brother's wife told me my letter freed him from his guilt. By sharing my weaknesses, he found more compassion for his own shortcomings. By combining the knowledge I gained in my inventory work with the strength I received from my support group, I allowed my brother to see who I really am. I found the courage to be vulnerable and let go of the outcome, which the warden tried to sabotage in his efforts to create a bad ending to a wonderful story. Through these tools, we have a better relationship today than ever before.

An inventory allows me to see clearly the personal struggle going on between my old belief system and my new belief system. An inventory also allows me to achieve greater self-awareness. It affords me the opportunity to recognize how people in my life needed me more than I needed them; to see how I was always playing caretaker instead of caring for myself. As I began to grow in awareness, it became clear that some of my greatest career strengths were also my greatest obstacles to personal growth. The self-reliance and willpower that led to my financial success weren't helpful qualities when it came to internal growth. This is why it is so important to find self-acceptance, because my strengths in one area are my weaknesses in another.

Self-Reliance

Relying on myself was an essential part of my business success. I had to do things my way, which in many instances resulted in success. In my healing process, my self-reliance was killing me. It constantly put me on the same path of destruction. When I started to rely more on others, I eliminated the false notion that everything would only work out if I was in total control.

Willpower

Willpower is another great quality for survival and success in business. I never gave up on anything. During my healing process, I reached a point where I had to learn to give up doing things my way and admit defeat, because my way only brought pain and dissatisfaction. By refusing to surrender my willpower, I continued to run into the same wall. When I finally surrendered my willpower, I discovered new solutions to my problems.

I also began to see how my real and manufactured fears were obscuring my outlook on life. Some fears were healthy and kept me from taking harmful actions, but the fears manufactured by the warden had to be turned over to my support group. The amount of time I spent worrying about the future left me with little energy to take care of present matters. At other times, I spent too much time on the past, allowing the pain of childhood to predict my future. This prison sentence was determined by my injured past.

Finally, these written inventories allowed me to see that pain is a prerequisite for growth. I have heard it said, *If it feels bad it doesn't always mean it is bad, and if it feels good it doesn't always mean it is good.* I started to believe that I did not have to know what the future would hold in order to feel safe. Many changes in my thinking are the result of doing an inventory, staying away from bad behaviors, having a trusted support group, and developing a relationship with a loving, protecting Higher Power.

A part of me resisted changes. There were times when I fought going to a therapist, going to a group, making phone calls, or doing personal inventories. I did not notice the improvement at first, as the warden tried to hide my growth, reemphasizing that I did not deserve peace in my life. My life used to be filled with chaos and insanity. If everything was in total disarray, I had little time to focus on my own difficulties and shortcomings. I was used to playing the victim and blaming my problems on everyone else. My support group had to remind me of my growth, because I was unable to see it for myself.

The same thing happens with the people I help. I see the growth in them long before they see it in themselves. When old wounds are exposed, there will be pain as well. Facing these childhood injustices takes courage. Sometimes I remind them of where they are today compared to where they were. They may not be where they want to be, but they are certainly moving in the right direction. As they start to express themselves, instead of shutting down, they begin to expose their feelings of pain and isolation. When I help someone whose spouse's name keeps coming up in their written inventories, I try to find out what the person is really afraid of. Usually anger masks their fears, and their fear covers their emotional wounds. Eventually, through the written inventories, their fear will be exposed. The next step is to communicate these fears without resorting to anger. It is more productive for someone to talk about their *feelings* of fears, rather than their *objects* of anger. I use another exercise when a spouse's name is continually repeated in the inventory. This exercise is in the form of a balance sheet. On one side, I suggest they list the harms they have inflicted on their spouse, and on the other side list the harms their spouse has inflicted on them. Comparing harms on paper is a valuable way to reduce victim thinking and self-righteousness.

Suggestions for Struggling Couples

True intimacy is not possible with an active addiction going on in the relationship. Addictions nullify intimacy, because the addict will always choose addiction first. Healthy emotional connections will never be achieved with the addiction sitting between the partners.

Sobriety must always be the priority to the recovering addict. However, if someone has achieved long-term sobriety but is still going to Twelve Step meetings almost every day—at the expense of the relationships in his or her life—then this must be looked at. The fear of intimacy can be so powerful and insidious that even Twelve Step meetings can be subconsciously used as a way to avoid intimacy with a spouse and children.

Sometimes couples need to separate from each other for a period of time in order to clarify what needs fixing in their relationship. Some people are unwilling or unable to look at themselves unless this happens. If the relationship is characterized by blaming one another for its demise, self-righteous anger is difficult to surrender while living under the same roof. Each partner may see his or her spouse as the single problem in the marriage. If each spouse feels like a victim, neither will have the ability to listen to the needs of the other. Separation might be the only way of viewing his or her issues without the distractions of the partner. This offers the opportunity to connect with people who have walked through similar problems and found healthy solutions. With the help of therapists, groups, or some other support network, the person may look at the baggage he or she brought into the relationship without also looking into the partner's suitcase. Sometimes when there are difficulties in a marriage the spouse has to let go for the time being. This does not mean giving up on the relationship; it means working on one's own stuff and leaving the spouse's stuff alone for awhile.

Guidelines for Forming a Support Group

Perhaps you are interested in forming a support group. If so, let's start with the word *support*. Support can mean to hold up, reinforce, or sustain others who are experiencing trials or problems. A support group can be two or more individuals who lend support or reinforcement to the members. A group can meet in a church, school, or someone's house.

Everyone can benefit from a support group. With the help of others, we can feel strengthened to accomplish tasks that might otherwise be impossible to tackle alone. Groups are comprised of people from all walks of life, with the common denominator that all must be willing to unmask their feelings in a group situation. There will always be fear of the unknown when a new group starts.

A group must choose a leader to enforce the guidelines suggested in this book. As the group evolves, it will take on a life of its own with its peaks and valleys. It is imperative that the guidelines in this book are adhered to so healthy boundaries are in place. The meeting can begin by discussing each other's goals and the obstacles that block these goals. Usually your warden will be there to magnify any of your fears or uncertainties.

Goals for the group can range from increasing one's intimacy with family to finding the courage to say no to parents or others.

Goals can include asking your boss for a raise or finding a new job. Even finding support to clean one's house can be a goal brought up in group. Whatever the goal is, the support of others can help you free yourself from the warden's commands. It takes time to trust others and find the courage to act in our own best interests.

In order to run an effective group, it must adhere to certain principles to prevent it from becoming a social atmosphere. The rules for forming a group follow.

Trust and Safety

The most important elements of a support group are trust and anonymity. Whatever is shared must not be discussed with anyone outside the group. One of the ways support group members bond is by sharing their darkest secrets. Sharing painful experiences means the person has to be vulnerable to others, which takes a great deal of courage. In many instances the experiences that they are reluctant to share are the ones that truly help identify and define them as belonging to the group. In contrast, keeping secrets or sharing them selectively is harmful to the group, because they form a barrier between those who are in on the secret and those who are not.

Talk about Your Life Challenges

Each member should discuss his or her challenges in life; for example, a troubled relationship is a raw nerve for many of us. There is a shared identification in our challenges in life, which creates unity within the group and eventually contributes to personal growth among the members. It is helpful to share feelings of anger, defectiveness, inferiority, or invisibility, even though it is difficult to do at the beginning. However, you will find that once you eventually disclose these feelings, others will share their own experiences, strength, and hope, which further increase each member's connection with the group. Talking about each other's warden is a way to bring group unity. Remember, it is important to talk about the things that you do not feel like talking about.

Helping Others Feel Accepted

The group depends and thrives on mutual support. Each member should enjoy the acceptance of the group to help them overcome their daily struggles. Mutual compassion is also important since it helps validate each person's membership in the group. Asking for and giving help will build the unity of the group.

Reaching Out

The commitment to phoning each other is important. If a member faces a difficult challenge, a phone call can make all the difference in the world. Each member depends on the power of the group to help him or her face and overcome fears. An example is confronting a spouse, a parent, or a boss when you don't have the nerve. We all suffer from our own demons, but learning to face them so they don't hold us back is critical. A support group can empower us to face these difficulties head on, then move on. The next plateau will have a new set of challenges that can be shared, and from which all can benefit. Phone calls to a trusted individual help to reduce anger while fostering acceptance of the situation. The key is to give ourselves permission to quit doing things our own way and to seek the guidance of others. A phone call by the members of the group, before and after a difficult task, can make a tremendous difference to the individual.

Talk about Solutions

Healthy feedback builds confidence and can direct people away from self-righteousness and resentments. The goal is to pave the way for acceptance and forgiveness.

Allow Your Voice to Be Heard

Wounds inflicted early in life can remain tender. We protect these wounds by being oversensitive or avoiding conflict, but in the process we also avoid standing up for our own convictions. If we grew up feeling invisible as children, we may exhibit similar behavior in the group. This type of distorted thinking must be rooted out. You must commit to sharing whatever is bothering you; otherwise, those secrets will continue to fester. Each group session is a process that establishes accountability, where each group member holds him- or herself accountable to another with the goal to not resort to old ways of thinking. The function of the group is to empower its members to voice their innermost thoughts and problems.

In the first few sessions the members can discuss the ways they identify with each other or feel different from one another. Confrontation is also healthy for the group as long as it is done in a nonjudgmental way. When the members have healthy confrontation, using "I" statements and avoiding judgments allow their feelings to surface. Disagreements are a part of life and group dynamics. At any time, a member can say they do not want feedback and this request must be honored.

When a member feels stuck and is afraid to share, they can be asked to complete the sentence, "I am afraid of (name the situation)." By putting fears into words, this may be a way of starting the member's engine.

Bottling up feelings is a sure way to ignite your resentment, which can occur when one member feels less important than the others in the group. By bringing fears to the surface, the member builds integrity, knowing that he or she did not let their fears shut them down. Also, by expressing these fears and angers, the member can release some of the pain harbored inside. When the member finally breaks through his or her protective shell, he or she experiences a new sense of freedom, a personal victory previously unknown.

The group process brings unforeseen opportunities. At times a member could see their parents' characteristics in another member. They may also recognize behaviors in other members that resemble their children, siblings, fellow workers, or employers. Therefore, a support group can become a training session where members can improve the relationships in their lives while in the safety of the group setting.

The more the members become comfortable with each other, the more they will pull away from discussing the details of their past experiences and lean toward discussing the feelings of the present.

Eventually the members will take the lessons and new techniques they learn in group and apply them to the outside world.

Chapter Nine: Old Beliefs Versus New Beliefs

*A war can exist between the warden and a person's new belief system,
but as the person follows the actions suggested by their guides and support
group, the balance of power slowly shifts away from the warden.*

℘℘ℂℛ

The warden may be quiet for a while, but if we don't maintain
our new behaviors his voice will come back to sabotage our happiness.
Even when our lives improve, the warden sits in the background
waiting to mess up the situation. I have received calls from those
who have made great strides in their lives. They have found sobriety,
are back with their spouses, are building better relationships with
their children, and have improved their working environment.
Nevertheless, they start to sabotage their progress by pushing people
away with anger again. When love and closeness grow, so does the
fear of intimacy. As fear grows, we are reminded again that we don't
deserve happiness. This is why we mess up the situation for no
apparent reason. Sometimes our spouse will do the same. When we
take a step back in our lives, instead of beating ourselves up, we can
use these experiences to heighten our awareness and make better
choices in the future. We also gain a greater respect for the warden's
power, and that respect increases our willingness to maintain the
healthy connections in our lives.

My father ingrained in me that *your occupation defines who you
are.* This became part of my belief system. In the days my father acted
out his addictions, he believed that his business was the only thing
that he could depend on. His philosophy was that people would come
and go, but his business would always be there for him.

I was troubled when I had to lay off people; I felt that I let
them down. As the warden's voice increased in volume, I neglected to
talk to my support group about it. I was setting myself up again as the

victim. Eventually I returned to my therapist, who reminded me of the danger in listening to this voice and not talking about it with others. Rather than face my problems squarely and share them with others, I suppressed the pain and ignored the wounds. I had to admit that part of me was angry over business failures. I felt like a failure. Once I started to do my written inventories again, I began to lose the victim thinking and was able to turn down the warden's volume. By accepting the way things were, instead of fighting them, I eventually developed a sense of gratitude. I also started to accept that things change and that I had another calling in life—to help those that needed help.

To help show the differences between new and old beliefs, I compare two thought processes in the following table. The first column lists the negative voices and distorted belief system from the past. This thinking is self-centered, implying that new information will not work and only result in more difficulty. The second column identifies a thought process that is open to new beliefs and attitudes. It is people centric, embraces patience, and avoids immediate gratification. As we allow newer information into our belief system, we start to build integrity and self-esteem. We begin to feel that we deserve happiness.

The Old Voice (The Warden)	New Inner Voices
No one can do for me what I can do for myself.	My best thinking brought isolation and loneliness into my life. Now I can try open mindedness
People aren't safe; they will hurt me.	The people in my life today are not the same people I grew up with.
Why bother to share my feelings with my wife? If she really cared she would know what I'm thinking.	My part is to share my feelings with my wife in a safe way and let go of the outcome.
I don't need any more therapy, groups, or meetings.	I need people to do for me what I can't do for myself.
It is hopeless. I'll never get better.	Think about all the ways my life has gotten better when I allow people into it.
I'm afraid things won't work out the way I want them to so I think I must control it.	I need to find faith in people who truly care for me. I can allow myself to let them help me make my decisions in life.

The Old Voice (The Warden)	New Inner Voices
I want what I want when I want it.	What can I do for someone else without expecting something in return? Learn to be patient.
Everything happens to me. I just have bad luck and it's not fair.	What part did I play in the situations that happened today?
I do not deserve happiness.	I deserve to be happy.
I cannot say no to people. Saying no would make them think less of me, and that would be painful.	When I say no to someone, it causes pain. Find other people who I trust who can guide me through this pain.
Everyone should think the way I want them to; after all, I have to always prove I'm right.	I do not have to be right; instead, I can find closeness by listening to the feelings of others.
I have a sense of self-righteousness; I'm better than him. Look what he's done.	Help me to see that person with the same understanding and compassion I want from others.
The more money I make, the happier I will be.	Remember my past. Money never fixed my wounds before, and it won't now.
I don't deserve happiness.	If I cannot find a voice of compassion within me, then I will find this kindness from my support system.
If I discipline my kids, I will lose their love.	If I feel like a bad parent let me seek the support of others to help me through this pain.
Don't ever share fear or emotion because this is a sign of weakness.	Let people see my weakness as a part of who I really am.
I'm afraid of asking questions because people will think I'm stupid.	Help me accept myself exactly as I am. I am not perfect.
I can't trust a spiritual power, because I've already been judged as a bad person.	A loving spiritual power will accept all of me, the good and bad.
I am not good enough to write this book. Who do I think I am?	Help me find the courage from my support system to share my experiences and hopes with others and let go of all the fears that will try to stop me from moving forward.

Old information from childhood was not intended to hurt us, but this was the only information our caregivers had at that time. Without the willingness to let new information into our thinking, it becomes difficult to change. There is still an internal collision going on between the two belief systems trying to control our thinking and dictate our actions. We should reach out the most when it becomes the most difficult. Isolation becomes the warden's greatest weapon, and gratitude is the warden's greatest nemesis.

As we begin the step of maintenance in our lives we begin to feel free from the chains of the old behaviors. As our belief system changes we start to see the distorted reality from the past. We become aware of patterns in our thinking that were driven by self-centered fear. Our new belief system slowly convinces us that we are good people who deserve to be happy. The more we feel that we deserve happiness, the less likely we will do things to sabotage this belief. Peace of mind comes from *accepting* certain things in life rather than *expecting* them.

By changing our view of reality, we also change our behavior. We find ourselves reacting far less to outside circumstances.

As we heal and grow emotionally, we lose self-centeredness. However, if we are too busy protecting our wounds and only thinking of self-survival, it leaves little room for anyone else. When we start to heal, the people we love get the attention they deserve. Sometimes others see the change in us before we do. We don't want to be a slave to our addictions or a slave to what other people think of us anymore. The more we grow, the more our integrity builds. We find ourselves less concerned over other people's actions. All of these actions become easier as we start to feel comfortable in our own skin for the first time. We can't forget about our past, but we don't have to let the past have a negative effect on our lives today.

The trust I have placed in people has helped me the most. Even with spiritual growth, I still need guides to continue my healing. There are many wonderful institutions that offer all kinds of support to people who suffer from a wounded past. Bookstores are full of self-help literature that fosters self-awareness. All these things are helpful, but self-knowledge is not enough to battle the warden in all of us. Actions and beliefs are so ingrained, whether harmful or not, that change occurs only when we accept three important elements in our lives: awareness, positive actions, and maintenance.

The first essential is *awareness*. It is essential to become aware of the ways our old belief system created this warden, which fought anything that disagreed with it. Even though this guy with the bat on our shoulder was hurting us, we still listened to every command. If the caregivers in our childhood hindered us from trusting others, the rebirth of trust in our lives is the stepping stone to healing our past. This is the reason any self-help procedure must be reinforced with a support system of trusting people.

The second essential involves the *positive actions* we need to incorporate into our daily affairs. If we stick to the disciplines in this book, we can slowly change our old belief system. But the warden will not go away without a fight.

This is why we need the third essential, *maintenance.* If we don't keep ourselves connected to our support groups and do the written inventories the warden's voice will get louder. You will experience days when your inner voice, destructive as it may be, will be more persuasive then all the compassionate voices you hear from your support network.

I can relapse into old ways of thinking which tell me I can go it alone without help. If I hold onto old resentments and stop talking to others about these feelings, I can get myself in trouble. We receive some kind of payback from all our actions. Even resentments have a payback. Resentments keep people at bay, pushing away those we need in our lives. The voice of self-righteousness can come back to tell me that being right is all that matters, which further disconnects me from everyone else.

Taking the steps to heal our wounds by confronting the warden can be painful at times. This journey is paved with peaks and valleys. We will stumble at times. Stumbling and slips are tools for growth and learning; they are a part of the journey. The key is to stay on that path by putting one foot in front of the other.

Review the diagram of the old belief system below. Then, view the new belief system on the next page. It offers powerful freedom from childhood wounds.

Old and New Belief System Stages

The first stage of both the old and new beliefs starts with wounds and the messages that developed from these wounds at an early age. These messages create the inner voices that determine the fears in the second stage of both pyramids.

The Old Belief System

Guided by Wounds and Destructive Messages

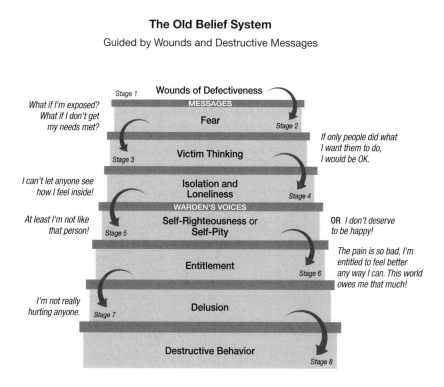

The key to freeing someone from the imprisonment of these wounds and messages begins in stages three and four in the New Belief System. This process starts by the person's willingness to stop the victim thinking in stage three of the Old Belief System.

With the aid of the warden's voice, victim thinking quickly gains momentum. It must quickly be replaced by healthy behavior, including reaching out to others and making a commitment to do written inventories on issues that create turmoil. If these actions are not taken, fears may build up to an overwhelming level and victim thinking will emerge. This may lead to a dangerous place called isolation. Written inventories bring us awareness of our responsibility. The connection we form with others allows our blind spots to be brought to the surface. Acceptance, forgiveness, and spirituality free us from the old recordings which kept us stuck in destructive thinking and behaviors. In time, the wounds in stage one slowly heal which creates less fear in the person. As the warden's voice becomes less frequent and more quiet we slowly free ourselves from the harmful roles we were set up to play.

The New Belief System

Guided by Healthy Information and Beliefs

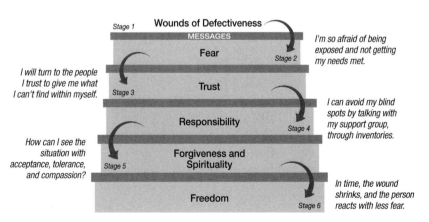

Stage 1 — **Wounds of Defectiveness**
MESSAGES
Fear — Stage 2
I'm so afraid of being exposed and not getting my needs met.

I will turn to the people I trust to give me what I can't find within myself. — Stage 3
Trust

Responsibility — Stage 4
I can avoid my blind spots by talking with my support group, through inventories.

How can I see the situation with acceptance, tolerance, and compassion? — Stage 5
Forgiveness and Spirituality

Freedom — Stage 6
In time, the wound shrinks, and the person reacts with less fear.

Chapter Ten:
The Most Precious Gift of All, Our Children

I cannot give my children what I don't have inside, just as my parents could not give me what they did not possess themselves.

ℰᏅℭℛ

Children need accountability and predictability from their caregivers in order to feel safe. Consistency in parenting enforces a child's self-esteem. Without consistent dependability the children feel anxious and uncomfortable, never knowing if their needs will be met. If children cannot count on this from their caregivers, they will become accustomed to chaos and create this chaos in their adult life.

The first time I went to a therapist, he asked me about my relationships. It wasn't until he inquired about my children that I became emotional. Thinking of my children reopened the wounds of my childhood.

Years later, I went to a workshop where I participated in a psychodrama. One therapist, using my infidelity to my wife as the subject and playing the role of my son, asked me why I was hurting him and his mother. He kept repeating, "Dad, how could you do this to me and Mommy?" Every time he said this, the pain cut deeper. My only thought was to hug and console this person, as if he really was my son. I was so taken in by the emotion that I approached him, and three other people were instructed to hold me back and let the role-play run its course. Nevertheless, I broke through their blockade, and I hugged the therapist, convinced he was my son, telling him everything would be OK. My only thought was to protect him and make him feel safe. I'll never forget this experience and the power it had over me. I'm sure this connected to the little boy in me who always wanted to be protected and loved by his father.

Children need caregivers who they can trust. It establishes

a foundation that allows the formation of a healthy belief system. This belief system permits the child to express his or her feelings without fear of losing the love of their caregivers. Love, they learn, is unconditional. If the child feels special, a sense of security will be established in his or her belief system. These caregivers do not necessarily have to be the parents. They can be grandparents, priests, rabbis, aunts, or uncles. Once they accept unconditional love, the children develop a sense of self-acceptance so that later, as an adult, they will have no need to wear a mask or medicate their feelings. Conversely, if love is conditional, children learn they are loved only when they are good. Unconditional acceptance is the key. Children whose needs are unmet don't usually act out until adolescence, at which time their handcuffs are loosened and their newfound freedom leads to destructive behaviors. Some of these behaviors are aimed at retaliating against their parents, although they may not be aware of it. These might include overspending, especially their parents' money, engaging in anti-social behavior, using drugs and alcohol, or doing the exact opposite of what their parents tell them to do. It is a subliminal way of torturing their parents.

As a parent, my new belief system was often at odds when it came to making important parental decisions. The most important action I could take for my children was to create a safe environment where they knew I would be there for them no matter what happened. I didn't want my children to experience the uncertainty and loneliness I felt as a child. A tool I use is to go back and think of the words I needed to hear from my parents when I was young. These words are not what I *wanted* to hear but what I *needed* to hear to feel safe and confident.

Today I make sure to share with my children all the things I wanted to hear from my parents. I tell them they are special and can confide in my wife and me without being judged. They don't have to be who I want them to be; they are free to determine their own destiny. Still, it isn't so much *what* I say as what I *do* that matters most. I can't expect them to ask for help unless I have the courage to seek help myself. I can't expect them to stand up for themselves if I'm failing to stand up for myself. The bottom line is this: *I cannot give my children what I don't have inside, just as my parents could not give me what they did not possess.* As a parent, I was no better or worse than my parents were; I could only draw from the information available in my belief system, just as my parents had done. Regardless of the love I have for my children, if my worldview is distorted, I cannot expect my children to view the world in a healthy way.

It is *healthy information* that must be passed on to our children. Four years after my father's death, my son had been chosen to play on an all-star little league team. My wife said, "Papa would have been so proud of you." His to-the-point reply was, "Papa was always proud of me." My son's remark showed that he felt accepted and loved unconditionally by my father.

My son's reality was much different than mine. My inner voice expressed a message conveyed long ago by my father, telling me that I wouldn't measure up unless I made lots of money. Similarly, messages from my mother told me that unless I made her happy, *first,* I wasn't good enough. These messages imprisoned me until I recognized how distorted my thinking was. As a result, I began to allow new, healthy information to replace the old. This new information originated from messages received from therapists, support groups, retreats, and many workshops. I learned it was OK to show anger in a healthy way. If I argued with people it did not mean I would lose their love. To disagree with someone was part of being human; it didn't mean the relationship was over. The new messages provided the building blocks for a more nurturing, self-accepting belief system. I soon recognized that the havoc of my former life was influenced by my old way of viewing the world. When I gave my children mixed signals it was because I was mixed up myself.

At one time, I didn't know how to express intimacy. Since intimacy meant pain as a child, I substituted destructive behaviors instead. As with my father, addictions came first, because they were linked to my survival. It was not because I was a bad father, but rather a discouraged father who needed help to get better. My problem was that I tried so hard to be different from my father that I went to the opposite extreme. I was unable to distinguish between acceptable discipline and parental abuse. Personal guilt prevented me from taking disciplinary action and establishing boundaries with my children.

Today I realize that avoiding conflict is just as harmful as creating conflict. There are times I will initiate conversations with my wife that are uncomfortable, yet doing so is healthy for our marriage. The one motivating thought that keeps me from avoiding this is the desire I have to stay away from going back to the person I used to be. Eventually my wife and I had to decide whether we each wanted to be married or not. If we decided to be in the marriage, this decision, like all other decisions in life, had to be followed by action. This meant getting outside help and doing what was necessary to heal our marriage.

I have stood clear of my old destructive behaviors and freed myself of the shame and self-hate I carried my whole life. In return, this has allowed me to see the damages caused by the warden's voice. While my inner voice is usually obvious, sometimes it is less detectable. I need people in my life to help me with that. I have this urge and need to control and protect my children from everyone and everything in the world. I don't want this message handed down to them, so that their fear of others paralyzes their lives.

I had an advantage that others didn't. This advantage stemmed from the realization that my childhood did not supply me with the tools I needed to be a healthy parent or husband. This awareness supplied me with the willingness to seek those that did have these skills. Eventually I gained insight and wisdom from other fathers. My identification with them brought unity and strength. We supplied each other with positive information that we didn't have in our childhood. The need to be liked by my children, combined with the guilt of my past, created situations in which saying no to them was excruciating. Simultaneously, I had to establish boundaries and talk to my support group when I felt like a cruel parent, especially when I needed to enforce consequences or properly enforce discipline. However, as was the case with my individual growth, the more I practiced awareness, action, and maintenance, the easier it was to say no to the voice inside my head. Willingness, open mindedness, courage, and desire to be the best parent possible got me through the tough times.

I remember the first time I told my father that I was going to get help for my compulsive gambling. He begged me to do something to cut the chain of insane behaviors that was passed down in our family from generation to generation. However, it was not only the behaviors that concerned me. It also was the character defects that were passed down. If I don't share my feelings in a healthy way, then my children won't. If I allow the warden to swing his bat at anyone who gets close to me, then my children will learn to do the same.

The Freedom to Cry in the Arms of One's Father

Several years ago we had to put our dog to sleep. Our oldest son was the same age as the dog, and he was very attached to her. As we returned from the veterinarian's office, I noticed our son was sad and withdrawn. I asked him if he was OK. He said, "I'm fine, Dad." I asked again, "Are you alright?" He replied, "I'll be alright." Instead of walking away, I hugged him. His tears started to flow as his grip on me tightened. At that moment, I knew I was providing my son a safe haven for him to cry. The message I relayed to him that day was it is acceptable to cry in the arms of his father. I never had a safe place to go as a child, but my son does.

Sometimes when I speak with my children, the feedback I receive makes me scratch my head. Accepting where my children are in their lives—instead of expecting them to share my views—can be difficult at times. As they get older, I realize that lectures only push them away. I try my best to keep identifying with my children instead of trying to get them to see things my way. They have their own path that will be paved with obstacles, and they will have the opportunity to learn from their mistakes. I can warn them not to put their hand in the flames, but I can't always keep them from doing it. Eventually, they will make a decision and learn to accept the consequences of their actions, their successes, and their mistakes. As a parent, one of the hardest actions to take at times is to take no action at all. If our relationship is healthy, they will return and share their failures and victories with us, without a warden's bat hanging over them.

Today, I teach my children to trust other people and ask for help when needed. It took me years to accept help, but if I pass this blessing to them at their young age, then I have given them a special gift. I do not always have to comply with my children's wishes, but I want them to know their opinions are heard. I do not want them to feel invisible. One of the ways my wife and I connect with our children is by taking one of them out to eat each week. Our intention is to have one-on-one conversation with each child, separate from the other children. They pick the place for dinner. When our children were younger they only wanted chicken nuggets. Now their tastes have become more expensive.

I share my weaknesses with them by explaining how perfectionism and controlling behavior hurt me. I tell my children about the value of mistakes, and how they can be used as a learning tool rather than a form of punishment. Today my children also see me pray. It is no longer something that causes me shame. Praying is not a sign of weakness; praying is a sign of strength because it takes courage to ask for help from a spiritual source.

As I allowed help into my life, it became easier to ignore the warden's commands. Today I have a chance to stop the victim thinking and voices of hopelessness that had been handed down from generation to generation. My children do not need to hear the warden's negative recordings that I grew up hearing. I am now free to love others and to be loved by my children and wife, the lights of my life.

Chapter Eleven: Forgiveness And Spirituality

The God of my youth was angry, resentful, and vindictive.
I often prayed, Please don't hurt my family for the actions I did.

ℰℭℛ

Everyone has his or her own beliefs and ideas about forgiveness and spirituality based on the way they were raised and their circumstances. The awareness of my wounds and the steps I took to heal became my path to recovery. The path is a lifelong journey. Along the way, I realized I would need to find a new solution when life did not go as planned. My deep wounds required a source more powerful than anyone, anything, or myself in order to heal. Spirituality, rather than addiction, would become my new solution when things got tough. To find my spirituality, I had to better understand my Higher Power. My written inventories helped me identify the answers to these questions: What do I believe? Where did my beliefs come from? Why was I so afraid to depend on any authority figure, including sponsors, coaches, support groups, and even a Higher Power?

My inventories suggested the God of my youth was angry, resentful, vindictive, and not forgiving of my weaknesses. My childhood and adolescent perceptions were of a spiritual power who would never forgive me if I did not behave according to the standards taught at home and school. How could a Higher Power love someone like me with such flaws and imperfections?

My biggest misconception as a child was that I had to be a good boy to be accepted. That put me behind the eight ball. I was not good enough to be accepted. These beliefs continued from adolescence to my adulthood. My perception was that I would be punished for the bad things I did. My perception was that God would take it out on my children. When one of my children got sick, I thought God was punishing me through my children.

Praying until I Got It Right

My support group suggested that I face my demons head on. I asked members of my group how they renewed their trust in a Higher Power. One of the first suggestions was to get down on my knees and pray each morning. So, I prayed. It was difficult at first. It was not a priority. If I overslept, I did not pray. I prayed sometimes while driving to work, or after I arrived, and never on weekends. I figured God didn't work on the weekends anyway.

When I prayed, my mind wandered. But, I kept doing it even though I thought it was a waste of time. Several times I would be on my knees praying when my one of my kids would walk in. Embarrassed and ashamed, I would quickly stand up. I learned later through my inventories that, as a child, I thought asking for help and forgiveness was a sign of weakness. This false message was keeping me away from what I needed most to heal. I struggled to find my spiritual connection. Each time I got on my knees, I felt paralyzed with shame and fear.

I started praying by pleading for the willingness, strength, and desire to stay away from my addictions. Sobriety was the most important thing to achieve. It felt comfortable asking for that. If praying would help me stay away from my addictions it was more than worth it. I prayed to believe that God truly existed, which I sometimes doubted. I prayed to save my wife and children from my anger and to help me feel gratitude. I prayed for the confidence to believe that I deserved God's love. I wanted to believe this Higher Power would be there especially on the days I felt alone and disconnected. Some days it was hard to fathom that a Higher Power could care for someone who did what I did.

It took months before I felt comfortable praying. Slowly, some of my shame and self-hate began to dissipate. I started to develop a relationship with a Power greater than myself. Sometimes I could not wait to pray, as if I was a little kid waiting to talk with my father. I thanked Him for giving me the perseverance to keep going until I felt a connection inside. Then I asked Him to remove the negative voice that caused so much turmoil in my life. I did not ask for any material possessions. I asked for help to accept the world as he meant it to be.

I let this Power know about those who angered me or those who I feared. I also prayed when the warden was beating me down.

Spiritual Fuel

I needed spirituality, and began to find it when I prayed. This gave me a sense of connection. I kept a journal and wrote to my Higher Power, asking for guidance and strength. I kept returning to refuel my spirituality. The key was to keep the door open for spirituality to enter. Over time, praying became more comfortable and important to me. I even prayed on weekends. If I was behind schedule, I still prayed and went to work late. Praying became my priority, and God showed up as long as I continued to seek him.

Asking for Forgiveness

My spiritual growth had to include the reconciliation of broken relationships with others. First, I needed to forgive myself. Since forgiveness begins with healing, I began to recognize the pain I inflicted on others. I wanted to make things right with others. I could never know the full extent of the pain that my infidelity caused my wife. The best way I could show her my sincere regret was to be the best husband and father possible. I demonstrated to my wife that she and our family are my first priority. I stress this to the people I guide. We identify ways to show our spouses and loved ones that we are not the same self-centered people we used to be. We can help with house cleaning or taking our children to school. Calling our spouses during the day reminds them we care and that our thoughts are with them. The best example I can extend to my children happens by showing care and love to my wife. I make it a priority to take time during the week to sit down and discuss our feelings.

There are times when atoning and making amends are not welcomed and even rejected. That is when I surrender the outcome to God and make certain that I do not punish myself. The key is to learn from mistakes and not to repeat them.

Forgiveness

Why forgive others? In forgiving others, we free ourselves from the poison of resentment. The act of forgiving can be difficult because it touches the core of our being and childhood wounds. What benefit are we gaining by not forgiving? Does this give us permission to stay stuck in our old ways of thinking and feeling victimized by others?

The first step is to acknowledge the pain. We must admit that we are wounded. It is our responsibility to find peace by self-healing. Step Two is to understand why we are holding on to those resentments that hurt us. What old beliefs are creating this pain? Are we afraid of losing something, or do we expect too much from someone else? Is our victim thinking causing us to harbor old resentments? I must constantly remind myself that the people with whom I am angry owe me nothing. If I expect them to repay a debt they are not capable of, then I am setting myself up for predetermined resentment. Many of these questions are addressed when we do our written inventories on anger.

Once we can identify the source of our pain, we can share this information with our support group, rather than expecting the people who caused it to change. This is where the power of prayer will become evident. Failure to forgive permits our scars to fester and leaves us in a state of victimhood.

The better we feel about ourselves, the more we accept others. I now can recognize positive qualities in people, instead of shortcomings. This was once a foreign concept to me. In the past, I settled into the victim role. The role of victim allowed me to focus on what others were doing wrong, rather than putting the focus on improving myself. I felt comfortable focusing on their weaknesses, rather than their strengths.

Allowing compassion to enter my life became easier when I reminded myself that I once was an innocent child of God. While I made poor decisions, I am still worthy of forgiveness. This goes for the people who wronged me. I ask, "Can I relate to their fears and angers?" People who react in anger to others carry a lot of pain inside. I ask my Higher Power to help me see them in a spiritual way. My perception of people changed as I began to see people as individuals who were hurting, rather than people inflicting pain on me. I no longer carried the belief that their goal was to harm me. Not everything in life is all about me.

Forgiveness can be nurtured by remembering that the people who harmed us were once innocent children of God. When I envision others as children, I have greater compassion, knowing they did their best with the belief system they inherited.

Forgiveness goes hand in hand with acceptance. I sincerely believe that acceptance is the key to problem solving. If we can accept people, instead of trying to control them, we will find greater peace inside. As we achieve self-compassion, we can be more empathic with others. But, if we are constantly at war with ourselves then we'll always be in conflict with others.

Forgiveness does not mean that we need to tolerate inappropriate or abusive behavior in others. Forgiveness frees us from the imprisonment of resentment, which poisons our entire being, disturbs our sleep, removes our joy, and injures our health. Resentment infiltrates all our relationships and can be passed down to our children and spouses. The power it has over our thinking cannot be ignored. Forgiveness is the only way to stop drinking the poison of resentment.

After I read my father's journaling in his cookbooks, I began to see him in a different light. As he wrote about his fears and the shame he carried his entire life, I saw him as a suffering, discouraged soul. He was not an indestructible, heartless person. He had to learn to trust others to help heal his pain, just as I did. If I could see him this way, then I could see others with similar compassion.

As I reflect on my past, I see how my perception has changed. In the process of healing, I had a choice. The choice was to change the world to fit my way of thinking, or to change myself. I chose the latter and discovered amazing results. No longer do I feel the world owes me something. I am grateful for the blessings that life has granted me. I do not allow others to dictate how I feel about myself.

There was a time when I hated to admit my weaknesses, but today I find comfort in this admission. I could not stop my compulsions on my own, and this defeat opened other doors of healing for me. The consequences of my actions ironically paved the path to intimacy, an emotion I never expected to experience. There was a time in my life when asking for help was an overwhelming task, but today I find it liberating. When I was finally open to receive help from others, it was like being given a beautiful gift. As the recipient of something precious, I felt it was my responsibility to share this blessing with others who struggle with their destructive behaviors and are not yet ready to trust others.

I had the opportunity to appreciate the true concept of forgiveness when a close member of my family had gambling problems. He was trying to stop his habit, and he needed employment. First, I sat down with my support group to discuss the matter of hiring him. I did not want to make a major decision without discussing it with them. All agreed that I would pay off his bills and deduct one-hundred dollars a week from his salary until he paid off his debts to me. He needed this lifeline immediately, because his electricity was shut off and he was about to be evicted. The arrangement with him started on the right foot; however, before the end of a year I sensed that he was in trouble again.

I knew something was wrong because he began to isolate himself. Then I discovered that he had taken my credit card and was using it. I fired him instantly. I yelled and screamed at him, and we came close to blows.

When I get this upset, I discuss it with my support group for advice. They agreed that I should have fired him, but they objected to my behavior. I thought that I was the victim and my anger and yelling at him was justified. But, his illness never entered into my mind. The group informed me that I owed him an apology for my rage. I didn't want to hear this but realized they were right. My ego was in the way. I had wanted him to apologize for his wrongs, but he was much too damaged inside to do this. I did apologize for my rage. At that moment, I felt great. I began to view this relative as a discouraged person who needed guidance, rather than someone who intentionally inflicted pain on me. What had been a horrible situation turned into to an opportunity to forgive. Forgiving him helped him to get back on track, which was only possible because I had left the door open to him with my apology. This lesson in forgiveness freed me from the prison of resentment.

My growth and improvement accelerated when I advanced from just believing in a Higher Power to fully depending on one. I now try to live in the moment by putting the pains of the past and the worries of the future into the hands of God. I seek guidance from God and from my support group. I am responsible to use the tools I learned to remove the anger and surrender to God. I now have a better understanding of what I can control and what I cannot.

Forgiveness is a spiritual process. To forgive others we must first forgive ourselves. It begins with self-acceptance and the belief that our Higher Power accepts our humanness, the good and the bad. As we forgive, we are forgiven. As we accept our shortcomings, we experience greater acceptance by others.

Three years after my father died I was shopping with my daughter who was looking for a Valentine's Day gift for her mom. As she searched for just the right gift, she spotted a pin with an angel. "That's it!" she said excitedly. When my wife opened the package, her eyes lit up. She asked if I had read the note that accompanied the pin. I said no, so she read it, causing my mouth to fall open with astonishment. The note said that this angel was born March 28, 1996, the date of my father's death. We stood there in stunned silence. That day I felt a spiritual presence that transcended my understanding.

My father had become a wonderful example of this spirituality. As I watched my father physically wither away due to his illness, his spirituality grew. He spoke of gratitude for the life he was given. My children always lovingly knew him as Papa.

Chapter Twelve: Parting Words

Falling off the path is part of the journey;
the key is to get back on the path if one stumbles.

ဆၢ

As I found the willingness to work on my character defects I constantly asked my Higher Power, *Please protect me from me. Help me keep my feet where they should be, where my family would want them to be.* As I continue to grow in my recovery, my attitude on life changes. This doesn't mean that life becomes any easier, it just means I don't view life through the same distorted lenses I once did.

I always had a need to prove I was right no matter what the expense was and I still feel this way at times. When this occurs I lose my ability to listen, be empathetic, or have compassion for the way others feel. Today I ask myself, *Do I have to prove I am right, or is it better to choose closeness and listen more?* Also in the past I expected others to read my mind and anticipate what I was thinking. Today I work hard at expressing my feelings and allowing others to express their feelings.

My Wife

When my wife criticized me in the past, my initial response was anger. The warden told me she saw through my mask and knew what a pathetic person I really was. I felt defective as a husband, and when my wife triggered this belief I used anger to protect myself. The warden's voice, programmed by my victim thinking, blocked out any empathy I could have for her. As I healed and accepted my shortcomings, instead of letting the warden beat me up unmercifully, I found empathy and sadness for my wife's pain. As my attitude toward her slowly changed, she began to trust me enough to help her with her pain. My attention had to be centered on accepting her exactly where she was, not where I wanted her to be. She was healing from a wound

I helped create. As much as I wanted her to forgive my injustices immediately, I had to accept that her healing would not be on my time frame.

She had a right to be sad, and I was able to tell her that her pain also saddened me. I could support her feelings, even if they weren't the feelings I wanted her to have. The more I worked on my written inventories, the more I realized the distorted ways I processed the words I heard. This awareness increased my courage to ask my wife what I could do to help her with her pain. Many times I felt scared to approach her in this manner, because I was being vulnerable, an uncomfortable feeling for me. I had to keep showing her that I cared even if it meant leaving me open to hurtful remarks. I would get through these challenging moments by reaching out to my support group for help. They would be there to hold me up when things got tough. I could not control my wife's feelings about the past, and all I could do was stay connected to the right people and do the next right thing. In time, her feelings shifted from resentment toward forgiveness.

My Children

My children do not always do the things my wife and I wished they would. Like most children, they can be demanding at times. And when they express their anger at me I want to reflect that anger right back at them. At times in my childhood I felt invisible and would react with anger if I felt invisible as a father. The warden's bat swung away at anyone, including my children, for not allowing my voice to be heard. It brought to the surface what I was trying to hide the most: my feelings of inadequacy. At the same time, my false pride led me to believe I'm entitled to have obedient children because of all the things I did for them. All of these character defects are self-centered, because they make every situation a personal one. They all revolve around me. Also, my children's anger is not always my responsibility to change. Not every disturbance they have in their life is due to something I did as a parent.

My children needed boundaries and rules, not anger. These boundaries are a sign of love, not an act of abuse. They needed privileges revoked, not to be humiliated by their parents. If I didn't have the courage to say no to my kids, then I had to find this courage through the support of others. My children also needed healthy attention so they knew their feelings were valid. This did not mean that I had to do what they said. It meant I had to listen to their feelings, even if I disagreed with them. By doing this, it helped build their self-esteem, so that they never felt invisible as a child. Most importantly, I realized that my children did not grow up in the same insanity I grew up in as a child. I needed this awareness so that I didn't overcompensate as a parent, which at times could be as harmful as undercompensating.

My job is to create a safe place where my children feel free enough to tell me their feelings in a respectful way. The only way I could create an environment like this was to show them that I was sympathetic to their needs, instead of always providing a solution. By listening to them, instead of judging the situation, I was able to bring them closer to me instead of having a war over who's right or wrong. If I cannot let go of my anger, then it is my responsibility to pause and bring it to my support group. Before I said something that I would regret, I had to bring it to the people who know me best. I could process the negative feelings with them before angry words came out of my mouth. My goal is to be close to my children, help provide healthy solutions, and let them know I am there if they fall. By talking to other people in my support group, I used their experiences to bring healthy information into my family. As I proceeded to work on my written inventories, I started to focus on my defects and wounds, instead of trying to mold my children into the person I wanted them to be. As I accept myself with all of my defects, it made it easier to accept them for where they were in their lives.

My Mother

In the past, I was unable to say no to loved ones. There will always be people, especially family members, who create guilt and shame when I establish healthy boundaries. I need to learn that pain is part of growth, and sometimes the right thing to do can be painful. The key is what I do with this pain. Do I medicate the pain with destructive entitlements, or do I ask my support group to help me?

My new belief system taught me to look at the good in people. My mother is a terrific grandmother. She is sorry for many of the things that happened between us. She always loved her children but was living in a battlefield with my father. Without guidance, I would not know how to ask for forgiveness for her or myself. Even with the willingness to forgive, it can be a long journey requiring patience and paved with small victories. Forgiveness takes time, courage, and the guidance of others. I had to do the actions and trust the people who told me the feelings of forgiveness would come later. Eventually, I found gratitude for what my mother did give me. I found sadness, instead of anger, for what she couldn't give me. She was a person in pain; she was not personally trying to hurt me. If I wish leniency for my injustices, then it is only fair I find compassion for hers.

God

I used to get angry at God, as He allowed my father to die just when we were beginning to reconcile our differences. My victim thinking wants me to believe that God did this just to hurt me. I cannot play God. It is not my decision to choose when people should die. The feelings that I had when my father died were understandable; however, judging God, myself, or others triggers a sense of destructive entitlement within me, one of my enduring character defects. Instead of trying to figure out God's reasoning, I need to pray for acceptance of whatever his will is. Acceptance can be so difficult at times, but for someone like me resentment will only hurt those I love and myself. When I find myself fighting the things I cannot change, then I have to go to my support group and allow them to help me change the things I can. If I am trying to figure out why things happen the way they do, then I am putting myself in the position of God, a place I don't belong.

Me

Whenever I made a mistake, the warden made sure that all the shame of my past bubbled up, reminding me what a defective person I am. Whether it is work, my wife, my children, or anyone else, the guy with the bat on my shoulder was always ready to pound away. I always focused on the things I could have done better, never on my accomplishments. My business failures became my failures as a person. The belief that I failed as a child was so painful that I felt hopeless whenever I stumbled as an adult. My expectations of myself were so high that failure was inevitable. I was the one writing the script for myself and everyone else. If I couldn't control the future, then I couldn't trust that anything would turn out OK. If I did something wrong, the warden would immerse me in shame and inadequacy. Self-compassion and self-tolerance were hard to find when the warden was hitting me over the head with a bat.

After doing written inventories for years, I started to notice the ways my thinking was self-destructive. By becoming aware of these patterns, I was given the opportunity to see what I needed to change. Inventories revealed how I interacted with people; this helped me see that the problem was my thinking. As I continued to do my inventories, I realized that my childhood wounds distorted how I saw situations—and how I heard things. If I felt rejected, worthless, inferior, or disrespected in my relationships, it touched off a lot of fear inside of me. This fear protected the pain of feeling small inside. A wounded animal can become vicious when it is scared. I was emotionally wounded, and I can be vicious when I'm scared. By doing inventories I began to identify the wound and separate my wound from the actual incident which triggered it. This enabled me to see the ways I let these old wounds influence my reactions toward others and how I have often overreacted. This also gave me the opportunity to talk about the old feelings I kept locked inside for so many years. Talking about these wounds is a much healthier approach than feeling rejected and shutting down. Now, instead of denying or rejecting who I am, I accept the part of me that was broken. Through acceptance and a new belief in a power that I can depend upon, I began to heal. These wounds are deep and have been there for a long time. They will get triggered at times, and it is then that I must take the right actions. Exposing my weaknesses becomes easier as the need to protect myself decreases.

When I look back on the destruction I caused there will always be a part of me that wishes I could take back the betrayal to my wife and the time and money I took from my family. However, there is more to my story. The relationships I have with my wife, children, and friends today would not be possible if my destructive behaviors did not open up a door of opportunity for me. This door gave me the chance to view a part of myself that would have remained buried. I would sabotage intimacy or happiness whenever it came my way. Those destructive behaviors led me to a place of healing which is where I started to believe that I did deserve happiness and the love of others. I was chained to the warden's messages which constantly sabotaged my intimate relationships. The healthy messages I bring to my children today would not be what they are if I wasn't brought to my knees by my destructive actions.

Today, after twenty-seven years, I have gone back to school for a Master's degree in social work at Rutgers University. God indeed has a sense of humor. My warden and all of his voices were at it again, telling me I'll never get through this. As before, I put one foot in front of the other, while continuing to allow others and my Higher Power to hold me up on the days I felt inadequate. I do not have to walk alone anymore, unless I choose to.

In closing, I want to leave you with a loving message from my daughter. When she was eight-years-old, she asked my wife if she could speak with her grandfather, her "Papa," on the telephone. My wife dialed the phone and handed the receiver to my daughter. "Papa," she said, "I love you. I love you not because of the things you buy me or the places you take me, but because you make me feel good every time I'm with you." Never before had he felt such profound love. It is comforting to know that the message my father left my children was one of unconditional love, a message they can pass on to future generations.

Appendix A

ೲೲ

Readers may photocopy these inventory templates.

The Aggressor	The incident	My initial reaction, aided by the Warden's voice	Old fears and wounds re-opened by event	A more mature & compassionate reaction that addresses my role in the incident

Who were your caregivers?	Messages received from those caregivers	Our inner voice created from the messages	The behaviors our inner voice commands us to do	What we need from our support system

About the Author

ஐ൫

Thomas Gagliano is a successful business owner and consultant who lives in North Brunswick, New Jersey, with his wife and family. For the past ten years, he has been a popular keynote speaker on recovery issues in the greater New York area. He has a Master's degree in social work from Rutgers University.

Gentle Path Books that May Interest You

A House Interrupted:
A Wife's Story of Recovering from Her Husband's Sex Addiction
Maurita Corcoran

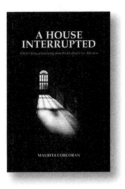

Maurita Corcoran's world collapsed when she learned that her husband, a successful physician, was a sex addict. She was suddenly submerged in a world of painful choices about how to rebuild a life for herself and her four children. This is an absorbing memoir about forgiveness, resilience, and hope. With the growing public awareness of how pervasive sex addiction has become, this memoir answers the questions that spouses must face in building lives of self-respect.

280 pp
Trade Paper | $16.95
978-0-9826505-8-5

Facing the Shadow, Second Edition
Starting Sexual and Relationship Recovery
Patrick Carnes, Ph.D.

Dr. Patrick Carnes' ground-breaking book, *Out of the Shadows,* introduced the world to his research on sexual addition. *Facing the Shadow* is the innovative workbook that helps readers understand how to begin meaningful recovery from an often misunderstood addiction. This book guides readers through the first seven tasks in Dr. Carnes' researched-based Thirty Task Model of treatment—the most respected therapy model available for treating sex addicts.

325 pp
Trade Paper | $29.95
978-0-9826505-2-3

Mending a Shattered Heart
A Guide for Partners of Sex Addicts

Edited by Stefanie Carnes, Ph.D.

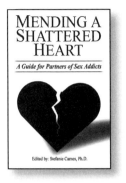

Hundreds of unsuspecting people wake up every day to discover their loved one, the one person who they are supposed to trust completely, has been living a life of lies and deceit because they suffer from a disease called sex addiction. Stefanie Carnes, Ph.D, brings together several authors to guide the reader through such difficult questions as "Should I stay or should I leave?" This comprehensive guide offers readers the best expertise available on how to begin the journey of personal recovery.

220 pp
Trade Paper | $19.95
978-0-9774400-6-1

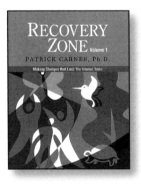

Recovery Zone, Volume 1
Making Changes that Last: The Internal Tasks

Patrick Carnes, Ph.D.

Recovery Zone, Volume One, picks up where *Facing the Shadow* leaves off, guiding readers through tasks eight through thirteen of Dr. Patrick Carnes' innovative Thirty Task Model. This book helps readers understand how to move beyond merely stopping addictive behavior. True recovery is achieved by learning to cope with difficult situations and emotions. Although there is no overnight solution for addictions, recovering people can learn how to achieve long-term sobriety by making decisions that suit their individual needs, devising a plan for living an optimal life, and becoming proactive leaders of their lives.

315 pp
Trade Paper | $29.95
978-0-9774400-1-6

Thirty Days to Hope and Freedom from Sexual Addiction

Milton Magness, D.Min.

Genuine healing is available to women and men who seek to restore their integrity and live in continuous sexual sobriety. Through a thirty-day approach, Milton Magness, D. Min., prepares readers for long-term recovery with essential advice on how to cope with isolation, dishonesty, secrecy, and what to expect from therapy.

290 pp
Trade Paper | $21.95
978-0-9826505-5-4

Surveying the Wreckage
A Guide to Step Four

John Leadem and Elaine Leadem

The course of addiction can cut a broad and deep swath through the lives of its victims. The Fourth Step, *We took a searching and fearless moral inventory our ourselves,* can be daunting, yet incredibly liberating. This guide helps the reader move through fear and doubt to successfully complete an inventory.

90 pp
Trade Paper | $14.95
978-0-9826505-3-0

Came to Believe
A Guide to the Second Step
Chet Meyers

In a world that seems increasingly violent, materialistic, and filled with problems, is it possible to believe in a Higher Power? Author Chet Meyers offers answers to this and other questions to help readers reframe their thinking on the nature of spirituality and faith. This is a thoughtful and nonjudgmental discussion of Step Two, *Came to believe that a Power greater than ourselves could restore us to sanity.*

90 pp
Trade Paper | $14.95
978-0-9774400-7-8

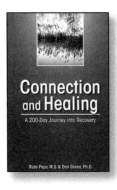

Connection and Healing
A 200-Day Journey into Recovery
Russ Pope, M.S., and Dan Green, Ph.D.

This guided journal provides two hundred days of inspirational writings on a variety of topics, including how to:

- reach out to family members and rebuild trust
- break habits of isolation and make the most of healthy connections
- experience the blessings of being truly known by others
- act in the true best interest of loved ones

430 pp
Trade Paper | $24.95
978-0-9826505-0-9

Hope and Freedom for Sexual Addicts and Their Partners

Milton S. Magness, D.Min.

Dr. Milton S. Magness offers sexual addicts and their partners step-by-step guidance on how to work through the phases of recovery. Readers learn about disclosure, celibacy contracts, relapse, and how to rebuild broken trust. This is a compassionate yet straightforward primer on how to end sexual addiction.

220 pp
Trade Paper | $19.95
978-0-9774400-5-4

Disclosing Secrets
When, to Whom, and How Much to Reveal

M. Deborah Corley, Ph.D., Jennifer P. Schneider, M.D., Ph.D.

Nearly every book on addiction recovery discusses the need for "coming clean" with loved ones, but this is the only guide that exclusively addresses this essential step in revealing sensitive secrets. Readers will learn what, when, and how to disclose information related to sexual and other addictions, as well as who to involve and what (if anything) to tell children.

290 pp
Trade Paper | $23.00
978-1-929866-04-5

Open Hearts
Renewing Relationships with
Recovery, Romance, and Reality
Patrick Carnes, Ph.D.,
Debra Laaser, Mark Laaser, Ph.D.

No relationship situation is hopeless. *In Open Hearts*, readers will learn how to overcome "coupleshame," fight fair, understand their family "epics," break free from the same old battles, form a spiritual bond, and renew their early passion. This book provides hopeful and helpful guidance on transforming one's most intimate bonds.

230 pp
Trade Paper | $19.95
978-1-929866-00-7

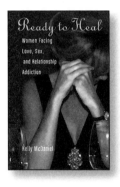

Ready to Heal
Women Facing Love, Sex,
and Relationship Addiction
Kelly McDaniel

Author Kelly McDaniel offers women compassionate yet direct assistance on how to change painful relationships. Readers will learn how to address patterns of choosing partners who are addicted to sex and substances, how to stop being involved in serial relationships, and what to do about anger and other painful emotions associated with intimate relationships.

190 pp
Trade Paper | $18.95
978-0-9774400-3-0

Gentle Path Press

Gentle Path Press was founded in 1998 by Patrick Carnes, Ph.D., a pioneering researcher, clinician, and author in the field of sexual and multiple addictions. Dr. Carnes' goal was to publish innovative books and other resources for consumers and professionals on topics related to addiction, trauma, and brain chemistry. Gentle Path books provide readers with the best research-based materials to help repair the lives of individuals and families.

Dr. Carnes' cutting-edge research and writing became widely known in 1983 with the publication of his book, *Out of the Shadows: Understanding Sexual Addiction.* It was the first book designed to help addicts deal with their sexual compulsions, and to examine the tangled web of trauma, love, addictive sex, hate, and fear often found in family relationships. His research, work with patients, and writing have continued over the past three decades.

Experts and consumers alike have come to embrace Dr. Carnes' 2001 book, *Facing the Shadow: Starting Sexual and Relationship Recovery,* as his most compelling and important work to date. *Facing the Shadow* introduced readers to Dr. Carnes' revolutionary Thirty Task Model for beginning and sustaining long-term recovery.

More information on Gentle Path books can be found at www.gentlepath.com.

International Institute
for Trauma and
Addiction Professionals

Institute for Trauma
and Addiction Professionals

Dr. Carnes also founded the International Institute for Trauma and Addiction Professionals (IITAP), which promotes professional training and knowledge of sexual addiction and related disorders. Sex addiction affects the lives of millions of people worldwide, and practicing therapists are on the frontlines treating this epidemic. IITAP offers three distinguished certifications to addiction-treatment professionals: Certified Sex Addiction Therapist (CSAT), Certified Multiple Addiction Therapist (CMAT), and Associate Sex Addiction Therapist (ASAT).

More information can be found at www.iitap.com.

Excerpt from

**Facing Addiction:
Starting Recovery from Alcohol and Drugs**
by Patrick Carnes, Ph.D.,
Stefanie Carnes, Ph.D. and John Bailey, M.D.

Introduction

For all addicts, a moment comes when they realize they have a problem. In this moment of lucidity, it suddenly hits home how out of control life is. Then the old rationales and cravings rush back in to blur reality. Think of an addiction as being caught in a wild and dangerous white-water stream. Those flashes of understanding enable addicts to regain stability. If they act quickly, there is a chance of escaping danger before they are pulled back into the roiling and thrilling current. Others recognize their peril and know they must get out in order to survive, but the stream is too strong and those lucid moments too rare.

There are some who have reached a point where they refuse to be pushed around any longer. They seize the opportunity and with courage and work manage to find tranquil pools or beaches. They pull themselves out and discover they had forgotten, or maybe never knew, a calmer, more ordered world. With perspective they realize the last choice they would make would be to spend their lives in the raging river. If you are looking at this book, you may be wrestling with the problem of addiction to alcohol or drugs. If you are, this doesn't mean you are bad or hopeless. It means you may have a disease from which many have healed.

If you are a normal addict, you have probably made the following statements to yourself

- Nothing will help.
- I am overreacting to normal things.
- Others (my family, my boss, my neighbors) are overreacting to normal things.

- I am worthless and too damaged to change.
- The problems will blow over.
- I can stop if I just try harder (as opposed to trying therapy or recovery).
- I will be OK if I just drink or use less.
- I will be OK if I can be more clever about my use so I will not be caught.
- The reason I do this is because of (my spouse or parents or work or religion or culture) _____ (fill in the blank).
- My situation is different.
- No one will understand what I do (or did).

If any of those thoughts occur to you, you are exactly where you should be. This is what most addicts think when first beginning to confront their addiction. If you are starting to acknowledge your problem, this is significant progress. You may be open at last to the possibility that hope and healing can enter your life. If you have reached the moment where you know that your drinking or drug use is out of control, this book is for you.

Fortunately, there are now many books on addiction. However, this is the first book that takes techniques used with thousands of recovering addicts and uses these to teach you step by step how to break free from the raging current of addiction and make your life better. Decades of research and clinical experience have shown that breaking recovery into defined tasks makes it easier to leave the addictive life. As recovering people perform these tasks, they learn specific competencies with which to manage their problems. Taken together, these skills form a map for success. If they follow the map, they will reach the goal of recovery. If not, they will end up back in the whitewater.

This book is the tool many of us now in recovery wish we had when we started. It is intended to be used as part of therapy, either in an outpatient or inpatient treatment program. It is also designed to support a Twelve Step recovery program such as Alcoholics Anonymous (AA) or Narcotics Anonymous (NA). (Look for a listing of such support groups on page 256 of this book.) Please note, the content in this book is not intended to replace conference-approved materials that are published by AA or NA for use in Twelve Step meetings.

Both therapy and Twelve Step support are keys to success. Your internal addict voice will supply rationales for not doing therapy or Twelve Step work, such as

- Therapy does not work.
- Therapists are crazy or they would not be in the business.
- Twelve Step groups will not work for me.
- I can do this on my own.
- I do not like the therapist, the group, the program, the Twelve Steps, the people there, talking about myself, or _____(fill in the blank).
- My situation is different.
- No one will understand what I do (or did).

It is at this point that addicts must try to see what is really going on because they soon will be caught up in the rapids again. That is why our first chapter explores, "What is Real?"

We have personally known many people who have died because of their addiction, and we have heard the stories of countless others who have met the same fate. Delusion is the deadliest part of this illness. Those rushing rapids kill. If you are in a moment where you can see them, we invite you to come out of the river.